Praise for Transformative Witchcraft

"*Transformative Witchcraft* by Jason Mankey finds the perfect balance between the core teachings of magical tradition and the fresh, cutting-edge magic of the modern witch. This well-researched book digs deep, exploring the foundations of witchcraft in a conversational and honest tone that makes the witchcraft mysteries accessible and current."

—Mickie Mueller, author of *The Witch's Mirror* and
Llewellyn's Little Book of Halloween

"A remarkable and refreshing exploration that is a must-read for anyone exploring contemporary Wicca and Witchcraft. Through a combination of in-depth historical research and charming personal narrative, Jason Mankey provides candid insight into important rituals and practices that are often glossed over or minimally explained in other texts."

—Laura Tempest Zakroff, author of *Sigil Witchery* and
Weave the Liminal

"Jason Mankey's *Transformative Witchcraft* is that rare work that covers the vital history of Wicca without being dry and thoroughly explains magical practices in ways that are both engaging and capture their core mystery. Digging into far more than the usual basics and not afraid to tackle the deeper work while remaining relatable and easy to read, this book is a unique entry on the subject and should be essential reading."

—Morgan Daimler, author of *Pagan Portals: The Morrigan: Meeting the
Great Queens* and *Fairycraft: Following the Path of Fairy Witchcraft*

T0351854

Transformative Witchcraft

© Tymn Urban

ABOUT THE AUTHOR

Jason Mankey has been a Pagan and a Witch for over twenty years and has spent much of that time writing, talking, and ritualizing across North America. He's a frequent visitor to a plethora of Pagan festivals, where he can often be found talking about Pagan deities, rock and roll, and various aspects of Pagan history. He is currently the editor of the Patheos Pagan channel and can be found online at his blog, *Raise the Horns*.

JASON MANKEY

Transformative

Witchcraft

THE GREATER MYSTERIES

Llewellyn Publications
Woodbury, Minnesota

FIRST EDITION
Third Printing, 2022

Cover design by Kevin R. Brown
Interior art on pages 48, 239, 250 and 251 by Wen Hsu. All other art by the Llewellyn
    Art Department.

Llewellyn Publications is a registered trademark of Llewellyn Worldwide Ltd.

Library of Congress Cataloging-in-Publication Data
Names: Mankey, Jason, author.
Title: Transformative witchcraft : the greater mysteries / by Jason Mankey.
Description: First edition. | Woodbury, Minnesota : Llewellyn Worldwide, 2019
  | Includes bibliographical references and index.
Identifiers: LCCN 2018044218 (print) | LCCN 2018049182 (ebook) | ISBN
  9780738758329 (ebook) | ISBN 9780738757971 (alk. paper)
Subjects: LCSH: Witchcraft.
Classification: LCC BF1571 (ebook) | LCC BF1571 .M36 2019 (print) | DDC
  133.4/3—dc23
LC record available at https://lccn.loc.gov/2018044218

Llewellyn Worldwide Ltd. does not participate in, endorse, or have any authority or responsibility concerning private business transactions between our authors and the public.

All mail addressed to the author is forwarded but the publisher cannot, unless specifically instructed by the author, give out an address or phone number.

Any internet references contained in this work are current at publication time, but the publisher cannot guarantee that a specific location will continue to be maintained. Please refer to the publisher's website for links to authors' websites and other sources.

Llewellyn Publications
A Division of Llewellyn Worldwide Ltd.
2143 Wooddale Drive
Woodbury, MN 55125-2989
www.llewellyn.com

Printed in the United States of America

Other Books by Jason Mankey

The Witch's Altar
(Co-author, Llewellyn, 2019)

The Witch's Book of Shadows
(Llewellyn, 2017)

The Witch's Athame
(Llewellyn, 2016)

DEDICATION

In memory of my grandparents, Mick and Marie Mankey. I know the two of you were not Witches, but you remain the most magickal people I've ever known. I love you, Grandma and Gramps!

CONTENTS

The Transformative Power of Witchcraft

Since I was a child I've been attracted to mysteries. In elementary school I was obsessed with undiscovered creatures such as Bigfoot and the Loch Ness Monster. That interest led me to other unexplained phenomena such as UFOs, ghosts, and the supernatural. Eventually I became interested in the occult, and while my peers were reading Choose Your Own Adventure books I was reading books on demons, vampires, and witches.

My interest in the unknown eventually led me to study religion in college, a subject that I found to be the biggest mystery of all. Why do some people feel called to deities like Jesus and others to the Hindu Shiva? Why do some religions thrive and others whither away? Why wasn't I experiencing anything magical or wondrous in my then Christian practice?

I often feel like a bad Witch for admitting it today, but I grew up as a Christian and practiced that faith until I was about twenty years old. I wasn't just a Sunday Christian either; I was president of my youth group and was actively involved in my church. Despite my involvement, I still felt like there was something missing in my life. Christianity simply didn't offer any mystery. It felt hollow, for lack of a better word.

At the age of twenty-one I picked up a book on Modern Witchcraft, and my life was forever changed. Within forty-eight hours of picking up that book I had added "the Lady" to my evening prayers and began to look at the world in a different way. Witchcraft presented me with a world full of magick and mystery, and it was undeniably alive. Rain falling from the sky wasn't just water, it was a literal gift from the gods, and the blowing wind contained messages from the Goddess and God. Jesus was quiet when I prayed to him, but the Lord and Lady were around all the time, no prayer required.

The biggest difference between Witchcraft and my previous path is that Witchcraft is *transformative*. Some of the rituals found in modern-day Christianity are meant to be transformative, but nearly all the mystery and wonder has been stripped from them. (Somehow Christianity has made the resurrection of Jesus—think about it for a second, it's a guy coming back from the dead!—boring.) Witchcraft ritual is flickering candles, chants, incense, and the promise of something awe-inspiring. Church is tired hymns or cloying worship songs, sermons about how bad we all are, and readings from a 2,000-year-old book.

Witchcraft's greatest mysteries fundamentally change the way we look at the world, and those mysteries make up the core of this book. During my time as a Witch, four different ritual experiences have turned my world upside down. The first of those mysteries was the *cone of power*, and though I didn't know what it was the first time I experienced it, from that point on I knew undoubtedly that magick was real. At the start of my second year as a Witch, I dedicated myself to the practice of the Craft and felt the power of the gods surround me while I did so. Several years later I was initiated into a specific Witchcraft tradition, and the way I viewed the world was never the same.

Perhaps the most life-changing event in my life was the first time I saw the Goddess descend into the body of a human being and then interact with those around her. This was probably what I dreamed about most as a Christian—direct experience with the divine—and is now something I experience with great regularity as a Witch (and every time it's just as awe-inspiring as it was on that first night). One of the women who drew down the moon that night would become my wife and magickal partner, and through the mystery of the Great Rite she and I have been able to become one in a spiritual and physical sense, at least for a little while.

The mysteries of Witchcraft are real and can be grasped if we are just willing to open ourselves up to them. And most importantly, they can be experienced by anyone. Witchcraft is about more than seasonal rituals and pentacle necklaces; it's meant to be a transformative path. Not every Witchcraft rite will change how you see the world, but the possibility for something so grand does exist in what we do as Witches.

The first public Modern Witch was a retired English civil servant named Gerald Gardner, and his work eventually opened the door to millions of other Witches. Witchcraft was such a transformative power in his life that the first section of this book shares the mystery of his alleged initiation back in 1939. Gardner most likely experienced all the things written about in this book, and they had the same effect on him as they've had on me.

Gardner went public with his experiences as a Witch in the early 1950s, and his first book on the subject, *Witchcraft Today*, was released in 1954. In this book Gardner claimed that Witchcraft was a religion and had survived in secret for centuries and, most importantly, still existed in 1954. The idea of Witchcraft as a pagan religion was not new, but the idea that it still existed in such a form was not only novel but revolutionary.

The Witchcraft that Gardner wrote about back in the 1950s is generally known as *Wicca* today (and even more specifically *Gardnerian Wicca*), but the word Wicca does not appear once in Gardner's work. Gardner believed he was documenting Witchcraft, and that's what he called the practice in his book. He called the individuals who practiced Witchcraft *Witches* and not Wiccans. He also sometimes used the phrase *Witch-cult* to refer to those who practiced Witchcraft either in his day or in the past.

This is important to me because there are some who claim that Wiccans are not Witches and that Wicca and Witchcraft should be seen as separate terms. One evening I came across a warning on social media to avoid any and all books that use Wicca and Witchcraft as synonyms. (The person who wrote that is going to hate this book!) Wiccan-Witchcraft is certainly not the only kind of Witchcraft in the world, but it is a kind of Witchcraft, and the two words have been used interchangeably since the 1960s, and I don't see any reason to stop doing that today.

Gardner does use the word *Wica* twice in his book *Witchcraft Today*, but not as the name of a religion. Instead, being of *the Wica* is the equivalent in Gardner's book of being part of an exclusive club. The Wica are "wise people" but are known both to themselves and to those around them as Witches and practitioners of Witchcraft.

In 1958, Charles and Mary Cardell (two very odd individuals who liked to pretend they were brother and sister) told the Spiritualist journal *Light* that they were "Wiccens."[1] The Witchcraft (or *Wicce*?) of the Cardells never really caught on, but a slightly different version of their term *Wiccen* did. In 1960, Margaret Bruce, a friend of Gerald Gardner and the owner of a magickal mail-order business, used the word *Wicca* in a humorous poem in reference to the Cardells:

> *We feel it is tragick*
> *That those who lack Magick.*
> *Should start a vendetta*
> *With those who know betta*
> *We who practice the Art*
> *Have no wish to take part*
> *Seems a pity the 'Wicca'*
> *Don't realise this Quicca.*[2]

By the early 1960s the words Wicca and Wiccan began to be commonly associated with the Witchcraft first written about by Gerald Gardner. Generally, use of the terms Wicca and Wiccan was limited to those initiated into the tradition of Gardner and its various offshoots. By the late 1980s the word Wicca was being used to describe any variation of Gardner's Witch religion, whether that tradition was initiatory or eclectic and homegrown.

---

1. Hutton, *The Triumph of the Moon*, 298–299.

2. Melissa Seims, "Wica or Wicca? Politics and the Power of Words," http://www
.thewica.co.uk/wica_or_wicca.htm.

The words Wicca and Witchcraft have been linked for countless centuries. According to the Oxford English Dictionary, the very word *witch* derives from the Old English words *wicca* (masculine) and *wicce* (feminine). What exactly *wicca* meant before being turned into *witch* is a matter of some debate. Some have speculated that it might mean "to bend or shape," and others have linked it to Germanic words meaning "awakener," "sacrificer," "adviser," or "diviner."[3] Advising, divining, and awakening are all things Modern Witches do, and there are still many who suffer from the delusion that Witches sacrifice things, so all four possibilities resonate at least a little bit with the word witch.

Whatever the word's early origins, by the time *witch* became a popular word in the English language it was mainly used to refer to negative magick users, with those practitioners most often being women. Not surprisingly, acts of negative magick and the people who were said to practice that magick were linked with the Christian Devil. In some instances "witches" were perceived as spectral beings, ghostlike entities that terrorized good Christian folks.

Gardner was not the first person to present Witchcraft in a sympathetic light. The word had slowly been gaining a degree of respect for several decades before him. Positive users of magick were even being called "white" Witches by some writers, but Gardner was the first person to publicly self-identify as a Witch. He's also seen today as the founder, revealer, and/or architect of the religion known as Wicca. Since Gardner and his later initiates used the two terms somewhat interchangeably, I do too.

The word Witch might not be a mystery, but it's use is often contentious. If a person chooses to self-identify as a Witch, more power to them—as long as that person doesn't tell everyone else that they are prohibited from doing so. The Witchcraft world is a large one, and there's enough room for the words Witchcraft and Witch to be used in a variety of ways.

---

3. Hutton, *The Triumph of the Moon*, 241.

A NOTE TO READERS

Many of the rites and rituals included in this book come directly from my own personal Book of Shadows. Since so many of those rituals were written with my wife, Ari, in mind (she's my ritual partner after all), they utilize the terms *High Priestess* and *High Priest* to indicate ritual leadership roles—but in no way am I looking to suggest that a coven must have a female and a male in such positions.

In our coven's practices we often do rituals with two High Priestesses or two High Priests. Writing "High Priest" and "High Priestess" simply reflects the fact that I do most of my rituals with Ari. These names are not meant to indicate any sort of defined role for a specific gender. (And since my wife is a better ritualist than I am, you'll see that the High Priestess part almost always gets the most lines in ritual.)

Women can call the Horned God and men can call the Triple Goddess, and ritual should also be welcoming to those Witches (and sometimes deities) who don't identify with any gender. My deities represent every facet of the gender spectrum, and that spectrum is long and varied.

Though I think this book can be enjoyed and understood by just about anybody, it's designed for readers who have had at least a little bit of experience with Witch ritual. For those of you new to the path, there's a glossary at the end to help with the words that might be unfamiliar to you.

Part One

The Origins of Modern Witchcraft

CHAPTER ONE

Gerald Gardner and the New Forest Witches

Nearly all modern religions have an origin myth. In Christianity that myth involves Jesus of Galilee dying on a cross and coming back from the dead. Islam begins with the prophet Muhammad praying in a cave, meeting the angel Gabriel, and then reciting the first verses of what would become the Koran. The founder of the Church of Jesus Christ of Latter-day Saints (the Mormons), Joseph Smith, also met an angel who revealed to him the existence of several "golden plates" that were then translated into the Book of Mormon.

Modern Witchcraft has its own origin story too, but one devoid of supernatural overtones and divine intervention. Instead of a story involving angels or other supernatural forces, Modern Witchcraft begins with a very human initiation in the year 1939. In September of that year it's alleged that a retired English civil servant named Gerald Gardner (1884–1964) was initiated into a coven of Witches near England's New Forest area.

Like most events that spark a worldwide religious movement, we have no way of knowing if Gardner's initiation was a real historical event. Despite what some believe, there are no contemporary accounts of Jesus's death and resurrection, and like Muhammad in his cave or Joseph Smith with the angel Moroni, we have no independent witnesses to corroborate Gardner's claim of initiation. Origin myths are often not about literal truths and are meant to be taken on faith. I believe whole-heartedly that Gerald Gardner was initiated into a coven of people who thought of themselves as Witches in 1939. It's not something that can be proven conclusively, but there's a lot of circumstantial evidence that gives credence to the argument.

The only source of information we have for Gardner's initiation is, not surprisingly, Gerald Gardner. In the 1960 biography *Gerald Gardner: Witch* (listed author: Jack Bracelin, see footnote),[4] Gardner gives his account of the event:

> Gardner felt delighted that he was about to be let into their secret. Thus it was that, a few days after the war had started, he was taken to a big house in the neighborhood. This belonged to "Old Dorothy"—a lady of note in the district, "county" and very well-to-do. She invariably wore a pearl necklace, worth some 5,000 pounds at the time.
>
> It was in this house that he was initiated into witchcraft. He was very amused at first, when he was stripped naked and brought into a place "properly prepared" to undergo his initiation.
>
> It was halfway through when the word Wica was first mentioned: "and I knew that which I had thought burnt out hundreds of years ago still survived."[5]

Gerald Gardner: Witch is not the only book Gardner was involved with that references his initiation, but it does contain the most information about it (and even that is scant). The lack of information about Gardner's initiation in print has a lot to do with the oath of secrecy he took during it. In his 1959 book *The Meaning of Witchcraft* he mentions this oath of secrecy: "But I was half-initiated before the word 'Wica' which they used hit me like a thunderbolt, and I knew where I was, and that

---

4. Jack Bracelin is listed as the author of *Gerald Gardner: Witch*, but most of the book is alleged to have been written by the Sufi mystic and novelist Idries Shah, a friend of Gardner. Gerald was intimately involved with the production of his biography, and I think it's safe to say that the story was told the way he wanted it to be.

5. Bracelin, *Gerald Gardner: Witch*, 165.

the Old Religion still existed. And so I found myself in the Circle, and there took the usual oath of secrecy, which bound me not to reveal certain things."[6]

While Gardner's recollections about his initiation don't reveal much, they do provide us with a little bit of information. The United Kingdom entered World War II in September of 1939, which means Gardner was probably initiated in September or October of that year ("a few days after the war started"). He also gives us a location, the home of "Old Dorothy."

There's one last tiny bit of information about Gardner's initiation from his published works: his initiation took place in the nude. This is not surprising, as later Gardnerian Witches would all work "skyclad" ("clothed by the sky"), which is a fancy word for naked. Before his initiation he was also "properly prepared," which means ritually cleansed.

We have one other source of information about Gardner's alleged initiation and it comes in the form of a letter from Gardner to English writer and occultist Gerald Yorke (who was then acting as editor of the book that would become *Witchcraft Today* in 1954):

> As soon as the Circle is cast & purified, they go round, what I call, evoking the Mighty Ones. To attend, to guard the Circle & witness the rites. These are meny. they are supposed to stand outside, & watch, seeing all is correct. Candidates for initiation are peraded round, introduced to them, & they are supposed to be satisfied all is in order. Also at certain rite, The, God, or Goddess Is invoked to descend & come into the Body of the Priestess or Priest, but first these are purified, & perade round so the mighty ones outside see all is in order, this we speak of as invoking. At ordinary meetings, the God & Goddess are not so invoked, the Priestess & Priest are simply their representatives, & are not the Gods themselves, I think I did not refer to this rite, if I did, I don't think theyll pass it.[7]

---

6. Gardner, *The Meaning of Witchcraft*. Originally published in 1959 by the Aquarian Press and by many other publishers subsequently. I'm quoting from a Magickal Childe edition published in the 1990s (there's no publication date in the book). This is from page 11.

7. Heselton, *Witchfather: A Life of Gerald Gardner, Vol. 1*, 215. The strange spellings, misspellings, and grammatical errors are from Gardner's original letter.

Gardner's letter to Yorke shines a bit more light on his initiation, outlining some of the ritual. Those components should be familiar to most Modern Witches and include calling the watchtowers (or quarters, generally the powers at the four cardinal points of the compass: east, south, west, and north) and possibly the ritual of drawing down the moon (see part 4 of this book). The language Gardner uses to describe these practices here is also what many Witches use in the circle today. "Goddess is invoked to descend and come into the body of the Priestess" almost sounds like it comes straight out of ritual.

Toward the end of this quoted passage Gardner writes, "I don't think they'll pass it," which is a reference to his initiators.[8] From the moment he went public with Witchcraft in 1951 until his death in 1964, Gardner often spoke of needing approval to publish certain things from the individuals who brought him into the Witch-cult. Originally he was "allowed" to write only a fictional account of Witchcraft (1949's *High Magic's Aid*) and then finally *Witchcraft Today* in 1954. Such prohibitions make sense in a religion with vows of secrecy.

Gardner's initiators, or lack thereof, are a big source of contention in academic circles. There's no concrete evidence that Gardner's initiation ever happened, and all we really have are Gardner's claims that it did. In addition, there are some issues with Gardner himself when it comes to whether or not he was initiated into Witchcraft. The passages quoted in this book make it sound as if Witchcraft was immediately fulfilling to Gardner, but history argues against that. In the years following his initiation, Gardner dabbled with several other magickal and esoteric orders, including Druidry, a liberal strain of Christianity known as the Ancient British Church, and English occultist Aleister Crowley's O.T.O. (Ordo Templi Orientis).

For me personally, Gardner's dabbling has always been hard to reconcile with the idea that he was initiated into a Witch coven in 1939. If Gardner was initiated in the days following England's entry into World War II, then he goes from getting hit "like a thunderbolt" to exploring

---

8. Gardner's letter was mistaken, too. Drawing down the moon does appear in *Witchcraft Today* and is referenced in regard to a Yule ritual.

several other esoteric paths in the span of about six to seven years. He would only "come back" to Witchcraft in 1949, ten years after beginning that journey.

For this reason, many modern Pagan scholars find the idea that Gardner was initiated into a Witch group in 1939 unlikely. I think their concerns are completely justified, and it's just not in the nature of academics to make wild speculative leaps with so little evidence. So we have to at least respect the idea that Gardner was not initiated all those decades ago. But as you may have guessed, I think he was initiated into *something*, and the New Forest area of England had just the right mix of occult elements to produce what today we call Wiccan-Witchcraft.

THE ELEMENTS OF
MODERN WICCAN-WITCHCRAFT

Despite the claims of some, there is no "unbroken chain" linking today's Witches to a public or underground Witch religion from ages past. While many Witches today feel a kinship with the innocents whose lives were lost during the Burning Times, those "witches" were not practicing the same things we are today. In fact, nearly all of them would have self-identified as Christians.

But just because today's Witchcraft is a relatively new belief system doesn't mean it lacks any ancient roots. I think it's safe to say that Wiccan-Witchcraft (and most other magickal paths of European descent being practiced today) is a part of the Western magickal tradition. While religions rise and fall, magickal practices generally remain. When most of Europe converted to Christianity, people didn't stop practicing magick—just the opposite. Magick remained an important part of their lives, and many of the greatest and most important magick books ever written were composed by Christians and attributed to legendary Jewish figures such as King Solomon.

When most of us say *abracadabra*, we think of it as a nonsense word associated with stage magic, but that's a misconception. The word has actually been used for over 1,800 years now, and for actual magick! Before being used on the stage, it was a staple in magick books and spells throughout Europe.[9] Many magick techniques and words have been Christianized over the years but often still date back to pagan antiquity.

The Western magickal tradition traces its history back to the ancient Greeks, and before that the Egyptians and Babylonians. After the emergence of Christianity, its wisdom was preserved in folk traditions and magickal grimoires. Eventually it gave birth to magickal religions such as modern Wiccan-Witchcraft and some forms of Druidry. Today's Witchcraft *is* ancient, just not in the way some hope for.

Within the Western magickal tradition there are several schools of thought and/or institutions that had a very large impact on the Witchcraft of today. We will be exploring many of these throughout this book. What's interesting is that all of these elements were present in the New Forest area of England back in 1939, when Gardner claimed to have been initiated.

Freemasonry

Nearly every modern tradition that contains an initiation ceremony owes something to Freemasonry. Most Wiccan initiation ceremonies share at least a superficial resemblance to Masonic ones, but Masonry provided Witchcraft with more than a ritual structure for initiations and other rites. Much of the language used in Witch circles also comes from the Masonic tradition. Words such as *charge* and *cowan* both stem from the Masonic tradition.

Masonry is at least three hundred years old, and probably much older. It's most likely a descendent of a Scottish "masonic guild" that helped design the huge cathedrals and castles of Scotland. Eventually it evolved into a fraternal society and thereafter inspired dozens of other "secret societies." Some of the earliest Druid orders were organizations very much like the Freemasons, and groups like the Horseman's Word (a group for individuals who worked with horses, including blacksmiths) took fraternal ritual to an entirely new level, as we'll see in chapter 7.

---

9. Hohman, *The Long-Lost Friend*, ed. Harms, 248.

Freemasonry exists in two very different worlds. For some Masons their organization is simply a fraternal order dedicated to fellowship and charity. For other Masons it is an esoteric one, with magickal and occult aspects. Masonic ritual is rich with symbolism and is open to anyone who believes in a "higher power." Most Masonic organizations are for men only, but Co-Masonry (a Masonic practice open to both women and men) was popular in Gardner's day and was practiced by people in the New Forest area.

The Grimoire Tradition

Books have been highly influential in the development of Modern Witchcraft, most specifically books dealing with ceremonial magick. Written spells existed before the invention of books, but the portability of books versus scrolls made them much more useful in magickal practice. Books as we would recognize them today first appeared in the third century BCE, though it would be several more centuries before they would become commonplace.

Most early grimoires were written in Greek, Latin, or Hebrew and were inaccessible to most people, but that began to change with the European discovery of movable type in 1450. Within a hundred years of that discovery, magick books in common languages began to appear.[10] While many today associate the ceremonial magick of the grimoire tradition with wealthy individuals, that wasn't always the case. Both rich and poor had access to books and reading by that time in history, and even rural cunning-folk were known to consult grimoires.

Though the grimoire tradition was originally Christian in nature, many of its tools and practices are familiar to Modern Witches. Grimoire-influenced magicians cast circles with swords and knives, and purified materials such as salt and water. Many of the most common Witchcraft rites come nearly word for word from the most famous and influential of all the grimoires, the *Key of Solomon* (know in Latin as *Clavicula Salomonis*).

---

10. I spend a lot of time discussing the history of books and grimoires in my book *The Witch's Book of Shadows*, published in 2017 by Llewellyn.

The high magick that came down through the grimoire tradition eventually influenced and inspired one of the most important magickal orders of the last two hundred years, the Hermetic Order of the Golden Dawn (founded in 1888). While the Golden Dawn generally thought of itself as a Judeo-Christian organization, it sometimes utilized pagan deities in its rites. The Golden Dawn, like the tradition that helped to give it life, would go on to influence Modern Witchcraft.

Cunning-Craft

For many centuries magick was a skill like any other. If you needed your grain milled, you went to the miller. If your horse needed shoeing, you visited the blacksmith. And if you needed assistance with negative forces or your fortune told, you went to a cunning-man or cunning-woman. Perhaps cunning-craft wasn't the most appreciated calling in the world, but it was certainly a part of most British villages, towns, and cities (and practically everywhere else, though every culture has its own name for it).

Many folks who practiced cunning-craft passed their knowledge down orally to students and family members. Oftentimes it was also preserved in books and other writings. Some of it was simply what today we might call herbalism, while other parts of it were influenced by the grimoire tradition. Cunning-craft was (and is) folk magick, which means it's a magickal system where the practitioner utilizes anything and everything that works. That might be an old spell handed down for hundreds of years, or it might be something out of a book like the *Key of Solomon.*

Sometimes practitioners of cunning-craft were called *witches*, to indicate that they were magick practitioners. However, that does not mean they were Witches in the same sense that you or I might be. Until recently, most (if not all) practitioners of cunning-craft thought of themselves as Christians, and often as Christians in opposition to evil witches.

The Theosophical Society

The Theosophical Society was founded in 1875 by Helena Blavatsky (1831–1891) and Henry Steel Olcott (1832–1907). Blavatsky was the driving force behind the group and claimed that she was in communication with a group of secret "Masters." The Masters (or *Mahatmas*) were said to have once been human but had achieved a higher state of wisdom due to their great knowledge and religious understanding. Theosophy was in many ways a mix of various religious traditions around the world, with the Blavatsky's Masters at the center of the truths revealed by those faiths.

Theosophy was never a mass movement, but it appealed to a great many occultists. The Golden Dawn had its own set of "Secret Chiefs" that were similar in many respects to the Mahatmas of the Theosophical Society. Theosophy's greatest gift to the world was its introduction of Eastern religious ideas to the Western world. Some of the ideas that many of us take for granted today in Witchcraft, such as karma and reincarnation, are most likely a part of our practice due to the Theosophical Society and its focus on spiritual ideas from places such as India.

THE MOST INTERESTING ELEMENTS (GARDNER'S INITIATORS)

In 1938 retired English civil servant Gerald Gardner and his wife, Donna, moved to the New Forest area of southern England. Before moving to New Forest, Gardner had spent most of his adult life far from England, in Borneo, Malaysia, Singapore, and Sri Lanka (then known as Ceylon). Gardner had spent most of his time in the East working as a plantation inspector (and possibly taking bribes), and when he returned to England in 1936 he was a fairly wealthy man.

Most of the pictures we see today of Gerald Gardner show him at the end of his life, well into his seventies and even eighties. But in 1938 Gardner was only in his early fifties and still retained much of his youthful vigor. He was a strong-looking, striking man with tattoos on his arms.

We have no idea when Gardner first became attracted to what we might today call "the occult," but it was certainly a passion he indulged in often as an adult. Not only did he enjoy reading about magick and the paranormal but he also actively sought it out during his adventures around the world. If there was a spiritual adventure to be had, Gardner did his best to partake in it.

A short while after moving to the New Forest area, Gardner joined an esoteric order and theatre company called the Rosicrucian Order Crotona Fellowship (often shortened to simply the Crotona Fellowship). The Crotona Fellowship was led by a man named George Alexander Sullivan (1890–1942), who claimed to be immortal and to change his identity every few decades. Gardner was introduced to the group through its plays (written by Sullivan), which were performed at the Christchurch Garden Theatre, a facility built exclusively for the Crotona Fellowship.

Gardner had very few nice things to say about the Crotona Fellowship or Sullivan in his biography, but he did find himself attracted to a small clique within the group. He called that group "the most interesting element" and added that they "had a real interest in the occult." [11] We will never know for sure exactly who all made up the "most interesting element," but there is one person we can be sure was a part of the group: Edith Woodford-Grimes (1887–1975), a divorced teacher of elocution and most likely Gardner's mistress. It's possible that they met even before Gardner began attending the meetings of the Crotona Fellowship.

Affectionately nicknamed *Dafo* by Gardner (this was not her magickal name), Woodford-Grimes remained a part of Gardner's life for nearly the next twenty years. We know with absolute certainty that Dafo was active as a Witch for at least a part of her life and enacted Witch ritual with Gerald. Due to Gardner's relationship with Woodford-Grimes, it's possible to speculate on the individuals who made up "the most interesting element," and it turns out that nearly all of them were Co-Masons, or at least ex-Co-Masons.

---

11. Heselton, *Witchfather: A Life of Gerald Gardner, Vol. 1,* 198.

The "element" was a part of Sullivan's group in large part because they had nowhere else to go. In 1935 Mabel Besant (daughter of Co-Masonry's founder and one of the leading lights of Theosophy, Annie Besant), who then held the title "Most Puissant Grand Commander of the British Federation" of Co-Masons, was "suspended" from Co-Masonry due to her anger over the group's Supreme Council reconciling with a French Masonic group exiled from the greater world of Masonry. (Yes, just like there are "Witch wars" today, there were "Co-Masonry massacres" in the 1930s.) In a show of solidarity with Besant, members of the nearby Southampton Co-Masonic lodge (ironically named Harmony Lodge) resigned from the group. Among those who resigned were Edith Woodford-Grimes and two other individuals we will get to know fairly well, Ernie and Susie Mason (who were brother and sister).

The Crotona Fellowship had built their theatre on property given to them by a woman named Catherine Chalk, who just happened to be a Co-Mason. It's likely that Chalk introduced Besant and her followers to the Rosicrucians. Gardner is very open about this in *Gerald Gardner: Witch* and even affectionately refers to Mabel Besant by the nickname "Mabs." [12] Exiled from the world of Co-Masonry, could Besant, Woodford-Grimes, and the Mason family have turned to Witchcraft? I think the answer is a very strong *possibly*.

Ernest "Ernie" Mason (1885–1979) is probably the most intriguing figure in the Crotona Fellowship when it comes to Witchcraft. An informant of historian Philip Heselton said this of Mason: "He was a witch, you know! The whole family were. They were mind control people. But he found the rituals too strenuous so he couldn't do it anymore." [13]

If there's a case to be made for Gardner being initiated into a tradition with some real roots in cunning-craft and other old magickal practices, it most likely goes through the Mason family.

Ernie, along with his sisters Susie and Rosetta Fudge (she took her husband's last name), were involved in many different esoteric and occult groups. Ernie was publicly a Co-Mason and a Rosicrucian, and he

---

12. For a much more detailed account of these goings-on, read pages 202–205 of Heselton's *Witchfather: A Life of Gerald Gardner, Vol. 1.*
13. Heselton, *Wiccan Roots*, 100.

might have inherited the teachings and traditions of the Crotona Fellowship after Sullivan's death, and at least practiced the tradition until the 1950s. Friends have also stated that he was a marvelous teacher and had his own set of mental exercises (which seem to somewhat resemble those of Modern Witchcraft) and was an amateur chemist.[14]

Susie Mason (1882–1979) was involved in all the same groups as Ernie but was also a part of the Theosophical Society, serving as a regional secretary from 1929–1934.[15] Rosetta Fudge (1884–1971) was the older sister of Ernie and Susie and married in 1903. Like her siblings, she was involved in Co-Masonry and Rosicrucianism and had also at least studied the works of occult writer Rudolf Steiner earlier in life.

So were the Masons a family of Witches? We will never know for sure, but as a family they were certainly at least very interested in occult and esoteric philosophies. I wish there was some sort of smoking cauldron linking them to a family magickal tradition, but so far that's proven elusive. With their broad array of unconventional interests, it's possible that people in their native town of Southampton might have called them "witches" or speculated on their magickal activities. Given the Co-Masonic ties between Edith Woodford-Grimes and the Mason family (they all resigned when Mabel Besant was "suspended" by the Co-Masonic Grand Council), I think it's likely that they make up a large part of what Gardner called the "most interesting element."

One of the major themes of early Witchcraft was reincarnation, and it seems to have played a large role in Gardner's 1939 initiation. Writing in *The Meaning of Witchcraft* in 1959, Gardner says this of his initiators:

> I was of these opinions in 1939, when, here in Britain, I met some people who compelled me to alter them. They were interested in curious things, reincarnation for one, and they were also interested in the fact that an ancestress of mine, Grizel Gairdner, had been burned as a witch. They kept saying that they had met me before. We went through everywhere we had been, and I could not ever have met them before in this life; but they claimed to

---

14. Heselton, *Wiccan Roots*, 106.

15. Ibid., 105.

have known me in previous lives. Although I believe in reincarnation, as many people do who have lived in the East, I do not remember my past lives clearly; I only wish I did. However, these people told me enough to make me think. Then some of these new (or old) friends said, "You belonged to us in the past. You are of the blood. Come back to where you belong." [16]

Perhaps the Mason family and Gardner's other initiators had only recently begun thinking of themselves as Witches, or maybe a memory of a past life sparked some sort of interest in Witchcraft. If they all felt some sort of kinship with Gardner that went beyond their rather recent association, it would explain why he seems to be their only initiate from that period of time, and the only one who was not a Co-Mason.

THE OTHER WITCHES

Before the publication of Ronald Hutton's *The Triumph of the Moon* in 1999, the name most associated with Gardner's 1939 initiation was "Old Dorothy." As we've seen previously, Gardner mentions her in the *Gerald Gardner: Witch* biography, but while doing so he makes no claims that "Old Dorothy" was his initiator or was even present during his initiation rite.

Later in *Gerald Gardner: Witch* she's mentioned again, this time in relation to Operation Cone of Power, a Witchcraft ritual constructed to keep the Germans from making landfall in the British Isles (see section 2 of this book). In this instance she's portrayed as the High Priestess of the Witch-cult:

> Old Dorothy called up "covens right and left; although by Witch Law they should not have known each other." And this was the start of "Operation Cone of Power," when the witches, as they claim, sent up a force against Hitler's mind. [17]

---

16. Gardner, *The Meaning of Witchcraft*. Originally published in 1959 by the Aquarian Press and by many other publishers subsequently. I'm quoting from a Magickal Childe edition published in the 1990s (there's no publication date in the book). This is from page 11.

17. Heselton, *Wiccan Roots*, 226.

It can be written with a large degree of certainty that the Dorothy being referred to in these passages by Gardner was Dorothy Fordham, better known to most Witches as Dorothy Clutterbuck (1880–1951).[18] Doreen Valiente, who was initiated by Gardner in 1953 and spent the rest of her life writing about Witchcraft, says that Gardner used to speak often of Old Dorothy, and apparently her last name was known to at least some of his initiates. In his 1980 book *A History of Witchcraft: Sorcerers, Heretics & Pagans*, historian Jeffrey Russell mentions that many Gardnerian Witches "tell the story that he was initiated by Old Dorothy Clutterbuck." [19]

For many years the very existence of "Old Dorothy" was met with a lot of skepticism both within academia and in the Witchcraft community. That changed in the early 1980s when Valiente was able to track down Dorothy's death certificate and prove her existence. She was much like Gardner described her in *Gerald Gardner: Witch*: wealthy and the owner of two large homes and at least one very expensive pearl necklace.

Clutterbuck is an especially vexing character when it comes to Gardner's initiation. She was not a former Co-Mason and was not involved with the Rosicrucian Order Crotona Fellowship. She and Gardner seem to at least have been acquaintances; he seconded her nomination to be president of the "Highcliffe Branch of the New Forest and Christchurch Conservative and Unionist Association" in 1940, but as of now that's the only known group that connects them.[20] It also seems unlikely that the "Conservative and Unionist Association" would have been a good place to talk about Witchcraft and other occult goings-on.

Despite her lack of involvement in any known occult groups or fraternal orders, Clutterbuck was highly unconventional. She had what was (most likely) a long-term and rather open same-sex relationship un-

---

18. In 1939 Clutterbuck would have been known as Dorothy Fordham, and later Dorothy St. Quintin-Fordham. Clutterbuck was her maiden name and Fordham her married name, and it was changed a third time after the death of her husband, Rupert, in 1939.

19. Valiente in Janet and Stewart Farrar's *A Witches' Bible*, 283. Valiente's essay appears as Appendix 1.

20. Heselton, *Witchfather: A Life of Gerald Gardner, Vol. 1*, 224–225.

til her partner passed away in the early 1930s. This was followed by her marriage to Rupert Fordham, who was still legally married when he and Dorothy held their nuptials. (Fordham's wife had previously been committed to a mental health facility, and they never officially divorced.)

Clutterbuck's parents had been wealthy, and she was able to live as a woman of independent means for her entire life, meaning she had plenty of free time. After her marriage to Fordham, she had even more money (he was the heir to a beer-brewing fortune) and certainly had the time to engage in a practice such as Witchcraft. In addition to her involvement in conservative politics, Clutterbuck dabbled in local theatre, generally as a wealthy benefactor. Because of that interest, it's not outside the realm of possibility that she visited the Crotona Fellowship when they staged a play.

As of yet there is no definitive piece of evidence that points to Clutterbuck's involvement in Witchcraft or the occult, but there are some sources that hint at it. During the early 1940s Clutterbuck kept a daily journal. This was not a diary but more like a daily meditation and/or art exercise. Dorothy's journals (there were three over the course of 1942–1943) contain poetic reflections and watercolor illustrations. Some of Dorothy's poems reflect a great love of the natural world, an interest that today we might call "pagan."[21]

Some of the more interesting passages include the personification of Christmas with a female (goddess-like?) figure and a poem about "the White Shepherdess," another figure that might be linked to a belief in a goddess. Clutterbuck's journals are light on Jesus and Christianity but do include thoughts on days dedicated to certain Catholic saints. I think that Clutterbuck's journals are a mixed bag and that if one looks through them searching for evidence that Clutterbuck was a Witch, it can be found. But conversely, the opposite is probably true as well.

So was Clutterbuck a Witch? Like everything in this chapter, the answer is *possibly*. She had the time, she was eccentric, and I don't think

---

21. Philip Heselton writes extensively about "Dorothy's diaries" in his book *Wiccan Roots*, and that book includes a few full-page photographs of Clutterbuck's work. If you want to learn more about Dorothy's books and read some excerpts, you should track down *Roots*.

she gave two shits what people thought about her, so why not? If she was a Witch, then Philip Heselton (Gardner's greatest biographer and the source of many of my footnotes) believes that Gardner probably didn't have much to do with her. Perhaps she was only around occasionally or lost interest in the practice after the start of World War II.

Ronald Hutton has suggested that the use of Clutterbuck's name by Gardner might have been a bit of a red herring. Perhaps in order to conceal the identity of Woodford-Grimes as his initiator, Gardner instead publicly used the name of the by then deceased Clutterbuck as a bit of a joke.[22] In addition to a lack of documented social interaction between Gardner and Clutterbuck, 1939 (the year of Gardner's alleged initiation) was an especially traumatic year for Old Dorothy. In May of that year, her husband, Rupert, died in an auto accident, an event that, according to Hutton, made her a virtual shut-in for the rest of the year.

While we will never know for sure if Clutterbuck was an occult practitioner, there is another name often linked to Gardner with strong magickal ties. While not as well known as Dorothy Clutterbuck, Rosamund Isabella Charlotte Sabine (1865–1948) might very well be the missing piece when it comes to Gardner's initiation and early Modern Witchcraft. Sabine is mentioned only once by Gardner, in a letter to his then friend Cecil Williamson.[23]

In that letter Gardner refers to the recent death of "Old Mother Sabine" and his inheritance of her dried herb collection. While there's nothing strange about that on the surface, a little digging reveals that Sabine died five years before Gardner wrote that letter in 1953![24] Much like with Clutterbuck, there's very little evidence linking Sabine directly to Gardner, and, like Clutterbuck, Sabine was not a part of Gardner's social circle and was not a Co-Mason or a member of the Crotona Fellowship.

---

22. Hutton, *The Triumph of the Moon*, 212. Hutton is the Craft's greatest historian, and he is rather dismissive of Clutterbuck as a Witch. He makes a good argument.
23. Williamson and Gardner opened a Witchcraft museum and then had a major falling-out. After their partnership fizzled out, Williamson opened a new museum, which has lasted into the present day. If you ever get a chance to visit the Museum of Witchcraft and Magic in Boscastle, England, I highly recommend it!
24. Heselton, *Witchfather: A Life of Gerald Gardner, Vol. 1*, 219.

However, earlier in life Sabine had been a member of an offshoot of the Golden Dawn, one of the most influential magickal organizations of the last two hundred years. And as late as 1930, Sabine was submitting articles to *The Occult Review*, then the United Kingdom's premier magickal magazine.[25] Sabine was clearly an occultist, and it doesn't take much imagination to think that as a fellow resident of the New Forest area, she might have hung out with the Rosicrucians of the Crotona Fellowship, even if there is no clear paper trail. (I'm sure I've visited groups without leaving too much in the way of a record.)

In the margins of Doreen Valiente's copy of *Gerald Gardner: Witch* there's a small note referencing a "Mother Sabine," with a question mark near a passage about the New Forest Witches. This indicates that Gardner spoke of a Mother Sabine with some regularity to his early initiates. It would be nice if there was a clear trail from Sabine to Gardner or even Woodford-Grimes, but all we have are these little tidbits.

Philip Heselton has speculated that perhaps Clutterbuck and Sabine were a part of a triad of Witches who were nominally linked to the ones from the Crotona Fellowship. He speculates that the two women, along with writer Katherine Oldmeadow (1878–1963), may have gotten interested in Witchcraft after reading an article about Margaret Murray's 1921 book *The Witch-Cult in Western Europe* in *The Occult Review* a year after the book's initial release. Oldmeadow and Clutterbuck were neighbors and were known to be friends, and Oldmeadow was interested in herbalism, as was Sabine. But linking the three of them together in connection with Witchcraft is, as of now, simply speculation.

Part of what makes a good mystery is not knowing, and such is the case with both Sabine and Clutterbuck. There's just enough there that the idea they may have been practicing Witchcraft can't be dismissed completely. As more research is done into the early days of the Craft, perhaps the missing link that connects all the dots will be found. And if not, speculation is part of the fun.

---

25. Heselton, *Witchfather: A Life of Gerald Gardner, Vol. 1*, 219. Heselton also writes about Sabine in his book *Gerald Gardner and the Cauldron of Inspiration*.

CHAPTER TWO

Theories and Other Witchcrafts

While the initiation of Gerald Gardner will most likely never be proven as an absolute historical happening, I still think it's likely to have occurred. The New Forest area of England where Gardner was living at the time had just the right mix of individuals with the required backgrounds to give birth to and/or refine the practice of Modern Witchcraft.

I don't believe that Gardner was initiated into anything that was more than twenty years old, but when it comes to religion, age is irrelevant. More than that, as we have seen, today's Witchcraft has an impressive history that goes back several centuries. Freemasonry, cunning-craft, and the grimoire tradition are all genuinely old and certainly worthy of admiration and respect as the cousins of today's Craft.

Besides Gardner, the most important player in this mystery is Edith Woodford-Grimes. She's the only one of Gardner's alleged initiators who we can say with certainty actually practiced Witchcraft with him. His relationship with Woodford-Grimes was probably a little more than friendship too; they were most likely lovers from the time of their introduction in 1938 until the early 1950s. Woodford-Grimes is the catalyst, the one who brought Gardner into the Craft and into the orbit of the "most interesting element" of the Rosicrucian Order Crotona Fellowship.

I'm of the opinion that the Witchcraft practiced by Woodford-Grimes and the Mason family was very fragmentary. Perhaps it was put together from various bits of Co-Masonic rituals, intuition, and other esoteric sources. I don't think this first coven of Witches met with much regularity, and they certainly would not have acted like a Modern Witch coven. They probably just enjoyed each other's company and the energy they raised together. With Co-Masonry denied to them, it's likely they were looking for a ritual system to fill in the gaps. They came up with Witchcraft.

Being former Co-Masons, they were well aware of just how powerful an initiation ritual could be, so they came up with one. And in Gardner they found a soul who was sympathetic to the use of the word *Witch* and was likely to get something out of the initiation rite. There's nothing to suggest that Gardner was all that close to anyone at his initiation other than Woodford-Grimes, so it's likely that she was the one who urged her comrades to initiate Gardner.

The initiation took place at the house of Dorothy Fordham Clutterbuck, but it doesn't seem as if she was present for the rite. Clutterbuck has always been one of the most difficult pieces to place on the board when it comes to the origin of today's Witchcraft. She, Katherine Oldmeadow, and Rosamund Sabine cannot be linked definitively to Gardner or the Crotona Fellowship. However, their interests don't seem incompatible with Modern Witchcraft (especially Sabine's), so it certainly remains possible.

The amount of time Gardner spent in a "coven" with his initiators was probably minimal. He only mentions being a part of two rituals with them: his initiation and Operation Cone of Power, which occurred just a little less than a year later. That the coven didn't meet during World War II is not surprising, but the absence of that coven in the postwar years is a bit perplexing.

It's possible that by the time the war ended, the New Forest Witches simply weren't practicing Witchcraft anymore. Their "Witch-cult" might have been just a passing fancy or a lark that was only indulged in a few times. Perhaps Gardner took it much more seriously than they did, and they ostracized him because of that.

Certainly by the late 1940s it doesn't seem as if Gardner is in any form of direct contact with his initiators other than with Woodford-Grimes. I believe there was some sort of estrangement between them and Gardner. His desire to talk and write about his experience as a Witch might have resulted in them showing him the door, or at least keeping him at arm's length. I believe this is the most likely scenario, as it would explain Gardner's interest in other magickal and esoteric orders in the late 1940s.

There's something about Gardner that makes me feel like he could have been easily duped. If Woodford-Grimes and her friends told him that their Witchcraft was a thousand years old, I think he would have believed it. I think we often simply *want* our occult practices to be old, even if they aren't. Having it be genuinely "old" might have been a form of wish fulfillment. Gardner probably thought he was practicing "the Old Religion," even if much of the ritual words were of a more recent vintage.

From 1946 to 1949 Gardner becomes a part of a mystical Christian sect, practices with Druids, receives a charter from Aleister Crowley to begin an O.T.O. camp, and writes for the English Folk-Lore Society. None of these sound like things a Witch absolutely dedicated to his practice would be doing. He seems to be searching for something to fill the void, and comes up empty. (Many Witches today are a part of groups outside Witchcraft, but what's striking about Gardner during this time period is just *how many* groups he becomes involved with.)

Eventually Gardner gives up on finding something else and starts recreating the Witchcraft he was initiated into back in 1939. Since he would just be working from memory, he borrows from a number of esoteric sources to fill in the gaps. It's also possible that he might have a written record of some of their rites. They might have also borrowed from and adapted grimoires such as the *Key of Solomon*. This would explain the magickal system used in Gardner's novel *High Magic's Aid* (1949) and the amount of similar material in what is now known as *Ye Bok of Ye Art Magical* (Gardner's first working Book of Shadows).[26]

---

26. That's not a typo. Gardner really did call his book a "bok," most likely in an attempt to make its contents feel more ancient than they truly were. *Ye Bok* is often abbreviated as *the BAM* by many Witches.

When Gardner doesn't find a spiritual home with the groups he was using to "fill in the gaps" since his forced departure from the New Forest Coven, he convinces Woodford-Grimes to begin practicing again, just the two of them, with perhaps Grimes's daughter Rosanne as a third member. Being an excitable sport, Gardner finds himself unable to keep his mouth shut about Witchcraft and starts talking to newspapers about it, and eventually writes a book on the subject that's published in 1954.

With the publicity, Gardner finds himself in a position where he has to create a Witch-cult quickly. He uses what he has from *Ye Bok*, along with an awful lot of material from Aleister Crowley (which he was possibly entitled to use due to his O.T.O. charter).[27] Second- and third-degree elevations are also written (although there's nothing to suggest that Gardner ever received more than one initiation, and certainly no elevations), adopting the Masonic model of three degrees. By the time Gardner gets around to creating a fully functioning Book of Shadows, he has several initiates, most notably Doreen Valiente, who would go on to write most of the best material not only in what would become the Gardnerian Book of Shadows but in all of Modern Witchcraft.

The publicity is probably too much for Woodford-Grimes, who seems to cease actively being a part of Gardner's life after the publication of *Witchcraft Today*. That probably wasn't all that big of a deal to Gardner, who was now firmly committed to sharing his version of Witchcraft with the world.

And share it he did. No one knows just how many Wiccan-Witches there are in the world today, but I've read estimates in the United States as high as two million.[28] While I think that number is probably an exaggeration, even just half that would still be impressive. We've come

---

27. I'm quite possibly underselling the amount of Crowley material that was used by Gardner, with some sources estimating that 80 percent of his Book of Shadows was borrowed from Crowley. For more, read "A New and Greater Pagan Cult: Gerald Gardner & the Ordo Templi Orientis" by Rodney Orpheus, http://rodneyorpheus.com /writings/occult/a-new-and-greater-pagan-cult-gerald-gardner-ordo-templi-orientis.

28. Although accurate numbers are hard to come by, the Religious Tolerance website has a series of posts making a good argument for there being two million Witches: http://www.religioustolerance.org/estimated-number-of-wiccans-in-the-united -states-7.htm.

a long way from Gardner's strange little initiation ritual nearly eighty years ago!

A Gerald Gardner Timeline

Gardner's life as a public Witch spanned only about fifteen years. During that period of time he would work tirelessly to promote the Witch-cult he loved. Before becoming the first public Modern Witch, Gardner had several experiences that helped prepare the way for that task. The following timeline is not exhaustive, but it does look at some of the more important moments in Gardner's journey.

Gerald Brosseau Gardner, 1884–1964

1884 Gerald Brosseau Gardner is born in Lancashire, England.

1888–1904 Gardner departs England with his nursemaid Josephine (Com) McCombie. Com would basically raise Gardner, and the two spent most of their time abroad. Gardner would stay overseas with Com (and later her husband) until 1904.

1904–1926 Gardner works mainly abroad in Borneo, Malaya, Ceylon (Sri Lanka), and Singapore.

1927 Gerald marries Dorothea (Donna) Frances Rosedale during a rare visit home to England. After a whirlwind courtship and marriage, the two head back east.

1936 Gardner's first book, *Keris and Other Malay Weapons*, is published. He and Donna return to England, though Gardner would continue to travel abroad with frequency for the rest of his life.

1938 Gerald and Donna move to New Forest.

July 1938 Gardner joins the Rosicrucian Order Crotona Fellowship.

September 1, 1939 World War II begins.

September 1939 (after the British join the war) Gardner is initiated into a Witch coven near New Forest.

December 1939 Gardner releases the fiction novel *A Goddess Arrives.* Most of the book was written before his initiation and tells the tale of a woman named Dayonis who becomes the inspiration for the goddess Aphrodite.

August 1940 Operation Cone of Power takes place. Gardner claims the ritual was done four times, but whether that was on four separate occasions or four times in one night is unclear (see chapter 6).

September 2, 1945 World War II ends.

Sometime in 1945 (or earlier) Gardner's estrangement from the original New Forest Coven begins. This would explain his involvement in various other esoteric orders before returning to Witchcraft in 1949. Perhaps he was kicked out of the New Forest group or was just given the brush-off.

1946 Gardner becomes involved in the Folk-Lore Society and the Ancient Druid Order and is ordained a priest in the Ancient British Church. He seems to be involved in everything but Witchcraft.

May 1947 Gardner first meets Aleister Crowley. After Crowley's death in December of 1947, Gardner theoretically becomes the head of the O.T.O. in Europe (though he would never really do anything with the position).

November 1947–March 1948 Gardner and Donna move to Memphis, Tennessee (USA), to live with Gerald's brother Douglas. We don't know what Gardner did while in the States, but he may have sought out practitioners of Voodoo (see chapter 12).

1949 This is the year when Gardner most likely begins crafting his own Witch rituals, attempting to recreate the ones he first experienced with the New Forest Coven. Gardner put his "new rituals" into a book that would come to be known as *Ye Bok of Ye Art Magical*, which served as a kind of "proto" Book of Shadows. Gardner's coven in 1949 probably consisted of him, Edith Woodford-Grimes, and Edith's daughter Rosanne.

July 1949 Gardner's *High Magic's Aid* is published in London.

1950 Gardner initiates Barbara Vickers and her husband, Gilbert, into the Wica. They are probably the first initiates into Gardner's Witchcult.

June 1951 The Fraudulent Mediums Act of 1951 repeals the Witchcraft Act of 1735, making it legal to call oneself a Witch in the United Kingdom. I think the importance of this act has been overstated, but it was still significant. Coinciding with the repeal, Gardner and Cecil Williamson open the Folklore Centre of Superstition and Witchcraft on the Isle of Man. The two would eventually have a falling-out in 1954, with Williamson selling the museum to Gardner and, shortly thereafter, opening up his own. (Williamson's museum is still in operation today and is now called the Museum of Witchcraft and Magic.)

July 1951 Gardner publicly states that he is a Witch in the *Sunday Pictorial* newspaper.

Autumn 1951 The first Gardnerian Witch coven is established at Bricket Wood, Hertfordshire, England. I'm being rather conservative with the date here, as there are some who claim that it might date back to the late 1940s. The Bricket Wood Coven is still active today.

1952 Gardner meets Doreen Valiente, whom he initiates in 1953. Valiente would go on to rewrite many of Gardner's rituals and compose the most well-known version of the Charge of the Goddess.

November 1954 The first nonfiction book about Modern Witchcraft is released, Gardner's *Witchcraft Today*. A second printing occurred in 1956.

May–June 1955 Several articles on Witchcraft are published in the *Sunday Pictorial*. Gardner is interviewed for the series, and his interview appears in the June 17 edition. (It is not flattering.)

1956 By 1956 Gardner had participated in the initiation of at least a dozen individuals, perhaps more.

March 1957 Doreen Valiente and several others leave the Bricket Wood Coven due to Gardner's "publicity seeking." Jack Bracelin and Dayonis would later take over as High Priest and High Priestess.

1959 Gardner's final book, *The Meaning of Witchcraft*, is published. In the latter half of the year, Gardner initiates and then elevates to the third degree a woman named Olive Green, who is acting as a spy for one of Gardner's detractors. Bits of her Book of Shadows would be published in 1964 in the pamphlet *Witch*.

May 1960 Gardner's wife, Donna, dies.

September 1960 The first Gardner biography, *Gerald Gardner: Witch*, is published. The book credits Bricket Wood Coven member Jack Bracelin as the author, but at least some of the manuscript was written by Sufi mystic Idries Shah (a friend of Gardner's) and much of it comes from Gerald himself. *Gerald Gardner: Witch* contains the story of Gardner's initiation and Operation Cone of Power, and is the only firsthand account of those two events.

February 12, 1964 Gardner dies while on a voyage abroad. His remains are then buried in Tunisia.

OTHER WITCHCRAFTS: LOOKING BEYOND GERALD GARDNER

Gerald Gardner was the first modern, public Witch to engage in and practice rituals we'd recognize today as Witchcraft. I think Gardner's version of Witchcraft has become the most influential in the Western world, but there are other kinds of Witchcraft out there, and many of those Witchcrafts claim to be older than Gardner's. I'm generally dubious of such claims, but I can't rule them out entirely.

Magick is tenacious, and it's not a tremendously big step to go from a family practice of magick to Witchcraft. I think many of the folks who have claimed to predate Gardner most certainly had a magickal background; I just doubt that they would have called themselves Witches until at least the 1920s, and probably not until after the repeal of the Witchcraft Act in 1951. There are no newspapers, books, or magazine articles profiling a living Witchcraft tradition until Gardner. Does that mean they didn't exist? Not necessarily, but it makes some claims more difficult to believe than others.

Wiccan-Witchcraft is both sensible and flexible. Its worldview is compatible with anyone who holds the natural world in awe, and it has room inside its circle for all kinds of magickal practice. I think people discovered Modern Witchcraft and added personal elements to it, and since those elements most likely predated Gardner, they began to think of their Witchcraft as somehow "older." The debates about what's older and what's more recent are rather pointless anyway. The smart Witch simply uses what works.

The following traditions and individuals are some of the "other" early Witch traditions and are sometimes said to predate Gardner's version of the Craft. Even if they aren't any older than the Witchcraft transmitted by Gardner, they've all made serious contributions to the Craft and are still practiced today. There are many branches on the Witchcraft tree!

The Anderson Feri Tradition

The most influential Witchcraft in the United States outside that of Gardner and his imitators/descendants is the Feri Tradition started in the San Francisco Bay Area in the early 1960s by Victor (1917–2001) and Cora (1915–2008) Anderson. In many parts of North America, the Feri Tradition is more of a whispered secret than a thriving tradition, but there are Feri covens in most large cities today, especially on the West and East Coasts.

Feri has mostly remained an initiation-only/oathbound tradition, but several Feri initiates have written some of the most well-known and beloved books of the Witchcraft revival. Starhawk (born in 1951), who went on to write *The Spiral Dance* (1979) and help found the Reclaiming tradition of Witchcraft, was a student of Victor and Cora's, and their tradition directly influences much of the Witchcraft she presents in her books.

The Feri Tradition as transmitted by Victor and Cora Anderson is a combination of many different elements. Cora, who was born in Alabama, came from a family of magick practitioners. Victor claimed to have been sexually initiated into Witchcraft at the age of nine and to have joined a coven at the age of fourteen (1932) in Ashland, Oregon.

That coven (named the Harpy Coven) was a unique blend of Huna,[29] folk magick, and Luciferian principles. The Harpy Coven did not honor a goddess, but only a male god who opposed Christianity.[30]

I'm not convinced that a magickal group would have identified itself as a coven in 1932, but the rest of Victor's story is certainly believable. The Harpy Coven as described by Victor seemed to focus on practical magick and less on ritual and theology. We even have a rough idea of who some of the members of that coven might have been thanks to the research of Bay Area High Priestess Valerie Voigt.[31]

While it's hard to imagine a nine-year-old Victor being sexually initiated in our world, one of the things that made him extremely unique as a Witch was just how often he traveled on the astral plane. Victor suffered from near blindness beginning in his childhood years, and as a result his experiences on the astral plane were often just as real to him as those in this world. It's possible that Victor had a sexual experience in that "other realm."

The Feri Tradition is often said to be a Witchcraft tradition that existed before Gardner, but Victor's own words seem to contradict that claim. When asked by journalist Margot Adler when he decided to form a coven, he replied, "It was when Gerald Gardner put out his book *Witchcraft Today*. I thought to myself, 'Well if that much is known ... it all fits together.'"[32]

Certainly the vision of the Andersons was unique when it comes to Witchcraft, as it looks nothing like the Wiccan-Witchcraft most of us are familiar with. It's also not a direct continuation of the practices of the Harpy Coven. I think it represents the summation of all the knowledge and experience soaked up by the Andersons during their lifetimes.

---

29. Huna is a magickal and philosophical system that was created in 1936 by novelist Max Freedom Long. Huna is often described as a "Hawaiian" practice, but it was actually created by Long and then given a pseudo-historical backstory. If Huna was incorporated into the practices of the Harpy Coven, then Anderson must have been a part of it for at least four to five years.

30. Kelly, *A Tapestry of Witches*, 29.

31. Ibid.

32. Adler, *Drawing Down the Moon*, 79.

Central Valley Wicca

California's Central Valley is a huge stretch of land located in the middle of California between the California coast and the Sierra Nevada mountain range. It's generally an agricultural region, though it's also home to Sacramento, California's capital. It's not the kind of place one generally associates with Witchcraft, but it's the birthplace of a unique Witch tradition that might possibly stretch back to the original New Forest Coven.

Central Valley Wicca was started in the early 1960s with a Gardnerian-style Book of Shadows, predating the "official" arrival of Gardnerian Witchcraft in the United States via Raymond Buckland in 1962. I've heard several different origin stories dealing with Central Valley Wicca over the years. The one most familiar to me is of a World War II–era serviceman becoming an initiate in Great Britain during the war, receiving a Book of Shadows, and then bringing the Craft back to the US. Other possible origins for the original Book of Shadows used by early Wiccans in the Central Valley include a schoolteacher from nearby Berkeley who openly claimed to be a Witch in 1961, along with an abandoned Book of Shadows (and some working tools) found by some individuals who used it to begin the tradition.[33]

What makes Central Valley Wicca so interesting is the claim that the Book of Shadows in use by that group closely resembles Gerald Gardner's first magick book, known today as *Ye Bok of Ye Art Magical* (and it also predates the Gardnerian Book of Shadows by several years). This has led some to wonder if Gardner and the author of the original Central Valley text copied their books from an earlier source. If that turns out to be the case, it's another piece of evidence confirming the existence of the New Forest Coven.[34]

However, the Central Valley Wicca Book of Shadows is oathbound, which means it's unavailable to most of us. And even those who have been allowed to see it can only talk about how it might resemble Gardner's *Ye Bok,* due to oaths of secrecy. It's all quite a conundrum. The

---

33. Kelly, *A Tapestry of Witches,* 52.
34. Magliocco, *Witching Culture,* 52.

Central Valley Book of Shadows could be a huge piece of the puzzle or simply another dead end. We will never really know for sure.

Cochrane's Craft

Robert Cochrane (1931–1966, birth name Roy Bowers) was an extremely influential Witch who rose to prominence in the early 1960s in England. Cochrane is the first person to be readily identified with the practice of what many today call *Traditional Witchcraft*. He also introduced several new tools and ritual practices to the Craft.

Cochrane is an extremely important figure but also an elusive one. He didn't write any books, and many of the letters and magazine articles he authored are deliberately written to confuse and mislead. He was also a rather combative figure, credited with coining the name *Gardnerian* to describe Gardner's initiates as a form of slander. He also once hoped to instigate "a Night of the Long Knives with the Gardnerians," which is just as awful and violent as it sounds.[35]

Despite his failings as a human being, Cochrane was said to be an amazing ritualist. Doreen Valiente credits Cochrane for giving her the opportunity "to take part in some of the best outdoor sabbats" she was ever a part of.[36] Letters from Cochrane to the American Joseph Bearwalker Wilson (1942–2004) became some of the core material that led to the establishment of the 1734 Tradition of Witchcraft and later the Ancient Keltic Church founded by Ann and David Finnin. Cochrane's original working group, the Clan of Tubal Cain, is still in existence, though I think much of their philosophy has shifted away from Cochrane's original vision. In many ways Robert Cochrane is more influential today than he ever was during his lifetime.

Cochrane claimed to be from a family of hereditary Witches, but that seems unlikely. One of Cochrane's nephews has denied that the family had any links to the Craft, and his widow later said that the "hereditary

---

35. Valiente, *The Rebirth of Witchcraft*, 129. Valiente's memoir is fabulous, and its most captivating chapter relates her experience with Cochrane.

36. Ibid., 125.

witch" stories were not literal truth.[37] Cochrane's rituals also shed some light on the "age" of his Witch practice. Though often strikingly original, many of the ideas in them are rather contemporary. Cochrane was deeply influenced by the book *The White Goddess* (published in 1948), written by English poet and novelist Robert Graves (1895–1985).

Graves is one of the most influential figures in the Modern Witch-craft revival, though he himself did not identify as a Witch (or a Pagan). *The White Goddess* was the first book to articulate the idea of the Great Goddess as a being in three parts: Maiden, Mother, and Crone. While Maiden, Mother, and Crone goddesses certainly existed in antiquity, they weren't generally seen as three parts of a greater whole. The fact that the idea shows up in Cochrane's rituals hints that they were con-temporary and not centuries old.

Though I doubt that the Bowers (Cochrane's legal last name) fam-ily had a long history of Witchcraft, there are parts of his practice that might have a firm grounding in folk magick practices. Cochrane and his wife, Jane, worked for a time on barges that traversed the narrow ca-nals in the Midlands of England. Certain families who are a part of that profession are said to be called "water witches" by some, and they very well may have had their own magickal practice or tradition that was absorbed by or taught to Cochrane in some fashion.[38]

I think another likely prospect for a bit of the "old and traditional" in Cochrane's Craft comes not from the magickal world but from the fraternal one. The Horseman's Word was a secret society for those who worked with horses in the British Isles that began in Scotland during the early nineteenth century. Many of their rituals contained elements that might be considered esoteric, and they included figures such as the Christian Devil and the Hebrew blacksmith Tubal Cain. Cochrane him-self worked as a blacksmith, and it's possible that he had some interac-tions with those who knew the traditions of the Horsemen. (It's also possible that his circle was called the Clan of Tubal Cain because of that work.) This is all just conjecture on my part, but I think it's an intriguing

---

37. Howard, *Children of Cain*, 48 and 56. Howard's history of Cochrane is essential reading.

38. Ibid., 42.

possibility. (In chapter 7 we'll look at the Horseman's Word in greater depth, and you'll see just how "witchy" their rituals could be.)

Though Cochrane greatly disliked Gardnerians, many of his ritual practices were directly inspired by them. The phrase *drawing down the moon* (see chapter 11) was completely unrelated to divine possession by a Goddess or God prior to its use by Gardner and his initiates, yet it shows up in the writings of the Clan of Tubal Cain no later than 1962.[39] There's also some evidence to suggest that Cochrane himself was a Gardnerian initiate or at least had dealings with Gardnerians before despising them.

In the end, the origins of Cochrane's Craft are immaterial. What matters is that they work. Today thousands of Witches use a stang in ritual and dance the turning of the mill, both ritual innovations begun by Cochrane. He was also one of the first Witches to work exclusively robed (instead of skyclad) and take Witch rituals from the parlor to the great outdoors.

Speculation is pointless, but I can't help but wonder what Modern Witchcraft would be like today if Cochrane hadn't committed suicide near Midsummer in 1966. With his coven and marriage in disarray, Cochrane drank a potion containing belladonna on the night before the solstice and died in a hospital bed nine days later. He left behind a suicide note, so his death was not an accident. By all accounts he was a deeply talented Witch and an intensely charismatic man. I think he would be happy with many of the things done today in his name.

---

39. John of Monmouth, *Genuine Witchcraft Is Explained*, 475. This is one of the best books ever put together on Cochrane and includes many of his rituals and coven notes. It's essential reading for Craft history nerds like myself.

$\mathcal{R}$ituals and the Literary Influence

We'll never know for sure just what the rituals of the earliest Modern Witches were like. However, based on the available evidence we can speculate a bit. We know which groups influenced and inspired Witches like Gerald Gardner, and we know which books first cast Witchcraft in a somewhat positive light. Two of those books, Charles Leland's *Aradia, or the Gospel of the Witches* and Margaret Murray's *The Witch-Cult in Western Europe*, not only were influential a hundred or so years ago but remain influential today.

Just like today's Witches use a variety of written sources to construct their rituals, our forebears did the same, only there were far fewer books to choose from. Using material from groups like the Freemasons, along with books such as *Aradia*, it's possible to create rituals as they might have looked a hundred years ago. I'm not arguing that the first Modern Witches were enacting rituals like the ones that follow, but they could have.

THE 1899 RITUAL AND CHARLES LELAND'S ARADIA, OR THE GOSPEL OF THE WITCHES

There are two books that stand above all others when it comes to reestablishing Witchcraft in the modern age. The first of those is *Aradia, or the Gospel of the Witches* (1899) by Charles Godfrey Leland (1824–1903). Leland's book allegedly contains some of the mythology, spellwork, and rituals of an Italian Witch-cult that is said to still be operating in Italy.

Leland's source for *Aradia* was a young woman known in his writings as Magdalena, though her real name was most likely Margherita.[40] We don't know much about Magdalena, but she most certainly existed, as some of Leland's friends attested to interacting with her. The material that makes up *Aradia* was written down by Magdalena and then given to Leland over the course of several years. Sadly, none of that correspondence exists today, but we do have some of Leland's notes translating Magdalena's Italian into English. *Aradia* does not contain all of the material she gave to Leland, but it does contain much of it.

Unlike today's Witchcraft, the magickal system written about by Leland is extremely adversarial. An early version of what would come to be known as the Charge of the Goddess concludes with the line "until the last your oppressors shall be dead." The mythology in *Aradia* is an interesting mix of both ancient pagan and Christian. The parents of the goddess Aradia are the Roman Diana (who has long been associated with witches) and a figure known to us from the Bible, Lucifer.

While Aradia has become a very popular goddess in Modern Witchcraft circles, she's completely absent from the written record before 1899. Some scholars have linked her to the historical figure Herodias (who was partially responsible for the death of John the Baptist), who was seen as a spectral witch-like figure in various parts of Italy. Legends of Herodias were often intermingled with those of the goddess of witchcraft, Diana.[41]

---

40. Leland, *Aradia, or the Gospel of the Witches (A New Translation)*, trans. Mario and Dina Pazzaglini, 30. This 1998 edition of *Aradia* includes a new translation of the text by Mario and Dina Pazzaglini, along with several essays that help to give the reader a better sense of Leland's world. This is the definitive version of *Aradia*, though sadly it now exists only as an ebook.

41. Magliocco, *Ten Years of Triumph of the Moon*. My brief paragraph summary here comes from Magliocco's article "Aradia in Sardinia: The Archeology of a Folk Character" on pages 40–58. The most comprehensive look at Aradia as an echo of Herodias can be found in this book.

There's nothing in the text suggesting that Magdalena's material is ancient. If it represents an Italian Witch tradition (which I think is likely), that tradition was no more than a few hundred years old by the time Leland wrote about it in the 1890s. There's also no evidence that Magdalena's witch group was widespread, and now 120 years later she remains our only witness to its existence. (There have been many authors who have claimed some sort of link to the Witches found in *Aradia*. I don't find any of those claims very credible, but I respect their work as fascinating reimaginings and additions to the original.)

Though evidence of Magdalena's witch group is a bit lacking, the magickal material found in *Aradia* is not unique to that work. Magickal systems often exist separate from religious tradition, and even today there are still individuals in Italy who are using spells and incantations similar to those found in *Aradia*.[42] I'm of the opinion that the Witchcraft found in *Aradia* represents a real magickal and spiritual system, though it may not be as ancient as some would like.

The antiquity or "truth" of *Aradia* is ultimately of little consequence. What's important is just how influential it's been over the last 120 years. I think it's one of the most important books of the Witchcraft revival, and people are still using bits of it in ritual. It's an often overlooked classic and directly influenced Gerald Gardner and the thousands (and now millions) of Witches who came after him.

THE STORY OF THE 1899 RITUAL

The 1899 Ritual is an attempt at creating a ritual that generally only uses material that was readily available in 1899 or earlier. I chose the year 1899 for this ritual because it's both the year *Aradia* was published and it simply sounded a lot better than the 1898 Ritual or the 1900 Ritual. I put it together with my friend Dr. Christopher Chase (who now teaches religious studies at Iowa State University) shortly after reading Ronald Hutton's *The Triumph of the Moon* (published in 1999).

---

42. Leland, *Aradia, or the Gospel of the Witches (A New Translation)*, trans. Mario and Dina Pazzaglini, 86–87. I cannot put into words how great and valuable this book is.

For this ritual I used the material found in *Aradia* and supplemented it with additional sources. It's certainly possible that there may have been a group of Witches or other magickal folk doing something similar to the ritual presented here, decades before Gardner. When I read about alleged Witch groups operating before Gardner, some of their goings-on sound similar to what I put into the 1899 Ritual.

Over the years I've tinkered with the ritual and eventually started presenting it at large Pagan gatherings. A friend of mine once said that everything in the ritual is similar to yet somehow different from everything we do in our coven, and I think that's an apt description. There are lots of parts that are familiar until they are turned on their head. The ritual includes footnotes indicating where the material in it can be found. Nearly all of it comes from the sources that influenced Gardner and other early Witches: Freemasonry, the grimoire tradition, and of course Leland's *Aradia*. Some of my favorite bits come from the poetry of the nineteenth century.

In the process of writing this book, someone asked me why anyone would want to enact the 1899 Ritual. It could be because of the workings, one for protection and one for good luck, but for me the ritual is mostly about connection. Even if there were no self-identifying Witches in 1899, the world was moving ever closer to that reality. The people in 1899 who were praising Pan in poetry, casting circles, and holding a Pagan worldview are at the very least our magickal cousins. This ritual is a way to connect with them and a chance to reflect on how far our rituals have come as Witches.

Ritual Roles

High Priestess/High Priest: These two individuals lead the ritual.

Guardian: Casts and releases the circle. Should look somewhat menacing.

Quarter Callers: One quarter caller each at the east, south, west, and north. All four have small roles in the ritual beyond summoning the elements.

Materials Needed

A red cord for the door

Sword

Altar

Shallow bowl full of small stones

2 bottles of wine

Candle

Scroll to be read for the god Pan

Cakes/bread

Cup/chalice

The ritual presented here was written for a large group, and in my mind's eye I imagined it being something like a group of Freemasons or Rosicrucians instead of Witches. Since most of us don't work with a circle of fifty people, I've also included a second working at the end of the ritual designed for a smaller group, called the Conjuration of the Lemons and the Pins.

THE 1899 RITUAL

Begin the ritual with silence and low light to quiet everyone in attendance. (If more light is needed, the lights can be turned on once the Guardian has sealed the door.) The altar should include one lit candle.

High Priest: *Are all here now a part of the Craft or those who would seek its mysteries?*

High Priestess: *They are. The door may be sealed.*

The Guardian seals the door with a banishing pentagram of earth, then lays a red cord over the door handles.

Guardian: *The door is sealed and now protected from all cowans and eavesdroppers. None shall pass through except for those who have permission from the High Priest or High Priestess.*

High Priestess: *So mote it be!*

Everyone turns and faces the east while the quarters are called.

East Quarter Caller: *As the sun rises in the east and pushes back the night, we give our first blessings to the spirits that dwell there. So mote it be!*

South Quarter Caller: *As the sun in the south at the high meridian is the beauty and glory of the day, we give blessings to the spirits that dwell there. So mote it be!*

West Quarter Caller: *As the sun sets in the west and joins in harmony with the moon and night, we give our blessings to the spirits that dwell there. So mote it be!*

North Quarter Caller: *As the moon rises in the north and is the magick and mystery of the night, we give blessings to the spirits who dwell there. So mote it be!* [43]

The Guardian picks the sword up from the altar and casts the circle clockwise.

Guardian: *When we enter herein with all humility, let the gods enter into this circle by the entrance of an eternal happiness, of a divine prosperity, of a perfect joy, of an abundant charity, of an eternal salutation. Let all the demons fly from this place, especially those who are opposed unto this work, and let the angels of peace assist and protect this circle, from which let discord and strife fly and depart. Magnify and extend upon us, O Lord and Goddess, and bless our conversation and our assembly. Sanctify, O ye gods, our humble entry herein, thou the blessed and holy ones of the eternal ages. So mote it be!* [44]

The Guardian wraps the cord around the handle of the door, symbolizing that it's locked. This can be held by the nearest quarter caller and

---

43. The entire opening bit and quarter calls were borrowed and adapted slightly from Masonic ritual, most notably *Duncan's Masonic Ritual and Monitor* by Malcom Duncan, published in 1866. The word *cowan* is used by Masons to signify a non-initiate. Many Modern Witches use it to refer to non-Witches.

44. Samuel Liddle MacGregor Mathers (translator), *The Key of Solomon the King (Clavicula Salomonis)*, first published in 1899. The copy on my bookshelf is the Weiser edition from 2016, with a foreword by Joseph H. Peterson.

handed to him, or he can wear it as a belt. When done with this, the Guardian puts the sword back on the altar.

High Priest: *There are many here who have gathered tonight to learn the secrets of Witchcraft and sorcery. My Lady, are those who stand before us worthy of the ways of the Witch and the Wizard?*

High Priestess: *Those gathered here this night have overcome many trials and tribulations to be with us. I deem them worthy candidates.*

High Priest: *Do all of you gather here tonight of your own free will and accord?*

All Participants: *Yes.*

High Priestess: *The mysteries are given unto you, but they are not yours to pass on. Great and terrible things shall be done to you in the names of the gods if you give up their secrets. Before we proceed, are there those of you unable or unwilling to accept the sacred trust we give you this night?*

Pause.

High Priestess: *If all here are true and honest men and women, then we shall proceed, and if you're not true and honest, your punishment shall be delivered CRUELLY BY THE GODS!*

Dramatic pause.

High Priestess: *Are all here duly and truly prepared for the horrors and blessings that may chance upon them from here on forward?*

All Participants: *Yes.*

High Priest: *Priestess, by what right do these candidates come forward?*

High Priestess: *By being born free men and women of good repute and well recommended.*

High Priest: *The names of our gods and our signs shall be revealed.*

High Priestess: *We worship the goddess Diana, she of the new moon and midnight groves, and we honor her with a kiss.* Hail Diana!*

*As the High Priestess says this, she places two fingers to her mouth and kisses them, then lifts them to the sky in a salute.

High Priest: *We worship the god Pan, earthly shepherd and guardian of the wild realms. We honor him with this sign* placed over our heart and then lifted toward the sky. Hail Pan!*[45]

* As the High Priest says this, he makes the sign of Pan (metal horns).

Sign of Pan (Metal Horns)

High Priestess: *Now we adore the sun who is King of all the Wizards.*

High Priestess: *As the sun sinks down into night we turn toward the west* (Pause, turn.) *to adore the sun, eternal source of light and life. Hail unto the sun who makes way for night! Hail to thee for the joy you bring and safe travels in your journey through the heavens. The sun shines down upon us, dispensing justice, wisdom, and power. Hail the sun!*[46]

High Priest: *Now we adore the moon, who is the Queen of all the Witches.*

---

45. The idea of using signs and symbols and wishing awful deaths upon people was borrowed from the Masons but was obviously adapted since they don't worship Pan and Diana. Diana was chosen for this ritual because she appears in *Aradia*, and Pan because he was the most written-about deity in nineteenth-century English literature.

46. Many Golden Dawn temples do some sort of sun adoration, and since I needed an invocation to balance the God and Goddess calls, I created this.

High Priestess: *When I shall have departed from this world,*
 Whenever ye have need of anything,
 Once in the month, and when the moon is full,
 Ye shall assemble in some desert place,
 Or in a forest all-together join
 To adore the potent spirit of your queen, Our mother, great Diana.
 She who fain Would learn all sorcery yet has not won Its deepest secrets,
 them my mother will Teach her, in truth all things as yet unknown.
 And ye shall all be freed from slavery, And so ye shall be free in everything;
 And as the sign that ye are truly free,
 Ye shall be naked in your rites, both men
 And women also: this shall last until
 The last of your oppressors shall be dead. [47]

High Priest: *In whose name and under whose symbol do we gather this night?*

High Priestess: *We gather in the name of Pan, and his horns are his symbol.*
 All who would worship him must make this sign* and hold it aloft, for it is
 dear to him.

* As the High Priestess says this, she raises her hand in the salute to Pan (metal horns).

High Priest: *I dare not sleep for delight of the perfect hour,*
 Lest God be wroth that his gift should be scorned of man.
 The face of the warm bright world is the face of a flower,
 The word of the wind and the leaves that the light winds fan
 As the word that quickened at first into flame, and ran,
 Creative and subtle and fierce with invasive power,
 Through darkness and cloud, from the breath of the one God, Pan
 We call the sun, that lit us when life began
 To brood on the world that is thine by his grace for a span,

---

47. Much of this call to the moon is better known today as the Charge of the Goddess, a text used in many Witch covens. This "proto" version comes directly from Leland's *Aradia*.

Conceals and reveals in the semblance of things that are
Thine immanent presence, the pulse of thy heart's life, Pan. [48]

High Priest: *In whose name do we also gather this night?*

High Priestess: *We gather tonight in the name of Diana, Queen of the Witches. It is she whom we adore, which is why her sign is the kiss. Blow a kiss to our Lady and then keep your arms raised and I shall summon Diana.*

All gathered blow Diana a kiss.

High Priestess: *I AM that which began;*
Out of me the years roll;
Out of me God and man;
I am equal and whole;
God changes, and man, and the form of them bodily; I am the soul.
Before ever land was,
Before ever the sea,
Or soft hair of the grass,
Or fair limbs of the tree,
Or the flesh-colour'd fruit of my branches,
I was, and thy soul was in me.
First life on my sources
First drifted and swam;
Out of me are the forces
That save it or damn;
Out of me man and woman, and wild-beast and bird:
before God was, I am. [49]

---

48. This part is an excerpt from Algernon Charles Swinburne's poem "A Nympholept," published in 1894 in the book *Astrophel and Other Poems*. It's a very long poem and this is just a tiny bit of it.

49. This is more Algernon Charles Swinburne, this time from his poem "Hertha," originally published in the volume *Songs Before Sunrise* in 1871. This is only an excerpt, but the whole thing reads just like this. It's great!

The Conjuration of the Stones

High Priestess: *All gifts come from her, she whom we call Diana, Goddess of Witches and Sorcery. She dwells in the east and in the west, and when she walks among the world of mortals, she gives many blessings. From the west there are the waters and the gift of her blood, the wine. We drink the sacred and purifying wine of Great Diana. From the east she brings us the very stone of the earth, the rocks that form the ground beneath our feet. In times of need she presents these gifts to us and we soak the earth in her blood to make it divine.*

The east quarter caller presents the bowl of stones to the High Priestess. The west quarter caller presents the bottle or decanter of wine to the Priestess, who then pours it into the rocks while shouting to Diana.

High Priestess: *The blood of Diana! The heart of the mother!*

The east quarter caller, still carrying the bowl of stones, presents them to everyone at the ritual, allowing each person to choose one wine-soaked stone.

High Priest: *Now blessed by the blood of Diana, we present each of you with a stone. Hold it under your tongue while the ancient magicks are recited upon it, speaking the words of the Priestess after she shares them with you.* [50]

(When my coven did this ritual for several hundred people, we also had an alternate bowl of stones soaked in grape juice. Also, watching everyone recite this very long incantation with a stone under their tongue is the best part of the ritual.)

In this next part, the High Priestess will say one line at a time and then pause to let all the participants repeat it.

High Priestess: *Stone, who by some wizard or some witch*
Hast certainly been buried long ago

---

50. This entire working was adapted from Charles Leland's book *Etruscan Roman Remains*, published in 1892. The spell used here originally called for the use of amethyst instead of a "stone," but that sounded expensive to me so I changed it to something easier. The original version does not call for placing the stone under the tongue either, but it's more fun this way.

Because thou wouldst not bring good luck to others
Now it is plain that thou hast repented
And has wished to recall it to me
And I know right well how to preserve it.
I conjure thee, O Stone!
I conjure this stone to ever bring me fortune!
And that it may free me from all evil.
Specially from foes
Who fain would cause me some deceit.
May this stone free me!
Should any wish to cause harm against me,
Whether by thought or deed
This piece of wine-stone shall ever be
My Wizard, freeing me from it!
I conjure thee, O stone!
I conjure thee, O stone!
I conjure thee, O stone! [51]

Each participant removes the stone from their mouth. If this is done deliberately by the High Priest and the quarter callers so that everyone can see it happening, there's no need to announce it.

High Priestess: *This stone shall now protect you from all those who would seek to do you harm. Keep it forever upon your person and you shall be safe from all sorcery. So mote it be!*

The Calling of Pan

The south quarter caller takes the candle from the altar and slowly moves around the circle clockwise as the opening invocation to Pan is read by the High Priestess. The north quarter caller now either picks up the scroll to Pan to be read by the High Priest or just has it upon their person, ready to give to the High Priest.

---

51. This is mostly how the conjuration appears in Leland's *Etruscan Roman Remains*, but I changed a few lines here and there to make it more intelligible. The original reads "Should any wish to intoxicate me, With wine, or other liquor," which I changed to "Should any wish to cause harm against me…"

High Priestess: *Deep within us the flame does glow, wild energies that*
  ebb and flow.
  Lust and passion and dark desire, the soul's eternal Pan-like fire.
  Let the flame awaken your lust, in his hands, O Pan we trust!
  This is the light and spark of Pan, tremble, weep, and take his hand.
  As his light spreads round the room, we leave this far too mortal tomb.
  Shout his name as his presence grows, We, the enlightened, those who
  know! [52]

At this point the participants in the circle should at least be whispering the name of Pan, and if not, the quarter callers should do this to let them know this is okay to do. The south fire candle caller should return to her place in the circle after the reading of the first invocation.

High Priestess: *And now the whispered promise of Pan comes to us from the*
  north. And what are those words that call to him?

The north quarter caller brings the scroll to the High Priest, who unrolls it and reads it aloud.

High Priest: *O goat-foot God of Arcady!*
  This modern world is gray and old,
  And what remains to us of thee?
  No more the shepherd lads in glee
  Throw apples at thy wattled fold,
  O goat-foot God of Arcady!
  Nor through the laurels can one see
  Thy soft brown limbs, thy beard of gold,
  And what remains to us of thee?
  And dull and dead our Thames would be,
  For here the winds are chill and cold,
  O goat-foot God of Arcady!
  Then keep the tomb of pagans past,
  Thine olive-woods, thy vine-clad wold,

---

52. This part here is not old. Alas, I wrote it simply to transition from one part of the ritual to another. If you think it sounds cool, good on me!

And what remains to us of thee?
Forgotten song rests silent an' vast
Sleeps in the reeds our rivers hold,
O goat-foot God of Arcady!
Ah, what remains to us of thee?
Oh, leave the hills of Arcady,
Thy satyrs and their wanton play,
This modern world hath need of thee.
No nymph or Faun indeed have we,
For Faun and nymph are old and gray,
Oh leave the hills of Arcady!
Come to the land of valley and sea
Where Witch and Wizard hold their sway
This modern world hath need of thee!
A people of spell and magick's key
Where enchantments faire seize the day,
The Country of bear and redwood tree
Loud our voices call for you to stay
This modern world hath need of thee
Then blow some trumpet loud and free
And give thine oaten pipe away
Oh leave the hills of Arcady
This modern world hath need of thee!
Oh leave the hills of Arcady
This modern world hath need of thee!
Oh leave the hills of Arcady
This modern world hath need of thee![53]
Ah, leave the hills of Arcady!
This fierce sea-lion of the sea,
This Golden State lacks some stronger lay,

---

53. Oscar Wilde's poem "Pan: Double Villanelle" was first published in 1909, but since Wilde died in 1900 it's a little bit older than that. It has been much adapted for this ritual. The setting for the original poem was in nineteenth-century England, but I included a few references here to California since that was where this version of the 1899 Ritual was being presented.

This modern world hath need of thee!
Then blow some trumpet loud and free,
And give thine oaten pipe away,
Ah, leave the hills of Arcady!
This modern world hath need of thee!
Ah, leave the hills of Arcady!
This modern world hath need of thee!
Ah, leave the hills of Arcady!
This modern world hath need of thee!
Ah, leave the hills of Arcady!
This modern world hath need of thee!

The last lines here are meant to be repeated over and over and turn into an energy-raising dance to welcome Pan back to the modern world. When the energy in the room has reached a crescendo, the High Priest speaks again to stop the chanting and dancing.

High Priest: *He is here, and we shall take his energy and Diana's gifts and embrace this night and this life. So mote it be!*

Cakes and Ale

High Priestess: *And now we celebrate the feast of thanksgiving, and in doing so we eat the body and blood of Great Diana.*

The High Priestess kneels before the High Priest, holding up the cakes. He holds the coven sword over the cakes.

High Priest: *We did not bake the bread, nor with it wine,*
  We did not cook the honey with the vine,
  We baked the body and the blood and soul,
  The soul of Diana who makes the years roll.
  She knew neither rest nor peace
  In cruel suffering no torments cease
  Until she granted what we most desired,
  The arch of magick growing ever higher.
  We begged it of her from our very hearts!
  And in that grace was granted by her mighty arts.

In honor of thee we hold this feast,
Feast and drain the goblet deep,
We eat this bread in our sacred hour
In the shadow of your moonlit power.
So mote it be! [54]

Cakes are passed around the circle. The High Priest takes the wine upon the altar and pours it into a cup or chalice, then kneels before the High Priestess while she picks up the coven sword and holds it against the lip of the cup.

High Priestess: *We thirst and to our knees we sink,*
  For it is the blood of Diana we drink.
  From the earth to the growing vine,
  Her blood has been transformed into wine.
  That blood shall give me good return,
  Diana handing us all we yearn.
  In drinking from this horn we drink her blood,
  The power that comes from root and stem and bud.
  We do kiss our hands in gift to the moon (All present blow a kiss
    to Diana.)
  And Diana who sits inside this very room.
  Should our fame and fortunes fall,
  It will be Diana that we call.
  Her blood is power, her eternal prayer,
  Goddess strong, wild, wicked, and fair.
  So mote it be! [55]

In the original version of this rite, we had a coven member sing a song from the era while the wine was shared.[56]

---

54. This blessing of the cakes and wine comes from *Aradia* and has been slightly adapted.

55. Not surprisingly, this is another bit from *Aradia*, again adapted to improve the rhyme.

56. During cakes and wine, a coven member of ours sang the song "The Pipes of Pan" by Adrian Ross (lyrics) and Edward Elgar (music), written in 1899. It's great having a music teacher in the family.

Closing the Circle

High Priestess: *Now as our ritual finds itself near the end, we bow toward the sun and he of the wilds, the Great God Pan.*

High Priest: *From its rays all life is. From his seed all life arises. With thanks and gratitude, we turn toward the south* (All present turn.) *and bow toward the sun as a symbol of our feelings.* (All present bow.) *Hail the sun! With thanks and gratitude, we now turn toward the north* (All present turn.), *the realm of Pan, and salute him once more with his symbol.* (All present salute with the sign of Pan.) *Hail Pan!*

Short pause.

High Priest: *Now as our ritual finds itself near the end, we bow toward the moon and she of the waves, the Lady Diana.*

High Priestess: *Her light is love, and from her touch all life arises. With thanks and gratitude, we turn toward the west* (All present turn.) *and bow to the moon as a way of paying homage to her light.* (All present bow.) *Hail the moon! With thanks and gratitude we now turn toward the east* (All present turn.), *the realm of Diana, and salute her with a kiss.* (All present blow a kiss to Diana.) *Hail Diana!*

The quarters are now dismissed clockwise, starting in the east.

East Quarter Caller: *As the sun rises in the east and pushes back the night, we give thanks for the blessings given to us by the spirits who dwell there. So mote it be!*

South Quarter Caller: *As the sun in the south at the high meridian is the beauty and glory of the day, we give thanks for the blessings given to us by the spirits that dwell there. So mote it be!*

West Quarter Caller: *As the sun sets in the west and joins in harmony with the moon and night, we give thanks for the blessings given to us by the spirits that dwell there. So mote it be!*

North Quarter Caller: *As the moon rises in the north and is the magick and mystery of the night, we give thanks to the blessings given to us by the spirits who dwell there. So mote it be!*

The Guardian walks around the circle counterclockwise twice, sword in hand as he releases the circle.

Guardian: *Be ye accursed, damned, and eternally reproved, and be ye tormented with perpetual pain, so that ye may find no repose by night nor by day, nor for a single moment or time, if ye share the secrets imparted upon this circle today! Those who break their pledge, we deprive ye of all office and dignity which ye may have enjoyed up till now; and by their virtue and power we relegate you unto a lake of sulphur and of flame, and unto the deepest depths of the abyss, that ye may burn therein eternally for ever.*[57] *By the virtue of those gathered here who have been obedient and have obeyed the commandments of our High Priestess and High Priest, all have now departed to their abodes and retreats. Be there peace between us and you. The license to depart has been granted.*

The Guardian takes the cord off the door and salutes the High Priest.

Guardian: *The circle is open.*

High Priest: *The door is now open to all cowans and eavesdroppers. All are free to enter and leave this place of their own free will. So mote it be!*

High Priestess: *I go mine, thou goest thine;*
Many ways we wend,
Many ways and many days,
Ending in one end.
Many a wrong and its crowning song,
Many a road and many an Inn;
For to roam, but only one home,
For all the world to win. [58]

~FIN~

---

57. This is again from the *Key of Solomon*, and the quarter dismissals are an adaptation from Masonic ritual.

58. That's an old Masonic goodbye.

Alternate Working: The Conjuration
of the Lemons and the Pins

If you are looking for an *Aradia*-style ritual that's a little simpler, then I suggest the Conjuration of the Lemons and the Pins. It doesn't require much in the way of tools, just lemons and pins. I'm lucky enough to have a lemon tree growing in my backyard, so we plucked our lemons directly from that tree when my coven did this ritual.

High Priest: *Tonight we perform the conjuration of the lemons and the pins. When thirteen colored pins are placed into a lemon and blessed by the goddess Diana, they bring good luck. We start our ritual by leaving our sacred space and journeying outside to the lemon tree, where we shall pick our fruits while invoking the Queen of the sun and moon—Diana!*

The following invocation should be read by the High Priestess while the coven members pick their lemons off the tree or pick them out of a bowl, if that's what you are working with. If you can move your bowl near a window so you can see the moon, all the better!

High Priestess: *At the instant when the sun had fled,*
   I have picked a lemon straight from the tree,
   I have picked a lemon to where I've been led,
   A lemon, yellow as the moon for all to see,
   Gathering with care this lemon for a boon.
   And while gathering I said with care:
   "Thou who art Queen of the sun and the moon
   And of the stars—lo! Here I call to thee fair!"
   And with what power I have I conjure thee
   To grant to me the favor I implore!
   By air, fire, water, and earth, come to me.
   Let thy presence be what I honor and adore!
   I have picked this lemon to bring me good luck.
   Held strong by my hand I present it to the sky.
   May it serve me well, magick's bargain struck,

My power to soar strong and high.
Queen of the stars! Queen of the World!
Diana, hear my prayers. [59]

After everyone has picked their lemon or chosen it from a bowl, the coven should head back to their ritual space and sit comfortably. I recommend putting the pins you'll be using for the rite in several small bowls scattered throughout the circle. The rite calls for pins of many colors, but the ones we use in our coven just have different-colored heads.

High Priestess: *Take many pins, and carefully stick them in the lemon, pins of many colors; and as thou wilt have good luck, and if thou desirest to give the lemon to any one or to a friend, thou shouldst stick in it many pins of varied colours. But if thou wilt that evil befall any one, put in it black pins.* [60]

The original version of this rite has the conjurer actively threatening Diana and invoking some pretty nasty stuff to an apparently very evil person. If that's your thing, the original text is easily found online. For my coven I wrote the following more benign conjuration.

High Priestess: *Goddess Diana, I do conjure thee,*
   And with uplifted voice to thee I call.
   Thou who gives peace and contentment,
   Come to our aid this night.
   For thee we shall pour a cup of wine in thanks. [61]
   Aid us in our magics of lemons and pins.
   Thirteen pins we shall place in this lemon,
   Pins for Lady, Lord, and the powers of this world.
   With the Witch's strength and power ,
   We shall bring about good luck. So mote it be!

---

59. The ideas here come from *Aradia*, but the words are my own.

60. Not surprisingly, this text comes directly from *Aradia*.

61. The original spell with the much more negative wording also includes a libation for Diana. If you say this line, be sure to pour a glass of wine outside for her.

The following couplets can be said by the High Priestess as each coven member inserts a pin into their lemon, or everyone present can read one, or couplets can alternate between participants.

Our first pin simply for luck,
Into the lemon it's now stuck.
Second for will that shall not break,
Our confidence to never shake.
Third for the power to overcome
Obstacles tall, wide, and fearsome.
Fourth for the sun that shines,
The Horned God and his signs.
Fifth for the moon high above,
The Lady looking down with love.
Sixth to the breeze of air that blows,
Ever increasing our luck to grow.
Seven is for fire, heat, and flame,
The Witch's power we reclaim.
Pin eight for the water and west,
We can overcome any trial or test.
The ninth pin for the sacred earth,
Eternal womb and cauldron of rebirth.
Ten pins now for the circle this night,
Home to the Witches' dance and delight.
Eleven is for our family chosen,
May the coven ever be unbroken.
Twelve is for darkness and this late hour,
As our spell is cast in moonstruck glower.
Thirteen is for Diana, goddess strong and fair,
Hear tonight our spell and listen to our prayer.
With power we have conjured upon the lemon,
The spell is struck and now our work is done! [62]

---

62. This part is not traditional in any way and was written by me.

When the spell is done, be sure to put your lemon in a safe place. When it starts to rot, bury it somewhere outside.

A RITUAL FROM MARGARET MURRAY AND THE WITCH-CULT

First published in 1921 (and pretty much continuously since), Margaret Alice Murray's *The Witch-Cult in Western Europe* (and its sequel *The God of the Witches* ten years later) is one of the most important books in the history of Modern Witchcraft. Murray (1863–1963) was a celebrated Egyptologist during her day but now is mostly known for articulating her views on Witchcraft and what's come to be known as the "Murray Hypothesis."

In *Witch-Cult* Murray argues that the people who were tried and executed as "witches" in the early modern period (1500–1800 CE) were practitioners of an organized Witch religion, or "Witch-cult." Murray's Witch-cult bears a lot of similarities to Modern Witchcraft, most likely because early Modern Witches were inspired by Murray! Murray's Witches celebrated esbats, operated in covens of thirteen, practiced magick, celebrated the natural world, and worshipped a horned male deity.

What Murray's Witches didn't do was worship or honor a goddess in any meaningful way, which is a big departure from the Witches of today.

The "witches" executed 500 years ago were mostly Christians, and while it's certainly possible that there were people who identified that way in the year 1500 CE, there's no credible evidence to suggest that they were an organized bunch. Murray's thesis has never been taken seriously by most scholars, but it's become a part of Modern Witch mythology. When I first became involved with the Craft twenty years ago, the idea that I was practicing a religion that had come down in an unbroken chain from at least the period of the witch trials was orthodoxy. Today we know better, but Murray's books still have some value.

Even though Murray's Witches weren't practicing an ancient pagan religion, her depiction of those Witches has continued to inspire. Like many other Witches, I feel a kinship with the unfortunate souls who were unjustifiably executed (murdered is a better word) by the ignorant all those centuries ago. Murray's books give life to those individuals, and they include bits of "witch ritual" that Modern Witches have been known to slip into their rites on occasion. (I put the "witch ritual" from Murray's books in quotes because it's hard to trust information that was gleaned from torture and threat of death. Many of the ritual bits shared during the witch trials most likely had very little to do with reality.)

Murray's books also describe Witchcraft as a positive religion and a true alternative to Christianity. Murray's books were some of the first popular books in English that would have made someone truly want to be a Witch. For that reason I think they are of tremendous importance. Not only that, but they also helped create the image of the Horned God that most of us honor today.

Murray took the very different mythologies of Cernunnos, Pan, and Herne and tied them all together, creating a horned and antlered god much larger and more universal than what had been worshipped before. She tied that deity to the Christian Devil but said people only worshipped him in that guise because they had forgotten his true form, as it had been corrupted by the Christian Church. Murray's "Horned God hidden in the Devil of the Witches" is a very provocative image, but I don't think it has much to do with history.

In addition to not having much to do with the Goddess, Murray's witch ritual differs from Modern Witchcraft in a number of other ways. Almost all of the ceremonial magick aspects that most of us are familiar with are absent, meaning there are no calls to the quarters (earth, air, fire, and water) or circle castings. The witch rituals that Murray writes about are generally focused on only a few things: fertility, orgies, dancing, feasting, selling one's soul to the Devil, and literal sacrifices (of children, adults, and sometimes the ritual leader). While I'm not opposed to orgies or feasting, they don't occur during ritual very often.

While trying to create a ritual from Murray's books, I chose to focus on the things that wouldn't get me in trouble with my High Priestess wife. So I chose dancing and an initiation rite. If you are curious about where the various bits of this ritual came from, those answers are in the footnotes.

Murray may not have been the most accurate historian when it comes to the witch trials of the early modern period, but she helped to inspire a lot of Witches in the present day. She was even a documented magick user! [63] I think she's probably immensely proud of the contributions she ended up making to today's Craft.

Were there self-identifying Witches who did rituals as described in Murray's books? We will probably never know for sure, but there's most certainly power in them. This ritual can be used as a coven initiation rite and/or as a way to connect with the power of the Horned God. It also makes a great Imbolc or Ostara ritual since much of it is built around the idea of waking up the earth after (or during) the winter.

Ritual Roles

Grand Magister: Murray's term for the High Priest. (Men led her witch rituals.)

Robin Goodfellow: Assistant to the Magister. Robin Goodfellow was sometimes used as an alternative name for the Devil.

Maiden: Another assistant.

If you choose to enact this ritual, it's not necessary to stick with these roles. I just wrote things this way because I thought it was the most accurate way to translate Murray's work.

Materials Needed

Two altars: one in the center of the ritual space and a second near the back for the signing of the book

A goat mask for the Magister, and animal masks for anyone else leading the ritual, if available

Bell

Book with a picture of the Horned God/Old Hornie in it

---

63. Hutton, *The Triumph of the Moon*, 200–201. Murray's use of magick wasn't always benevolent either. She once cast a curse on a colleague who then became so ill he had to change jobs. She cast her curse/spell in a frying pan in the company of two of her peers.

Quill pen and ink

Music

Communion wafers (or bread)

Wine with cup

Opening Procession

Ritual goers are led into the ritual area, forming a circle. At the front of the room stands the Grand Magister in full regalia, including his goat mask. After everyone has entered the room, the Maiden and Robin hush all in attendance and then move to stand a few feet in front of the Magister.

Robin rings the bell, focusing the attention on the front of the room.

Robin Goodfellow: *Witches all! Witches all! Attend to the Grand Magister, he who is the living embodiment of our god—he who is known as Old Hornie to the folk and by many other names. Great God, walk with us this night and lead us in your ways. Save us from oppression so that we might celebrate your earth. The path of the Witch is one of joy and fertility, and we humbly ask that you might lead us down that road.*

As the invocation is being read, the Grand Magister stands with his hands outstretched. After the words are read and the Magister has effectively "become the God," he should lower his arms, signifying the arrival of Old Hornie.[64]

Maiden: *Now that the God of the Witches has come, show your respect for his personage with either a bow or a kiss.*

Robin and the Maiden both bow to or kiss the Magister. Then, walking widdershins (counterclockwise), Robin leads the Magister around the circle, with each stopping to bow before the God.

---

64. Murray saw the Grand Magister of this ritual as the living embodiment of the Devil/Horned God, whom she sometimes calls "Old Hornie." Because he was the physical representative of the Witches' God, he was often deferred to in ritual, frequently including bows or kisses.

The Oath

Magister: *From the four corners of the earth we have gathered. From lands far and near we have come together to celebrate Witchcraft. There are those who would seek to destroy our fellowship, to deny my children the right to worship me and honor the ground beneath their feet. To that I say nay!*

Witches heal, Witches are most certainly real, and Witches will also curse those who stand in their way. Separate thee from the coven? Again I say nay, with all the power of heaven and hell behind my words. My children are free, free to come and free to go, and free to go where their soul wills after death. But to know that you are my children, that you are true Witches and sons and daughters of the Horned One, I need you to recite my oath. Before we begin, do all of you come to this place of your own free will? [65]

Ritual goers: *Yes.*

Magister: *Again, do you come here of your own free will?*

Ritual goers: *Yes.*

Magister: *Place your left hand atop your head and your right hand on the sole of your right foot to show me just how much you all love me.* [66] *All of that space, from hand to foot, is how much you have to adore me to be a true Witch! Now, as I am a loving master, place your arms down near your sides and simply repeat after me.*

The High Priestess pauses after each of the following lines to let all participants repeat it.

That is how much I love thee,
Horned One, who sets me free.
Free to laugh, love, lust, and thrust,

---

65. The words here are my own, but the sentiment is expressed in Murray's writings. As she writes on page 83 of *The God of the Witches*, "No contract was signed without the free consent of the contracting parties."

66. This rather odd placement of the hands is meant to show how much the initiating Witch loves the Horned One, and it's taken directly from Murray: "A variant of the vow of fidelity much used in Scotland was that the candidate placed one hand on the crown of her head, the other under the sole of her foot, and dedicated all that was between the two hands to the service of her god." *The God of the Witches*, 78.

Within Witchcraft I place my trust.
And to Old Hornie I swear
For the old gods, hear my prayer.

Magister: *And now you must seal your devotion with a kiss. In this book you shall see a picture of me. When it is brought your way, you must kiss it to seal your pledge to me. You may kiss your fingers and transfer your devotion to my book, or you may properly kiss the image, for this is how oaths are sealed in the Witch-cult. For those who take their vows most seriously, you may sign my book at the end of this rite, committing your life, love, and allegiance to the Horned One.* [67]

The book with the picture of Old Hornie is carried briskly around the circle by Robin Goodfellow, with each participant kissing the image. As this is being done, the dance is prepared.

The Dance

Magister: *Witches all! Witches all! The reasons for our gathering this night are legion. We do not meet so that we might meekly bow down at the feet of a god who gives us nothing. We do not sing empty songs of praise or dirge-like hymns. We don't meet so that I may take your time, money, or treasure.*

We meet because we enjoy the companionship of one another. We gather as brothers and sisters of the Craft, not as sheep in search of a shepherd. The Witch-cult is a chosen family, not an obligation to be met grudgingly.

Some of us gather in order to flirt, find, and satisfy our urges. The pleasures of sex and bodily union are not mine to keep from you but are here to be given out amongst the willing. The Witch-cult is lusty and eager for those who love life and celebrate the pleasures of the flesh to their fullest. [68]

In this circle we step outside of the mundane world and into another place where we are transformed. We lose ourselves in dance and song, or

---

67. Signing the Devil's book is standard stuff in Murray's work, but her Witches were often required to kiss the buttocks of the Magister or write their names in blood in the book. Having the participants kiss a picture of Old Hornie with their fingers and letting them sign with ink seemed like a better alternative to me.

68. This is as close to an actual orgy as my ritual gets. Murray's Witches were never repressed!

perhaps in drink. For at the Witches' sabbat all can be overcome and the miraculous made real. Together we move between worlds and exist in a space unreachable to those of other faiths.

The Witch-cult celebrates fertility! Fertility of the mind! Fertility of the body! Fertility of the soul! And fertility of the earth. We gather to push the seasons forward to bring about new life, and sometimes death. We are not separate from the earth, we are a vital part of the earth![69]

The idea here is to say anything and everything about why Witches might meet and to bring the energy level of the room up.

Magister: *We dance to awaken the earth and to awaken the inner Witch within ourselves. Lose yourself in the dance, the music, the ecstasy of being and being with one another! As we dance, let your energy flow into the earth and awaken all that sleeps there, and as you send out also receive what comes in so that it might awaken all that is passionate and true within you.*

Robin Goodfellow: *As we dance we will chant! We will chant in honor of the Horned One, who has brought us all together tonight. Our chant is just three lines:*

"Horned One, Horned One, dance here, dance here.
Horned One, Horned One, play here, play here.
Rise up, rise up, sabbat, sabbat!" (Everyone chants this.)

Now turn to your right, face forward, and place your hands on the shoulders of the person in front of you and prepare to dance in a celebration of Witchcraft!

The Maiden and Robin Goodfellow should lead the dance, one on each side of the circle. The dancing should be frenzied. Whoops and yells are appropriate too. The point is to let the energy build as high as possible. In the middle of the dance, the Grand Magister may begin instructing everyone on things to do while dancing, such as jumping together. Plan

---

69. Often expressed in Murray's work is the idea that the Witches danced in order to make the crops grow. So those orgies were about the earth's fertility, in addition to being about orgies.

on about seven minutes of movement, enough to make a few people a bit ragged. As the energy reaches its peak, the Magister signifies the end of the dance, counting down (3, 2, 1) and bringing his arms downward as an unspoken instruction for everyone to let go of the person in front of them.

Grand Magister: *And release! Awaken, Earth! Awaken, Witches all!*

The Supper

Robin Goodfellow: *And now let us eat the bread and drink the wine that was taken from us. May our goblets be full and our larders never empty!*

The Grand Magister holds the communion wafers[70] upon a platter while Robin Goodfellow leads everyone in a blessing for them.

Robin Goodfellow: *Witches all, repeat after me:*
(Robin pauses after each line so that all the participants can repeat it.)
We eat this bread in the Horned One's name,
With joy and truth and never shame.
We shall overcome the lies and deceit
And watch our opponents fall down in defeat!
Let all good now come to the fore
As we ever respect the Witches' lore!

Maiden: *May our goblets be full and our larders never empty!*

Robin Goodfellow passes out the communion wafers. As the wafers are being distributed, the Magister holds up a cup of wine to be blessed by the Maiden.

Maiden: *Witches all, repeat after me:*
(The Maiden pauses after each line so that all the participants can repeat it.)
We drink this wine in the Horned One's name,
Imbibing truth and never blame.

---

70. During the witch trials, Christians believed that Witches were continuously stealing their communion wafers, so I use those in this ritual instead of bread.

We are free to do us as we will,
And ever our own fate to fulfill.
He is not shepherd and we are not sheep,
What a Witch sows a Witch shall reap!

The cup of wine is passed around the circle and shared by all.

Closing

Grand Magister: *Witches all! Witches all! Well have we met and well have we gathered! We have celebrated the mysteries and joined with each other, and now we must depart from our sacred gather! Take with you the joys of the cult, the pleasures of the flesh, and the blessings of I, Old Hornie! Keep quiet our secrets, but always stand proud as a Witch and as a follower of the Horned One! We make our place in this world, and we are both masters and servants of it. Until our next sabbat!*

Robin and the Maiden stand before the Magister. The Magister hands his book to Robin Goodfellow. Robin carries the book to a back table, where it is left open for all who might wish to sign its pages. Alternatively, if the ritual is small, the book can be signed during the actual rite.

Robin Goodfellow: *I place this here so that those with true courage might sign their name in the Horned One's book, marking them as a true Witch!*

Maiden: *Great God, you have walked with us this night and led us in your ways. Until we meet again, Old Hornie, I say this sabbat is complete! Witches all! Witches all! Go forth now into the night knowing that you have now experienced Witchery most true! Our rite is at an end.*

The Maiden removes the goat mask from the face of the Grand Magister, and the ritual is over.

Magister: *Merry meet, and merry part, and merry meet again!*

Part Two

The Cone of Power

CHAPTER FOUR

Energy and the Magick Circle

When I made my initial foray into Witchcraft, almost all of the books I read included the instruction to "build a cone of power," but none of them included any information on just how to do so or even what the cone of power was. The result of this was that for many years I suffered under the delusion that I was missing out on some great secret of Witchcraft. Lacking a teacher at the time, I didn't have anyone to ask about the cone of power either, and talking to my friends about it seemed embarrassing. My solution to this problem ended up being to ignore the cone of power completely.

I never did find a book or a teacher to truly explain the cone of power to me. Instead, I began experiencing it during ritual. My coven would start chanting and dancing, and I'd feel our ritual area swell and pulse with energy. That energy would begin swirling around our circle, and as it circled it would become narrower at the top, looking like a cone point-side up or an upside-down tornado. There is no great secret to building a cone of power. It's just something Witches do, often without realizing it.

The cone of power is simply the energy that Witches build up while engaging in ritual. In a well-cast magick circle, that energy will spiral upward in a clockwise direction, forming something like a cone. Generally that energy is then directed toward a specific purpose, such as finding a new job or a place to live. In my own practice I've directed the energy raised in circle toward a variety of purposes, from finding employment to healing my friends to protecting society's most vulnerable members.

There's another name for the cone of power too: *magick*, because that's what it is. When Witches gather in a circle to try to create change, they are engaging in a magickal practice. The cone of power is one of those fundamental magickal practices. Though any Witch or coven can create a cone of power (and will often do so without even knowing it), there are ways to make that power more effective and a variety of things that can be done to create that power during circle.

Just What Is Magickal Energy and Where Does It Come From?

One word that is constantly referenced in regard to the cone of power is *energy*, but what does that mean exactly and where does this energy come from? Since the magickal energies we use to create a cone of power can't be seen, there are varying interpretations of what they are exactly and where they come from. To better understand how to manipulate energy, these are important questions to ponder, even if we won't all agree on the answers.

The simplest way to feel energy is to clap your hands together and rub them until they start to get warm. Once they are warm, pull your hands apart and notice the power radiating between them. The power you feel between your hands is what most Witches call energy. You should be able to feel that energy become more concentrated when your hands are closer together and feel more spread-out when they are farther apart. You should also be able to shape this energy using your hands, turning it into a ball or perhaps stretching it like taffy. We usually can't see energy, but it most certainly can be felt.

Energy in its raw form is neutral. Witches then bend, shape, and mold it to fit their desires. If we raise energy and concentrate on successful employment and financial opportunities, we infuse that energy with those qualities. If we raise energy while hurt or angry, those emotions will become a part of the energy. Raising energy is only half the equation; it's up to us as Witches to infuse that energy with our intentions. Once we've changed the energy we raised into something that reflects our needs, that energy is then cast out into the world to manifest the change desired. The cone of power is especially effective in magick because it is a concentrated eruption of that energy, and the more energy you have to throw at a particular problem the better! That's what makes the cone such a powerful tool.

If that sounds magickal, it should—energy is the building block of magick! Magick requires us to do more than draw a symbol or recite a few words; it requires us to raise and release energy. The more energy we raise, the more likely we are to achieve our desired outcome. Most human beings raise and release energy but have no idea how to harness that energy for productive purposes. Sporting events are great examples of this. You have thousands of fans yelling and cheering, and raising energy as a result, but they rarely know how to direct it toward anything positive. The energy is simply raised and released. Witches take all of that energy and direct it toward a specific goal.

The most well-known definition of magick comes to us from the English occultist Aleister Crowley, who wrote that magick is "the Science and Art of causing Change to occur in conformity with Will." Crowley's definition is a fine one, but it lacks an explanation of what causes that change. Certainly our will plays a large role. Magick can help us obtain what we truly desire and not just what we articulate, but in order to achieve change we can't just desperately want something or leave everything up to our will; we have to direct energy at the problem. Magick to me is "the science and art of causing change to occur with the use of natural energies in conformity with will."

I believe that energy comes from a variety of sources, some of which are easier to tap than others. What follows are some of the most common sources of magickal energy. You may find yourself disagreeing with some of them or being open to all of them. I'm not sure that it ultimately matters where energy comes from as long as we put it to use.

Energy from the Physical World

The earth and the universe have their own energies that we can utilize in our magickal practices. The energies of the earth are the energies that cause the seed to sprout and the wind to blow. They are the energies of life and death and are constantly swirling around us. To use them, we have only to reach out to them and draw them inward.

The easiest way to feel earth energy is to sit outside on the ground, with your back straight or possibly resting against a tree. Visualize your spine being in alignment with the earth and then reaching out from your body and into the ground below you. Once your spine has tapped into the earth, begin to imagine your body drawing energy up and out of the ground. Within a minute or two you should be able to feel the earth's natural energies inside of you.

The energies of the earth will often vary from place to place. You might feel a burst of wild energy when conducting this little exercise in a forest, or get a peaceful feeling if doing it at the seashore when the ocean is calm. This exercise can also be done in reverse if you are trying to tap into something above you. It's possible to draw in the violent energies of a thunderstorm by standing with your arms out over your head and concentrating on bringing that energy inside of yourself.

The green growing things tap into the earth's natural energies, and we can often feel those energies inside of living things. Try hugging a tree and opening yourself up to the energy it throws back at you. If the tree is healthy, you'll most likely feel love and contentment. I think trees are one of the easiest ways to feel the world's natural energy around us.

In ritual I'm usually not in a forest or at a beach, so I draw the earth's energy inward from my feet. Anytime I begin a major magickal operation, I imagine my feet as the roots of a tree going deep into the earth. Using those roots, I then pull energy up and out of the earth and into my own body. (My wife despises guided meditations that begin with "Imagine your feet are the roots of a tree" because it tends to be completely overused, but I find this to be an effective visualization while in ritual.) As the energy comes up through me, it then mingles with my own, creating a powerful magickal force.

Besides our blue marble of a planet, there are other celestial bodies that offer energy for us to tap into. The moon and the sun are obvious examples. Sunlight is an intense energy to work with and is fiery, just like its origin point. The moon is a bit more calm and measured, and its monthly cycle of waxing and waning offers abundant energies to use in magickal operations that require growth or getting rid of something. Even farther afield, the energies of the stars, galaxies, and other planets can be worked with too (though because of their great distance, their energies can be harder to harness).

The world we reside in is alive and teeming with energy and power. These natural forces are among the easiest to work with and utilize in ritual. They also work well in conjunction with the energy that resides inside ourselves.

Human or Personal Energy

There are a variety of ways to tap into and create energy through our own bodies. Some of these involve our magickal will, while others utilize physical processes. Most Witches eventually combine these two ways of raising energy because it makes our magick even more powerful than it would be otherwise (and most of us do this without even thinking about it).

The easiest place to start is with energy we create through mundane or physical means. Clapping and rubbing our hands together is one way to tap into this power, but there are other techniques that are just as effective, if not more so. One of my favorites involves the muscles in my hands and arms.

This is an easy exercise. To start, hold your arms out in front of you, with your elbows bent. Now squeeze your biceps and ball your hands into fists. As you flex your muscles you should feel the energy pulse in your arms, and when you release your muscles you should feel that energy move out of your body, gathering in front of you near your hands. The longer you squeeze and release, the more energy you'll raise and gather in front of you. If you practice this little exercise long enough, you should feel the energy in front of you. (Generally this feels like the air around you is heavy.) This energy can then be used for spellwork.

If I'm using this technique for a personal spell, I'll completely open up my hands and push forward with my arms as I relax my muscles for the last time. As I push the energy away, I'll visualize it going out into the world and working to help me reach whatever goal I raised it for.

The hand and arm squeeze is a great way to feel the energy we can create with our own bodies, but it's just the start when it comes to using our bodies to create and release energy. Nearly any physical act will release energy from our bodies, which we can then use for magickal purposes and building the cone of power. Breathing, dancing, and clapping will all work, though you may not feel things as directly as you can by squeezing your muscles.

There's another source for our own energy though, and that's our magickal will. Our will is the sum total of all our experiences, our emotions, and our interactions with other people, deity, and the world around us. I think of it as my inner furnace of magickal energy, and it's where I draw some of my most powerful energy. Our magickal will doesn't exist in any specific place in the body (there's no organ or gland that stores our magickal energy); it exists within our soul. Our will doesn't spend time contemplating the nature of the universe either; it's a repository of our purest emotions.

When we feel something passionately, we are feeling our will. Think for a second about one of your most emotional moments. If you are like me, those moments were full of energy, which probably hung like a cloud around you for as long as you were emotional. I remember one Yuletide season when my now wife and I were a bit estranged. For the first time ever in our relationship, I was on the outside looking in. The love that I suddenly knew I had for her was not being returned. I spent that Sunday afternoon wailing and crying harder than I had ever cried before. I remember just how powerful my sobbing was; I had never felt pain like that in my life. My bedroom turned into a cloud of doom and despair. That was me releasing my will, and that particular day my will was completely shattered.

We can tap into our will when we are passionate about something, and that passion will most likely release energy that we can use for magick and to create a cone of power. When I gather with my coven, we often raise energy and direct it toward those who are the most vulnerable in society. Social justice issues are important to all of us, and when we all tap into those emotions, a great deal of energy is released.

If you are having trouble finding the will inside of you, find a comfortable place and close your eyes. Let your mind drift for a bit before asking yourself one question: *What do I care most about?* A few images will most likely appear in your mind's eye. When I do this exercise I see my wife, my friends, my Craft, the natural world, and often a few of my most powerful memories. After the images have passed, focus your consciousness inward and reach out toward the source of those feelings.

Eventually you should be drawn to your inner magickal furnace, your will. I tend to visualize it as a blue-white ball of energy, pulsing, vibrating, and powerful. Once you've found it, try to pull a little bit of energy out of your will and then allow it to run through your entire body. As you feel the energy enter your arms, open up your hands and push the energy out of you. The more you work with this, the easier it should be tap into your own reservoir of personal power.

We also create energy in what often feels like mundane circumstances. If you've ever been to a sporting event with thousands of yelling, clapping, and stomping fans, you've been around a lot of really wild energy. That energy usually isn't directed at anything specific, but it can certainly be felt and experienced. I often joke with Ari that if we put a well-trained High Priestess in the middle of every football stadium in the fall, we could solve a lot of problems! I've felt the same kind of energy at raves and at concerts, and it can be tapped into in a coven setting as well.

Any large group of people who are all focused on the same thing will produce a lot of ambient energy. If you are dragging, this energy can be tapped into to raise your own energy level, and sometimes it can be used to fuel your magickal work as well. Let's say you are out shopping over the holidays and everything is wild and chaotic. You could gather that energy up and focus it on something more positive in your own life. Coven spells work so well because everyone in the coven is giving off energy when a working is decided upon.

When we focus on our desires in ritual, the inner and outer parts of ourselves will start working in tandem. The passions we have will flow through our bodies and will shape the energy we create with our movements and breath. When the physical and the spiritual parts of ourselves work together, we reach our greatest potential as Witches.

Energy from Deities

Most of us conceptualize deity in our own way. Some Witches see the gods as natural forces that work with the earth to keep everything humming and spinning along. Others see all the different deities that have ever been worshipped as real and distinct beings that just happen to be greater and more powerful than we are. Some see the individual gods as reflections of a greater power, like the idea that there is one Goddess and all the other goddesses throughout history are a part of that larger whole.

No matter how we look at deity, there's no denying that when deity is invited into circle, it brings its own power with it. If you call to Aphrodite (the Greek goddess of love) and she chooses to show up at your ritual, your circle will fill up with her energy, and it's an energy that will most likely make you feel loved, sexy, and perhaps a little amorous. The gods have energy and power, and when they step into our circles they add that power to whatever project we are working on.

The goddess Aradia is a goddess of justice, and if my coven is building a cone of power and we ask Aradia to be in our ritual and she shows up, she'll add her energy to what we build. It can be like having an extra Witch in the circle, except in this instance that Witch is a goddess! Her energies will mingle with our own, creating something even more powerful than we could have built otherwise.

When the gods step into our bodies during the rite known as drawing down the moon (see part 4), we can tap into their energy and release it from our physical selves. Most people involved in ritual don't draw down the moon, but anytime the gods are invoked (and show up), they can be a source of energy and a partner to a Witch or coven in their rites.

Energy from Other Sources

The first Pagan book I read as an adult was D. J. Conway's *Celtic Magic*.[71] In it, Conway writes that ritual magic

> is merely the taking of energy from another plane of existence and weaving that energy, by specific thoughts, words, and practices, into a desired physical form or result in this plane of existence. The whole idea of magic is to contact various energy pools that exist in a dimension other than our own.[72]

Conway's conception of magickal energy was an important one when I was younger. When I was first starting upon the path of the Witch, I used to visualize pools of energy existing in places just outside of our own world and then reaching into them for energy in my rites and rituals. As I've grown as a Witch, I've mostly abandoned the idea that our energy comes from other dimensions, but I suppose it's possible.

This visualization certainly worked for me when I was younger, and I'm sure there are still many Witches who use it today. If it's an idea that works for you, then you should utilize it. Ultimately we can only theorize where energy truly comes from, and other dimensions don't sound completely out of the question.

While I don't subscribe to Conway's theory today, I believe there are still some instances where we use magick from outside of our known world. I believe in the fey, for example, and think they exist just beyond what we know of the natural world. Since the fey sometimes lend their energies to the rites of Witches they like, I suppose that when this happens we are tapping into energies from outside our plane of existence. Ultimately, building a cone of power and working magick is about tapping into energy, regardless of where that energy comes from.

---

71. *Celtic Magic* is not a book that has held up particularly well (it contains some serious issues with history), but I will always treasure it because of the impact it had on my life.

72. Conway, *Celtic Magic*, 6.

Setting Up a Magickal Space

A cone of power can be built nearly anywhere, but some places are more advantageous than others. When engaging in Witch ritual, I have two preferences when it comes to location: outdoors in a secluded private area, or an indoor space set aside primarily for ritual. Wherever you end up holding ritual, the most important thing is that it's in a space where you won't be disturbed. You don't want people watching you like you're an animal in a zoo, and you don't want roommates or family members interrupting your magickal goings-on.

I live in one of the prettiest areas of the country, California's Silicon Valley, but it's teeming with people and there are very few outdoor locations in my immediate vicinity that provide any measure of privacy. Even my backyard is visible to several neighbors, so I do most of my work indoors. My indoor ritual space (or temple room) doubles as a guest bedroom when friends arrive from out of town to visit, but it's mostly set aside for Witch activities. Before turning our guest room into a Witch room, we did most of our rituals in our living room.

Most of us probably don't have a separate room to dedicate to Witch activities, and that's okay. What's important is transforming your common space into something more magickal. If you're stuck doing ritual in the family den, put a tapestry over the television and bring in some extra candles instead of using a lamp. If your space feels more magickal, it will be more magickal.

Building a cone of power often requires a bit of space, especially if you're practicing with a coven or circle of Witches. A traditional Witch circle is nine feet in diameter, which is the perfect size for a coven of thirteen Witches to run around in, though there's really no right or wrong size. You'll need a bit of room to move around in, which is why bedrooms usually don't work very well for ritual—the bed just takes up too much space!

Once you've settled on a spot for ritual, you'll want to cleanse the area before raising any energy. Cleansing is both a mundane and a magickal practice. If you're bringing other Witches into your space, it should be tidy and clean. I always sweep and mop the floors of my house before every ritual. There's nothing less magickal than stepping on a nail while building a cone of power! If my ritual is outside, I make sure there's nothing that anyone might trip over in the space we'll be using.

Magickal cleansing is a part of many Witch rituals and is generally performed at the start of most rites. It involves the removal of any and all negative energies that might be in your ritual space. What exactly is negative energy? In its simplest form it's any energy in you or your space that doesn't serve your working. Most often it's an energy that feels icky or adversarial. Have you ever walked into a place that just gave you a bad feeling? That's negative energy, and allowing it to remain can have harmful effects on the energy you raise and on your own psyche.

Negative energy can come from a variety of sources. I once bought a house where a stabbing had taken place, and the area where the event occurred made the hairs on my neck stand up (even before I knew what had transpired there). The energy generated during that event required cleaning up, and once my wife and I took care of it, our basement returned to normal (though it took some work). Examples like a stabbing in a basement are extreme cases though. Most of the time the negative energy in our ritual spaces doesn't come from past traumatic events, it comes from us!

My house is generally a pretty cheerful place, but my wife and I both spend a lot of time worrying about work, politics, and a thousand other things. That "worry energy" rolls off us and into our home, and when we feel that energy it serves to amplify those feelings in us, or perhaps causes us to start worrying when we shouldn't be. Even worse are the energies that come from anger, jealousy, and rage. Though we don't spend a lot of time in our Witch room outside of ritual, those energies still manage to find their way into that space.

Magickal spaces also attract all kinds of entities who are curious about what we are doing. If you've got a ghost in your house, it most likely spends a lot of time hovering around your ritual area. Casting a magick circle attracts curious forces who would otherwise probably ignore us. Getting rid of those energies (and entities) is vital for casting a strong circle and raising energy.

Removal of negative energy before building the cone of power is vital. Allowing negativity to remain in sacred space will pollute whatever energy you conjure up, transforming it into something else. Negative energy acts much like a drop of ink in a clear glass of water. The ink doesn't stay in one place; it affects all of the water in the glass, turning something clean and pure into something else entirely. Negative energy has the same effect if it's not dealt with.

The most common way to remove negative energies from a ritual space is through censing and asperging,[73] a process that generally utilizes salt water and lit incense. Salt has long been known for its purifying effects, and mixing it with water allows it to be more easily sprinkled and shared in the ritual circle. Incense smoke has been used for millennia as a form of purification and can still be found doing that job today in the Catholic Church. An alternative to incense that still utilizes smoke is the smudge stick. Smudging is a Native American practice that most often utilizes sage and cedar for their cleansing properties.

Incense smoke and salt water eat away at negative energy, breaking it into little pieces until it's basically dissolved. When censing and asperging my ritual space, I like to pay special attention to the corners, along with the doors and windows. Negative energy is most likely to collect in forgotten corners, and it most certainly enters our spaces through mundane means such as through doorways. I always spend a little extra time purifying any area that feels icky or uncomfortable to me.

Before being used for cleansing, the salt, water, incense, and flame are generally ritually blessed, with the first two materials being cleansed by the athame. There are many ways to perform this ritual, and I suspect many of you reading this already have such a rite. If you don't have a rite for cleansing and consecrating the elements, such rituals are easily found in most Witchcraft 101 books and on the internet.

---

73. *Asperging* is not a real word, though it's used with some frequency by Modern Witches. It's a variation of the word *asperges* (often spelled with the *s* in the United States), which is a Catholic rite involving the sprinkling of holy water. According to the Oxford Dictionary, *asperges* is a Latin word that literally means "thou shalt purge."

Salt water and incense aren't the only materials that can be used to cleanse a magickal space. One of my favorite tools to use for this purpose is the broom (or besom). Using a broom to get rid of negative energy is much like using a broom in daily life, but instead of sweeping up dust you'll be sweeping up energy. As you sweep, visualize any negative energy in your ritual space being swept, and don't forget the areas up off the ground. When I use my broom to cleanse a room, I also sweep the walls and/or ceiling if I think they need it. Since the broom won't break up negative energy like salt water does, I usually sweep all the negative energy that I've gathered up and out of my house.

Once your ritual space has been cleansed, you will be ready to cast the circle that will help create your cone of power—that is, as long as everyone in your circle is ready. Many Witches also ritually cleanse themselves before and during the setup of their magickal space.

CLEANSING THE SELF

We humans create more negative energy than probably any other force on the planet, and in order for our magick to be effective it's generally wise to get rid of this before building the cone of power. Many covens require all of their members to shower (often with salt or certain herbs) before ritual or to wash their hands with salt water. I think showering is a little extreme, but the method of cleansing the self is really up to each individual and not so much the work of the coven. However, there are a few tried-and-true methods that can be used with a group during ritual to help deal with unwanted energies.

The first method is to breathe out all of the negativity inside of us. This method works best at the very beginning of ritual, as everything we've expelled from our bodies has to be dealt with. Start by taking a big inhale, and as you breathe the air in, visualize it as strong and cleansing. Hold the air in your lungs for several long seconds, and as it's inside of you, imagine it collecting all of the negativity within. Pour all of your anger, worry, work garbage, relationship problems, and whatever else into that air. Then as you exhale, visualize that energy leaving your body.

My coven generally opens every ritual with this technique. It helps to calm and center everyone in the circle and is an effective way to get our bodies and minds ready for ritual and magick. Breathe in and out several times, taking in big breaths, holding them, and then slowly releasing the air and anything inside of yourself that is unwanted.

The only downside to this technique is that it leaves a lot of negative energy hanging in your ritual space. (The bad energy has been expelled from your body but has not been taken out of your ritual space.) This negative energy can generally be dealt with through censing and asperging, which is one of the reasons we lead off with the cleansing breaths instead of saving them for later. Many covens cense and asperge the ritual participants as they prepare their sacred space, an especially wise practice after taking a few cleansing breaths. (The ritual broomsweeping is an equally effective way to deal with this psychic residue.)

In my coven we also ritually purify everyone in the circle after taking our cleansing breaths. We ask the participants to visualize whatever negativity they have left inside of them gathering in their hands. (If you do this, feel all of the tension in your body rising up and collecting in your hands.) We then pour scented water over everyone's hands using a large pitcher and bowl, blessing and cleansing them in the names of the Lord and the Lady. The negative energy is washed off them by the water and then collects in the bowl, staying there until we dump that water outside at the end of ritual.

THE MAGICK CIRCLE

Circle casting is one of the essential components of creating a cone of power. To put it simply, no circle (or a poorly cast circle) equals no cone of power. Circle casting is something every Witch should learn to do well, and it's a practice that is often overlooked in books and by many teachers. A circle is more than where a Witch works in ritual; it's a tool in its own right. Well-constructed circles are a necessity for effective spellcraft.

Circles have been used in spiritual settings for thousands of years. Before conducting a sacrifice, the ancient Greeks used to mark out a circular space. That space included the sacrificial animal of course, but also all of the participants, the altar, and all of the tools that were to be used during the ceremony. The Greeks created a circle for one of the reasons Modern Witches do today: to differentiate the sacred from the profane.[74]

The Modern Witch's circle derives from ceremonial magick and the grimoire tradition, where circles were generally constructed for protection. Beginning in the Middle Ages, many magicians practiced magick to gain control over entities such as demons and angels. Because these magicians were attempting to bind and violate the free will of sentient beings, they often operated with a great deal of fear. They cast circles to keep out unwanted entities and to provide a layer of protection between them and the demons they were summoning.

Circle casting became a part of magickal orders such as the Golden Dawn, where it was used to facilitate spiritual experiences and to provide a safe place to practice magick. When Modern Witches began using magick circles, they incorporated the circle's traditional uses (sacred space and protection) and added a third use: as a vessel to store energy. This is a unique characteristic that initially was found only in the circles of Wiccan-Witches.

When casting a circle, it's important to remember that the circle exists for the following three reasons.

Sacred Space

The circle is a liminal space between our mundane world and the realms of the gods. While it might physically look like it's located on this plane of existence, the circle exists "between the worlds." It's a space where we can freely feel the energy of goddesses and gods and call upon those who have left this world, both our beloved and our Mighty Dead.

Witchcraft rites can be conducted outside a circle, and it's not necessary to cast a circle to feel the soul of a departed loved one or the energy of a deity, but the circle makes such things easier. I can talk to my wife if she stands behind a closed door, but it's more difficult for me to hear

---

74. Burkert, *Greek Religion*, 56.

her. The circle is an open doorway into another place that helps to facilitate communication with entities and powers greater than ourselves.

Protection

Circles are still used for protection by most Witches. A well-cast circle can help to keep any unwanted spirit, deity, or other entity out of your sacred space. It's also a shield that keeps out and repels any negative energy that is being directed at you or your coven or that just happens to be floating through your ritual space.

I've also found well-cast circles to be extremely effective at keeping out the mundane world. When doing ritual outside, I've seen non-Witches (sometimes called *cowans*) in the vicinity either completely overlook the ritual I'm doing or go out of their way to avoid my sacred space all together. Phones have trouble ringing inside a well-cast circle, and other electronics will often malfunction. At an Imbolc ritual many years ago, my old landline phone started ringing the moment we took the circle down, and not a second before. This was especially surprising since I shared the house with six people and our phone rang almost all the time!

Storing Energy

All of the energy that's raised in a circle will stay there until it's directed to leave. This is what allows us to create a cone of power, and it's a unique characteristic of many Witch circles. When the energy is released, it generally leaves through the top of the circle (the tip of the cone), and I often visualize it like a volcano exploding.

A well-cast circle will often result in your ritual space feeling like soup. The air will get heavy, and if you are sensitive to energy you can feel it rushing around you. During a rather intense series of initiations several years ago, my friend Angus was charged with "cutting" a doorway in the circle so he could leave our ritual space and bring in each individual waiting to be initiated. As the night went on, he began to comment on how hard it was to cut open the circle. So much energy had gathered (and was being raised) that it was difficult to get through, and it had nowhere to go since we hadn't released it from the circle.

Oftentimes the temperature in your ritual space will go up after your circle is cast. This is no doubt partly due to having a bunch of people in close proximity to one another engaging in magickal work, but it's also simply due to the fact that the circle is keeping all of that heat energy inside of it. The moment my coven releases our circle, the temperature in our ritual space goes down about ten degrees, and this is long before we've opened any door.

The ancient Greeks physically drew their circles upon the ground, as did many ceremonial magicians, and there are still some Witches today who do the same. If you wish to draw a physical circle to designate sacred space, there are several options for materials to use, with the two most common being flour and salt. Salt is especially effective because it adds to the protective power of the circle. Flour doesn't provide that benefit, but it's easily available and can be found in most homes. I rarely build a physical circle during ritual, but I sometimes do for initiations. In those instances I generally use dried leaves and/or flower petals. There are also Witches who have circles constructed out of wood or other materials that they put down in their ritual space. (I think such things look really cool but sound like way too much work to build and store.)

Having a physical circle (with the exception of one made out of salt or perhaps red brick dust) is really only a cosmetic consideration, and I believe that creating one only adds a level of confusion to what a magick circle essentially is, for while we use the term magick *circle*, our circles are actually spherical! They extend over us, under us, and all around us. They aren't a wall, and they generally extend a bit outside of any physical boundary we might construct. (If they didn't, they'd never be quite tall enough, and our heads would most likely poke out of the top of the circle near the perimeter.)

Most Witches cast their circles with either an athame or a sword, but those aren't the only tools that can be used. There are some Witches who use a wand and a few who use a stang,[75] and I've seen people use

---

75. The stang is a tool that was first popularized by the English Witch Robert Cochrane (see chapter 5), though it's generally used as a focal point for ritual and not as an energy-wielding tool.

axes and spears as well. Nearly any tool capable of directing energy can be used to create a circle, and this includes natural tools such as our fingers. For many years my "athame" was my right index finger. Anything will work for casting a circle, but in my experience athames and swords produce the best results.

In addition to being practical, magick circles are seen by many Witches as symbolizing some of the universe's great forces. The circle is sometimes compared to the womb of Mother Earth, and due to its circular nature is sometimes equated with the Wheel of the Year. With no beginning and no end, the circle has long been symbolic of unity and perfection.[76] It's not necessary to see a circle as symbolic of anything, but such associations can give your rituals a deeper meaning if they resonate with you.

CASTING THE CIRCLE

Casting a powerful circle is about more than saying a few poetic words and waving a sword around. It requires concentration, will, desire, intent, visualization, and energy. The circle is where the work of the Witch is done, and its casting and creation should be taken seriously. Not every ritual will require a well-cast circle, but anytime the cone of power is built, circle construction becomes a major point of concern.

Most Witch circles are cast deosil, or clockwise. There is some argument over where exactly to start a circle casting, but generally it begins in the east (or possibly the north). I'm partial to the east because it's the direction of the sunrise, so all of my circle castings begin and end there. Moving from east to south (and onward) and using a clockwise direction just feels natural to me. It's also the direction that energy generally seems to move in, especially in the Northern Hemisphere.

On certain occasions there are Witches who cast their circles widdershins, or counterclockwise. This is usually done to accomplish a specific magickal goal such as cursing or hexing a troublesome individual. (Not every Witch believes in absolutely "harming none.") Even if the energy raised from your cone of power is being directed toward a some-

---

76. Guiley, *The Encyclopedia of Witches & Witchcraft*, 217.

what aggressive purpose, I recommend against a widdershins circle casting. It might be fine for certain types of spellwork, but I don't think such a configuration lends itself to the cone of power.

Circle casting is about 50 percent mental and 50 percent physical. It requires us to visualize the energies we are sending out and to imagine the physical construction of the circle in our mind's eye. The energies wielded by Witches are invisible to everyday vision; I believe they can be felt and sensed but not necessarily seen. In order to use these energies most effectively, we have to be able to picture them as visible things.

The first Witchcraft book I ever read as an adult recommended seeing the energies used to cast a circle as a blue-white light. I still use this image when casting a circle, but I know some Witches who see the energies they raise for circle casting differently. I know some who see the energy as fire-like, and others who visualize it as resembling the color of the sea or sky. Just how you visualize circle-casting energy is immaterial; what matters is that the visualization you use resonates with you. If blue-white light makes sense to you, by all means go ahead and use it, and if not, pick something else.

Effective creative visualization is important in circle casting because you are most likely going to get whatever it is that you see in your mind's eye. Visualizing the energies being used will allow you to create well-defined boundaries for your circle. Seeing your circle as whole and complete will allow it to hold more of the energy you will be raising within it. (You certainly don't want your circle to have a hole in it!)

When starting a circle casting, begin at the altar by taking a steadying breath and picking up your athame or sword (or whatever other tool you are using). Approach the east from a clockwise direction, and point your athame downward, projecting energy from inside of you out toward where you want your circle's boundaries to be. Slowly begin walking around the perimeter of the circle, visualizing the energy leaving your athame while focusing your mind on the kinds of energies you are projecting outward.

During a circle casting there are a lot of things to process inside of our head. We are visualizing the energy leaving our body and actively creating the circle, but we are also concentrating internally on the *kinds* of energy we are manifesting. When I'm casting a circle, I concentrate internally on the three reasons for doing so: protection, sacred space, and holding energy. The energy that leaves our body during a circle casting is raw; it's up to us to shape it and give it purpose. When we define what we are using that energy for, it will take on those characteristics.

I always cast my circles three times, pointing my athame downward on the first pass around the circle, at shoulder height during the second pass, and then upward during the third one. I do this to remind myself that I'm creating a sphere, and with each of my three passes around the circle I'm building another part of that sphere: from bottom to middle to top. A circle is not a brick wall, and the energies we use to create it will move around, rotating clockwise, much like the energy that we will soon pour into it.

Using a three-times-round casting technique also serves as a reminder of the three reasons why we cast a circle. Depending on the time of year and the operation the coven will be engaging in, I might add more protective energy to a specific circle casting or dedicate more energy to sacred space. At Samhain, for instance, I'm often worried about unwanted spirits showing up, and less so at Beltane.

The energy I use for a circle casting comes from two places: from inside of me and from the earth. When I cast a circle, I push energy outward from inside of myself, and since my feet are on the ground while I'm walking around during the creation of the circle, I attempt to draw energy up and out of the earth to add to my own. I think this gives the circle I create a more organic feel and helps to link that circle to the natural world.

With all of the things that are going on internally when I'm casting a circle, not to mention all of the things I'm doing while wielding a sword, saying something during a circle casting can be problematic. I've been a part of many circles where the circle caster was more worried about remembering a specific line than casting the circle effectively. If words are just going to get in the way, they don't have to be said, or they can be said by someone else in the circle. At many rituals I will let someone else do the actual circle casting yet I will recite the words used to cast the circle.

The words we use in such instances can help to provide a degree of focus. Verbalizing our intent can add to the effectiveness of magickal operations, but it should never come at the cost of half-assing the actual magickal work. Most of us eventually learn to internalize most of the processes utilized in effective circle casting, which makes adding a layer of words on top of that pretty easy, but until that point is reached there's no need to worry about the ritual script.

When coming up with words for a circle casting, I like to choose words that accurately reflect what I'm doing while casting the circle. There are no specific Witch words for any operation, though I suggest always using something that captures what your circle casting is trying to accomplish. All of the words I use in my circle castings are similar to this:

In perfect love and perfect trust I conjure thee, O circle of power! Let only truth and joy remain in this space as we cast out all wickedness and evil. Thou art a shield against the forces of wickedness and evil that would disrupt our rite, and an entryway into a realm between the worlds—where both gods and mortals tread! Thou art a vessel for the powers and energies we will raise together! So therefore I do bless and consecrate this space in the names of the Lord and the Lady. The circle is cast. So mote it be!

Since this is designed as a circle-casting rite for my coven, all those assembled are meeting in "perfect love and perfect trust," but this is harder to ensure in public circles. The phrase "in perfect love and perfect trust" might be one of the most overused tropes in Witchcraft, but it should be reserved for when it's an accurate statement of fact. A circle with ten people I've just met for the first time who may or not even be Witches is not a place of perfect love and trust.

My circles are places of "truth and joy" and are actively created to keep out "all wickedness and evil." I double down on this idea by calling the circle a "shield." While most Witches scoff at the existence of demons, there are all sorts of entities in the magickal and spiritual worlds that are not fans of humanity. Our ancestors were mortally afraid of the fey, and for good reason! While most entities from the fairy realm are rather benign, there are some who like to play tricks on humans and others who are downright hostile. The same goes for spirits: the unenlightened in life do not suddenly become paragons of virtue in death. Best to be careful.

The circle as a "realm (or world) between the worlds" is a common turn of phrase in many Witchcraft circles, and for good reason. To me the idea of standing between the worlds is one of the things that makes Witchcraft unique in the modern world. Churches may be holy to Christians, but they don't exist in a space between heaven and earth—our circles do! Gods and goddesses can walk wherever they please, but it's easier for them to interact with us in the land between the worlds.

Many of the rites I use for circle casting leave out any information about the circle as a place to gather energy, but I've included it here as a reminder of that third point. The circle is a "vessel for the powers and energies" created by Witches, and while sentences about that function lack a certain poetic grace, verbal cues have a lot of power. Saying things aloud is a spell all its own and helps to manifest what we desire in life and in ritual.

Taking down the circle at the end of ritual is just as important as creating it. You and I can simply walk out of a circle when ritual is over, but other entities may find themselves trapped inside of it if it's not taken down. There's also the problem of energy just sitting in a specific spot and not going back out into the natural world where it belongs. If we truly believe in the power of the circles we create, then we also have to believe in uncreating them.

Releasing a circle is much like casting a circle, only everything is done in reverse. The process starts in the east, with the sword held high, but this time you want to move widdershins. Walking counterclockwise helps to break up the energy in the circle and disrupt its natural flow, making it easier to send it on its way. I do three passes to take down the circle, visualizing it unraveling as I move around the circle.

While I often feel as if I'm channeling the energy used to create the circle back into my sword and therefore myself, there are others who view this operation differently. Instead, they see the uncasting as a breaking up of energies, with those broken energies then being free to return to where they previously were. I like the idea of drawing a little energy back into my sword or athame so it's there for the next time I cast a circle, but there's no absolute right or wrong way. As long as the energy is collected and/or dispersed, the circle has been taken down properly.

More important than any words said during the deconstruction of the circle is the act of taking apart the circle. As the circle comes down, you should visualize the energy used to create it dissipating and your ritual space returning to the mundane world. In my mind's eye I visualize all of the powers called to during ritual departing from my temple room, and all of the energies that have been called up sent to where we desired them to go. After my three passes around the circle with my sword or athame first held high, then held at shoulder height, and then pointed at the ground, I make a show of placing my sword or athame back on the altar to signify the close of the ritual.

When verbalizing the circle uncasting, one of the most important lines I use is this:

All will be as it once was, and all that was here has been dismissed in the names of the Lord and the Lady.

I want all those I'm circling with to know that the gods, spirits, ancestors, and any other entities have been sent away and have moved on from our ritual space. This helps not only those I'm circling with but also possibly the spirits and deities themselves. We aren't the only ones who need a verbal cue every once in a while.

The words I say when taking down the circle are similar to the ones I use to cast it, but I like to add that taking down the circle brings us back to a mundane space from a magickal one:

I cast this circle of power in perfect love and perfect trust, creating an entryway to the world between the worlds—a land where both gods and mortals may tread. You have served us well, O circle, and have protected our rite. I now take down that power, and all will be as it once was, and all that was here has been dismissed in the names of the Lord and the Lady. So mote it be!

The exact words are never as important as the intent. What's most important is making sure to take down the magickal space that you've created.

CIRCLE ETIQUETTE

Too many Witches see sacred space as an imaginary construct and not a real power. Respecting the energies that give our circles power only helps to make our magick more effective and our interactions with deity more powerful. To maximize the power of your circle, there are a few easy things to do.

Only walk deosil while in circle. Since the energies of the circle move clockwise, walking counterclockwise while in circle disrupts those energies. Moving in a clockwise direction connects you to the circle and the energies raised within it. It may seem silly to walk all the way around the altar instead of just going a few feet counterclockwise to pick up the cakes and ale, but your circle will be all the better for it.

Not only should every Witch walk deosil while in circle, but everything should be passed around that way too. Anything that moves should take advantage of the energy current swirling clockwise around the circle. (My friends often laugh at me during circle because I've been known to let out a loud hissing sound when seeing *and feeling* someone walk widdershins during ritual.)

Cut a doorway in and out of the circle. Of course we can just walk through a circle if we want to, but that's not good for the circle, nor is it fair to the other Witches around us. When we just walk through the perimeter of the circle without respecting it, we are disrupting its energy and getting in the way of the job we've created it to do. Emergencies happen, and sometimes we simply forget a lighter or whatever else, but when that happens, cut a doorway in and out of the circle.

Cutting a doorway in a circle is a relatively simple task. All it really requires is an athame. To cut a doorway, feel the power of the circle moving along its perimeter. Once you've found that, just cut a doorway into that circle, going clockwise again. In my mind's eye I sometimes see this as cutting the threads that hold the circle together and creating a breach in it. The rest of the circle's energy should continue to flow clockwise, with the door acting like a big rock in the middle of a stream.

Once the individual leaving the circle has stepped out of magickal space, close the circle behind them. In my mind's eye I use the thread analogy, but this time I use my athame to stitch those severed threads back together. When the departed individual returns, repeat the process of opening and closing the circle.

There are some Witches who believe that doorways are best utilized in certain directions, but I tend to build them wherever it's most convenient. The primary concern should be getting the individual Witch in and out of the circle as quickly, easily, and unobtrusively as possible. In my coven that means cutting a doorway in the northeastern part of the circle because that's where the mundane door to our ritual room is located.

Having the person who cast the circle cut the doorway is generally optimal, though anyone can cut a doorway. I suggest using the circle caster to let people in and out of magickal space because they are probably most "in tune" with the circle's energy since they played an outsized role in creating it. Covens and Witches who have worked together for an extended period of time probably all know how to work with each individual's energy, so this is probably less of a concern with established groups.

What Energy Can and Can't Do (and How to Take Advantage of It)

Magickal energy is not a cure-all. It cannot cure cancer, get you a job, or make someone fall in love with you all on its own. If this sounds like I'm pooh-poohing magick, I'm not. I've seen it work too many times to discount it, even when my rational mind doubts its power. However, energy is a part of the natural world, and therefore it has to play by those rules.

Raising energy for a sick friend won't instantly heal them or reverse a major disease, but it can be helpful. Energy raised and sent for someone battling a serious medical condition can provide comfort or give them a little bit of personal energy that might help them get through their day or, even better, fuel their fight. A friend of mine had a very serious case of lymphoma (a cancerous blood disease), and for months our coven raised energy for him. He told me that after our first energy raising he could see little golden parachutes full of energy descend from the ceiling and fall on him and his hospital bed.

We didn't tell him we were doing anything for him, but he recognized our energy when it came to him. That energy didn't fix all of his problems, and it would be another eight months before he was even ready to go back home, but it did make him feel better and gave him some strength to keep fighting. While raising energy, we visualized our friend: we pictured him healthy, happy, and not in pain. His doctors deserve far more credit than our coven for him being alive and back in the mundane world, but we gave what we could and he says that it helped.

I got my first book contract with Llewellyn (the publisher of this book) two weeks after a major job spell my wife put together. In that ritual we raised energy and visualized ourselves doing the kind of work we most desired to do. I saw myself in front of my computer typing for several hours a day. Two weeks later I got an email asking if I would be interested in writing a book. (There was a major happy dance after that email!) But the magick we sent out didn't exist in a vacuum. I had been blogging for several years by that point and was a frequent workshop presenter at several large Pagan festivals. I had been doing the groundwork to write a book for years. The energy we raised that night didn't get me a book contract all on its own; it was the final push in a long personal quest I had been engaged in for years.

Over the last several years we've seen a rise in hate crimes in the United States, and that has me worried for many of my friends. Because of this, at almost every ritual our coven raises energy directed to protect society's most vulnerable folks. That energy is not going to end racism or transphobia, and we know that. We raise it and send it out into the universe so it can find its way to people who are being harassed, violated, and hated just for being themselves. The hope is that our energy will find its way to people when they need it most.

When preparing to build a cone of power, there are a few things you should consider to make sure the energy you are sending out will do what you want it to do. This is especially important when working with a group of Witches because everyone probably has their own idea of what sort of energy to raise if it hasn't been truly specified.

Be Specific. All magick works best when we are specific about what we want and our goals. The first love spell I ever did was focused on me falling in love, which sounded great on the surface, but I should have asked for that love to be reciprocated! I fell pretty hard for a friend, but that love wasn't returned. If you are raising energy to find a job, it's best to envision doing something that you want to do instead of just thinking "job."

One Bad Apple Can Spoil the Whole Bunch. If you're trying to build a cone of power with someone who is distracted or angry at the world, things are not likely to go well. Their energy will most likely pollute whatever you are trying to accomplish. The cone of power works best when everyone is equally focused on building it. If someone you work with doubts the reality of what you are doing, that will hinder your results as well.

Stay Focused. Sometimes what we do as Witches ends up being funny, and there's nothing wrong with responding to such things with a laugh. However, when someone continually tries to be funny in circle or lets out an uncalled-for quip in the middle of an energy raising, it's not funny—it's distracting. Building energy requires concentration and focus. Trying to be the center of attention or not taking what's going on seriously isn't conducive to effective magickal work.

Luckily most Witches are well aware of the challenges involved in building the cone of power, and behave and act appropriately. If you run into someone who has issues in that area, try speaking to them before or after ritual. The circle is no place to try to correct someone, and doing so there might result in some hurt feelings. The Witches I've known over the years always try to get things right and are generally open to constructive and positive criticism.

CHAPTER FIVE

Raising the Cone of Power

Building the cone of power is pretty simple on the surface. A magick circle is cast and then filled with energy. The energy spirals around the circle, moving upward and clockwise, looking much like an upside-down tornado or a funnel. When the energy in the circle has peaked, the energy is allowed to leave the circle and go out into the mundane world, where it will do the will of the Witches who raised it.

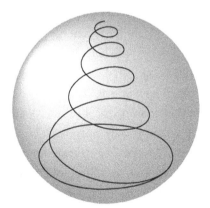

The Cone of Power

Energy raising can be accomplished in several different ways, and there's no right or wrong way to do it as long as everyone is focused and ready to do the work. Various ways of energy raising can be combined, spliced up, or adapted, and clever Witches are constantly figuring out new, more effective methods. This section contains some of my favorite ways to raise energy and why they work. They may not appeal to everybody, and that's okay. Anytime we raise energy, the process we use should make sense to us. If some of the techniques I outline here don't resonate with you, don't use them.

Just as important as raising energy is releasing it out into the universe. Regardless of how you fill your cone of power, the energy you've raised has to be allowed to leave the circle or it won't do a whole lot of good. (There are exceptions to this, such as raising energy for a particular individual in the circle.) In most instances you are going to want to visualize the energy you've built up erupting out of your cone of power like lava exploding out of a volcano.

There's no need to cut a hole into the top of your circle to release energy either. Circles generally respond to our needs and desires, and a circle purposefully cast to hold and release energy will do just that. Circles are tools, and like any good tool, they will work as intended if crafted properly.

DANCING AROUND THE CIRCLE

The most common way to build up energy in the circle is through movement, most specifically some sort of circle dance. Sometimes the specific dance step will be specified, and other times it'll be a free-for-all, with varying levels of movement. There's no one way for Witches to move in a circle other than deosil. I've seen Witches waltz to raise energy and a few who simply walk purposefully. When moving especially quickly, my coven's "dances" sometimes feel more like a group of people running a race together, and that's completely fine. The whole point is just to move and whip up energy; the exact "hows" are inconsequential.

Dance is an especially effective way to raise energy because it allows us to tap into several different sources of magickal power. There's the energy we produce with our muscles by walking and the energy we release from inside of ourselves (our will), and because our feet are on and off the ground it's possible to tap into the energies of the earth as well. Dancing clockwise around the circle gets our energy swirling and pulsating in a hurry, which is why moving around in the circle feels so powerful and effective.

Dancing also allows us to connect to the people around us while we are circling. By holding hands, the entire coven can unite and share energy directly with one another. I've been in circles with and without hand-holding during an energy-raising dance, and I feel comfortable stating that being physically connected with everyone who is building the cone of power is especially effective.

There is no one type or kind of dance that has to be used while moving in circle, but there are a few practices that are more common than others and are worth mentioning. The first is a particular dance step known as the "vine" or "grapevine." This is the default style of movement for many Witches when moving to raise energy (though that doesn't mean we all get it right, me included!).

Looking up "grapevine" online will produce a myriad of results, which can make this particular dance step look more difficult than it really is. Start the grapevine in a comfortable stance. Begin by moving your right foot over your left foot and then stepping outward with your left foot. Your right foot then goes behind your left one before stepping out again with your left. This is then repeated until the dance is done. Generally, people hold hands while in the circle doing this step. Does this sound complicated? Perhaps, but I swear it makes sense when you do it and follow the instructions here.[77]

If a particular dance step has you or a coven member completely focused on getting the dance step right while ignoring the purpose of your energy raising, *don't worry about it*. I get the vine step wrong nearly every time I do it, and in twenty-plus years of Witchcraft no one has ever called me out on it or made me feel bad for dancing like a wounded

---

77. I'm terrible with dance steps, and my wife had to coach me through this while telling me over and over, "This is not that difficult." For more on the grapevine, you may want to consult Lady Sable Aradia's 2014 book *The Witch's Eight Paths of Power*, published by Weiser Books. She gives instructions on the vine step (with pictures!) on pages 163–164.

gerbil. It's all about our intent anyway, not how precisely we tangle up our feet!

Often done with a grapevine step, the *spiral dance* has become Witchcraft's most well-known dance. Popularized by Starhawk and the Reclaiming tradition in Northern California, the spiral dance is now enacted and celebrated the world over. The spiral dance begins with everyone in the circle holding hands, with the person leading the dance letting go of the hand of the person on their left. The leader then moves in front of the person whose hand she has just let go of and begins spiraling around the ritual space until she reaches the last person in line. From there she moves to her right, and should now be facing everyone she moves past. The spiral dance ends when the leader has returned to her original position.

The spiral dance gets its name from the dance spiraling in toward the center and then back out toward the edge of the circle. By the time the dance has ended, everyone engaged in it will have come face to face with each other. The spiral dance is a great way to build energy (even if you'll be moving widdershins for a time) and community since everyone will make eye contact with one another. There's no limit to how many people can be part of a spiral dance either. At Samhain every year, over 2,000 Witches gather in San Francisco to do the spiral dance!

When building the cone of power through movement, there often will be one Witch elected to stay in the middle and coordinate the energy raising. Because it can be difficult to signal just when to stop moving and release all the power gathered up, this person in the middle directs the intensity of the movement and signals when the rite is at an end. In most cases this is the coven's High Priestess or whoever is leading the particular energy raising. When energy is being raised for a specific individual who is not in the coven, the coven member closest to that individual might be the one in the middle.

In our coven it's most often our High Priestess (my wife) who stands in the middle and directs what we are doing. Her instructions are usually rather general, and she shouts things like "Faster!" and "More intensity!" Toward the end of the ritual she'll hold up three fingers, indicating to us that we'll only be moving around the circle three more times. From there she counts down our final rotations, and right before the end of that third and final go-round she'll usually give us instructions such as "Almost done, in 3, 2, 1, and done!" Her saying "done" is a cue to release all the energy we've collected and stop moving.

It's not necessary to place anyone in the middle of the circle to keep an eye on things, but I do recommend it if you are raising energy in a large public group where the participants are not familiar with one another. It's nearly impossible to hear or see instructions in a large circle when the person giving them is out on the periphery with everyone else. In a coven that has worked together for several years, having someone coordinate the energy and timing of things isn't always necessary.

CHANTING

Chanting is often used in combination with dance and movement when creating the cone of power. Chanting is an effective way to raise energy because, like movement, it utilizes two different approaches to raising power. First, there's a physical component to sound that we often overlook: our lungs, muscles, and mouths are all doing a lot of work when we chant. Second, those sounds are coming from within our bodies and are tapping into our collective will.

The power that comes from voicing our desires is an often overlooked magickal practice. If you get up every morning and tell yourself that you are worthless, you'll probably start to feel worthless; but if you tell yourself that you have value, you'll feel better about where you are in life. The simple act of uttering a phrase or mantra is a form of spellwork. Every time we verbalize something, we are putting those intentions, desires, thoughts, and energies out into the universe. Words are powerful, which is why many Witches are taught to speak out loud when it comes to their needs and wants.

I'm of the opinion that chants in the circle should be kept as simple as possible. I've been a part of circles where the chant we were instructed to recite was eight lines long, and I spent far more time worrying about saying the right words than creating the proper energies. The saying "Keep it simple, stupid" could have been created for chants!

A chant can be as simple as one word repeated over and over, or it can involve a line or two. If the idea you want to express in your chant is more than a few words long, you should probably try to make your chant rhyme. Rhymed lines allow everyone in the circle to maintain a sense of rhythm, which is especially useful if the chant is accompanied by movement. Rhymes are also more easily remembered and keep people from stumbling over words and wondering what it is they are supposed to say next.

Oftentimes the simple chants we come up with might feel juvenile or silly, but that's not what will be going through anyone's head while saying them during an energy raising. What's most important with a chant is not that it's clever but that the words being used reinforce the ideas and reasons behind the creation of the cone of power. If you are doing a job spell, the chant should be about jobs or financial well-being. There's no reason to have eight lines about eight things that are only marginally connected to the true intent of the ritual.

I think the most effective chants are simple and to the point. Here are some examples:

- Protection: *May we be safe from harm. Lady, power our charm!*
- Money or jobs: *Money, money, come to me. Let success be all I see!*
- Dealing with depression or sadness: *Let my problems flee. Happy may I be!*
- Searching for or feeling love for oneself: *Love be here. Love be near!*
- The sabbat of Samhain: *Samhain, Samhain, Witches' night. When our cherished dead take flight!*
- Dealing with depression: *Let this pain go away. Joyful may we stay!*

Though chants are often accompanied by dancing, a lot of energy can be raised from a chant all on its own. This is especially useful if you are leading a circle where there are a lot of people with mobility issues or you simply don't have enough space to move. A clever rhyming couplet accompanied by some clapping or stomping has a great deal of power, and it's something everyone will feel.

Words don't have to be chanted to have power. One of my absolute favorite High Priestesses once had her coven build the cone of power simply by telling jokes! Every laugh put more power into the circle, and that energy was charged with joy and humor. This can be a fun way to raise energy when dealing with a negative situation.

TONING

Toning is similar to chanting because it utilizes sound and our will, but it is often reserved for particularly vexing or emotional issues. Toning generally involves vowel sounds pushed out from the body, with the sound lasting until the individual Witch is out of breath. The most common tone sounds tend to be *Ahhhhhhhh*, *Eeeeeeeee*, and *Ohhhhhhhh*.

When toning, I envision my will in the area near my heart, and I see it as a pulsing reservoir of power and usually as a glowing warm color such as gold, brown, or yellow. I dig deep into that energy, pushing it out through my lungs and diaphragm. I hold whatever tone I'm using for however long I can until all of my breath is used up. I then take a big gulp of air and repeat the process for as long as needed. Generally, when a group of Witches tone, the energy they push out of themselves becomes more powerful and their voices grow louder as the rite builds.

It's rare for toning to be accompanied by dance, though there's often some movement involved with it. In my coven we all join hands while toning, and as the power builds we slowly raise our arms until they are above our shoulders. When the energy is at its strongest, we then release our hands and drop our arms, sending the energy raised out into the universe to accomplish its purpose.

Our coven tends to reserve toning for some of our most serious magickal work. When we have a friend stricken with a serious illness, we tone. The energy raised from toning tends to be very precise and focused, which makes it especially effective if the energy is meant to go to one specific person. Toning is also useful if space is at a premium or there's no way to truly put into words what your magick is being used for.

THE PULSE

My primary coven has about eighteen active members, but we meet in a very small space. Oftentimes dancing is not really an option for us because of where we meet. Inspired by a description of Operation Cone of Power (see chapter 6), I devised a way to raise energy with lots of movement, but movement that doesn't require a great deal of space. I started calling this method "the pulse," and it has become one of my absolute favorite ways to build the cone of power in ritual. I doubt I'm the first person to use the pulse method of energy raising (and if you call it something else, I apologize), but I've never seen it written about before, so I wanted to make sure to include it in this book.

My pulse rite involves everyone in the coven standing around the altar holding hands. Everyone should hold hands comfortably at about waist level, with a little bit of space between each participant. Before starting the rite, everyone should agree on what the energy is being raised for and encapsulate that desire in one word. We've generally done this rite for protection, so our word has been "safe," but other words and needs that might work here include health, job, love, respect, etc. This method of raising energy won't work with a big, long phrase, so deciding on a single word is a must.

Once the purpose of the cone of power has been established, the energy raising begins, with everyone holding hands and then stepping inward toward the altar, drawing closer to one another. As everyone steps in toward the center of the circle, they bend their arms at the elbow so their hands come up to about shoulder level. As they step in and raise their hands, they forcefully say whatever word is being used. (Step in, raise hands, say word loudly!) This is followed by everyone taking a step back, and lowering their hands as they do so. The process of stepping in and stepping back is then repeated until the High Priestess signals the end of the rite.

Much like with toning, the volume in the circle will likely increase as the rite gears up in intensity. We often find ourselves stepping in and out of the circle's center faster as our power builds. The pulse builds a solid energy from the movement, verbalization, and overall intensity of this energy raising. Curiously, I find that stepping toward the altar (which we tend to place in the center of our ritual space) results in our energy going straight up toward the tip of our cone.

Just like when we tone, we will sometimes slowly raise our arms as the rite progresses until our hands are nearly above our heads. By this time the energy has generally peaked, and on a signal from our High Priestess we drop our arms, let out one final cry, and push our energy up and out of the circle through the center of the cone of power. I find the pulse to be very intense and usually only reserve it for our most aggressive energy work (repelling curses, keeping people safe, pushing back against negative magick, etc.).

TREADING THE WITCHES' MILL

One of the central acts of Traditional Witchcraft is the energy raising known as the "Witches' Mill" (also called the "grinding of fate" by its chief architect). Since first being introduced by Robert Cochrane in the late 1960s, the mill has been adopted by a lot of Witches from a variety of traditions. Because it's become extremely popular over the last twenty years, there are several different versions of the technique.

The practice of "treading the mill" is both similar to the traditional cone of power and radically different from it at the same time. While most Witches today build the cone of power by moving in a deosil fashion around the circle, the mill is designed to be performed widdershins. In fact, one of Cochrane's students, Evan John Jones (1936–2003), wrote that the mill "is always widdershins and never deosil." [78]

English magician and occultist William "Bill" Gray (1913–1992), who actively participated in some of Cochrane's rituals, wrote in the Witch magazine The Pentagram that the most effective dance step in regard to the mill was "the dragging shuffle of the Lame. ... God performed energetically." Cochrane's heirs later referred to this step as the "stamp and drag" and used it in their group the Regency. [79] The "stamp

---

78. Jones and Cochrane, The Roebuck in the Thicket: An Anthology of the Robert Cochrane Witchcraft Tradition, 81. This book is a collection of previously published magazine articles and is a must-read if you are interested in Cochrane or his system.

79. John of Monmouth, Genuine Witchcraft Is Explained, 71–72.

and drag" step was in honor of blacksmithing gods (such as the Greek Hephaestus and the Hebrew blacksmith Tubal Cain), who were often lame.

In my own practice I find that the Witches' Mill works much like two gears moving. The energy of the circle moves clockwise, while the energy of the coven (or *cuveen*, a term sometimes used by Traditional Witches) moves widdershins. This grinding (like a mill) of the two flows of energy creates a unique magickal environment that gives the mill its power. The Witches' Mill is not a technique I employ often, but if the energy I need might benefit from some conflict or chaos, the Witches' Mill is a superb form of energy raising. Also worth noting is that some people report the circle getting colder during the treading of the mill, so if this happens to you, it's not because you're doing anything wrong. In fact, it's probably the opposite.

In addition to creating power, the Witches' Mill can also be used for trance work.[80] Cochrane's rituals often used a forked staff or pitchfork called a stang that acted much like a traditional altar. The stang would be placed in the middle of the circle, becoming the axis point for everything that happened in ritual. When the Witches' Mill was used for trance work, the stang then became the rite's focal point, with every eye focused on it.

When using the Witches' Mill to induce a trancelike state in ritual, start with everyone facing inward toward the altar or stang. Have everyone then turn to their right and place their right hand on the right shoulder of the person standing in front of them. The left arm should then be extended toward the stang and the turning of the mill begun. Due to the close proximity of everyone in the circle, the "stamp and drag" step is not advised. It's usually best just to have everyone walk widdershins at a relatively fast pace, with their faces all turned inward to look at the stang.

The results here can be dramatic, and I've found that this indeed does produce a powerful trance state. People who have used this tech-

---

80. Shani Oates, in the chapter "The People of God and the Clan of Tubal Cain" in John of Monmouth's *Genuine Witchcraft Is Explained*, 151.

nique have described strange energies visible to the naked eye, as well as appearances by the Horned God. If anything is seen or sensed during the mill, it's best to write it down somewhere and look at it again later.

Robert Cochrane believed that the Witches' Mill was best performed in silence but added that "if it pleases the group, a chant may be useful."[81] Over the years the most common chant associated with the mill is *Io Io Evohe* (pronounced "Yo Yo Evo-hey"). A song has been built around these words, called "The Witches' Mill," naturally. In my own practice I find that the use of a chant while turning the mill creates a much more hypnotic effect.

Whether you use the mill for raising energy or group trance, it's a wonderful tool to have in your witchy bag of tricks. In addition to my interpretation of the Witches' Mill, there are several other versions out there worth looking into. As Traditional Witchcraft becomes more and more popular, it's likely that we'll see an increase in the number of Witches using the mill.

LETTING THE ENERGY GO
(AND WHAT TO DO WITH ANYTHING LEFT OVER)

The climax of the cone of power rite is the moment when the energy raised in the circle is released out into the universe. It's hard to explain just when to release that energy, and for most Witches it's a skill that's developed over time through participating in ritual and learning how to sense energy. Things are further complicated by the fact that we all feel energy differently. What I think of as the "right" time may not be what the person standing next to me thinks.

Even with all of these difficulties, there are a few signs that it's probably time to release the cone of power. The most obvious one is pure exhaustion. If you are doing something physical to raise the cone of power and everyone in the circle starts lagging and running out of breath, the time has come to let the energy go. When the buildup of energy starts to slow down, you've reached the end point. Ideally the cone of power is released on a high note; the energy builds to a crescendo and is sent out before it starts to wane.

---

81. Jones and Cochrane, *The Robert Cochrane Letters*, 135.

Well-cast circles retain a lot of heat. Instead of the heat produced by the coven going out the window or door (or out into the woods), it stays in place and heats up the area contained within the circle. When the cone of power is being raised, temperatures increase even faster. When the circle has become unbearably hot and sweat has encircled the brows of your covenmates, it's probably time to expel the energy that has built up. There's also a point in ritual where the air around the coven can't (or won't) get any thicker than it already is. If it feels like you are suffocating due to the heavy air around you, it's time to release the cone of power.

Many of the reasons we have for creating a cone of power are personal ones, and as a result, a lot of physical and emotional energy is poured into the circle. When focused on a sensitive or personal issue, the energy raising can be emotionally exhausting, and sometimes while the body might be willing to continue, the heart has given all it can. When an emotional climax has been reached during the creation of the cone of power, it's probably best to let the built-up energy go out into the world.

A clean ending to an energy raising can be difficult to accomplish. It's possible to have everyone building the cone so focused on their work that they are oblivious to those around them. A staggered ending to an energy raising won't ruin everything that's been built up, but it can be a bit awkward, and the last bit of energy created might be something different from what was previously created. (When everyone starts looking at me in circle because I missed the cue to stop toning, the last tendrils of energy released from my body tend to be the energies of embarrassment. It's a situation best avoided.)

The easiest way to signal an end to the cone's building is with shouted instructions. Even a quick shout of "Just one more time!" won't break anyone's rhythm and will usually alert everyone to what's going on. Even better is an instruction such as "Three more times!" Letting everyone know that there are only three more turns around the circle or verses of a chant will encourage everyone in the circle to dig a little deeper and really build the energy in what little time is left.

Assuming everyone's eyes are open (and they often will close, especially when toning), hand signals are also effective. My wife will often count the coven down from three when we are finishing up the cone of power. Even better is a combination of the two (a hand signal and a countdown), just to make sure everyone knows what's going on.

Many covens like to end an energy raising with a dramatic physical gesture. There are some groups that will drop to the ground at the end of a circle dance, which is powerful but also has the potential for injury if not done right. In my coven we often end with our hands held high together, followed by a quick drop of our arms as we release our hands. A physical gesture signifying the end of the energy raising is dramatic and provides a solid ending for the cone of power. There's no absolute right or wrong way to end the cone of power rite; there's only what makes sense to each individual or coven.

Even when ending the cone of power through sheer exhaustion, it's possible to still feel charged with power. When we are raising energy, we may not initially expel all of it from within ourselves. It's also possible that not every bit of energy raised will go out through the top of the cone of power. That extra energy, within and around us, often feels exhilarating, but it's best to ground the energy before ending your ritual.

The process of grounding gets us back to our normal state, and while it's fun to walk around buzzing due to magickal forces, it's not in the best interests of our health. (Our bodies just aren't designed to carry that kind of energy around all the time.) Grounding rids us of whatever extra energies might be inside of us.

The rite of cakes and ale (sometimes called cakes and wine—see part 5) is an easy grounding exercise built into most rituals. The process of eating and drinking links us to the natural world, and when food and drink enter the stomach, they draw in energy so those substances can be processed. In most cases cakes and ale is more than enough to ground the body and bring it back to its normal state, but not always.

After cakes and ale, the most common grounding exercise is to drain any extra energy inside of the body into the earth. The process is simple enough. Just place your hands palms down upon the ground. Open up your hands to whatever energy is coursing through you and let it all pour into the earth. If it doesn't flow willingly on its own, you can force it out of you by visualizing that energy leaving your body and going into the surface beneath you and deep into the earth.

One of my favorite ways to rid my body of extra energy is to simply brush it off my hands. After releasing the cone of power, I will literally brush my hands together, removing any energy that's left over. Other times I'll flick my fingers toward the altar or the sky, pushing my leftover energy into the world. The energy will then do one of two things: go up through the cone of power or get caught up in the swirling energies of the magick circle.

If there's any extra energy floating around your circle when the ritual is at its end, it will generally dissipate once the circle is released. This might take a few hours or even a couple days, but eventually everything will be as it once was, though if you do ritual time and time again in the same place, that location or room will eventually build its own energy signature. Magickal power will be ever so slightly absorbed into the ground or walls of your temple space. This isn't a bad thing; it means you're doing everything right!

ENERGY ADD-ONS

In addition to the energy we raise from the natural world and from inside of ourselves, there are other sources of energy that can be added to the cone of power. The most obvious one is divine energy—that is, energy from the deities we are close to and invite into our circles. The energy of a goddess like Aphrodite would be complementary to a rite focused on love or acceptance, while the energy of a goddess like Athena would be ideal for a spell designed to help a coven member pass a test. Assuming the deity invited to the ritual shows up, their energies become a part of the ritual and the cone of power.

Nearly everything in the world gives off energy, and that energy often lends itself to particular objectives. When those items are added to the rites of a group raising the cone of power, those energies become a part of the circle. There are a whole host of stones, herbs, and incenses associated with things such as love, prosperity, peace, clarity, and nearly anything else you can think of. Such things add to the energy being raised.

One of the oldest adages in magick is the idea that like attracts like. Decorating your altar with things you associate with healing will bring healing energies into your circle, and the items placed there will also give off those vibrations. Colors can also dramatically change the energy in a circle and can be utilized for whatever goal you are working toward.

In the United States the color green is often associated with money (it's the color of the currency), and using green candles, green tools, green altar cloths, etc., will make a money-drawing spell even more powerful. Anything we associate with a particular idea or quality can become a fine source of complementary energy.

When planning to create a cone of power for a particular purpose, decorate your altar and ritual space with things that remind you of your end goal. If you work with particular goddesses and gods, invite them into the circle so they can add their energies to your work (provided they choose to, of course). When building the cone of power, we Witches make and stir the soup, but the more ingredients we add to it, the better and stronger that soup often will be.

THE SOLO CONE OF POWER

This section has mostly dealt with building the cone of power in a group setting. While many of the techniques described in this chapter work best with a coven or circle, the cone of power can also be built by the solitary Witch. Here are some tips when working alone.

Keep the Circle Small. This seems obvious, but it's easy to simply cast a circle to fit an entire room if one isn't paying a whole lot of attention. Because the energies raised by one person are not going to equal the amount raised by a group, the solitary Witch should keep their circle small and tight. Ideally the circle shouldn't be much bigger than the arm span of the Witch performing the operation.

When I'm working alone on the cone of power, I tend to center my rituals around my altar and cast a circle just big enough for me and it. The altar is often a focal point and has all my tools on it; I don't need much more magickal space than that. The altar in my office is a long bookshelf, and when I'm working there I'll often cast my circle as a bubble encompassing just me and the active part of my altar (generally just the middle third of the bookshelf's altar space). This means that my circle bisects a part of my altar/bookshelf, but it's a magick circle, so it can do that! I find it's best to concentrate my power into a small space.

Certain Techniques Just Work Better Solo. A Witch can dance, tone, and clap when alone in a circle. However, most of us probably don't do those things, and I'll admit that I often feel very silly dancing alone, and I'm so tone-deaf that making a lot of melodious sounds to raise power doesn't feel natural alone either (and it's hard to keep the circle small and tight if the working requires room to move around). I'm sure there are people who do both of these things, and more power to them, but it's probably not all that common.

What I find works best alone is to utilize my muscles in the way described in the "Human or Personal Energy" section near the beginning of chapter 4. I squeeze my biceps and clench my hands into fists and then release that energy with a little push when I relax my muscles. Some of this energy is undoubtedly coming from my will as well, as I often visualize that center of myself releasing energy along with my muscles. Once the energy is released, it begins to spiral around the circle, and all the usual things I associate with the cone of power (the air feeling heavy, the warm becoming noticeably warmer) tend to occur.

I usually pair the flexing to raise energy with an easy chant or a repeated word. Repeating a word over and over again has a kind of lulling quality to it and keeps me focused completely on the objective of my power raising. If I'm not in a place where I feel like I can chant or repeat a word over and over again, I'll put some music on in the background and time the movements of my hands and arms with the beat of whatever it is that I'm listening to. In such instances I try to pair whatever music I'm playing with the reason for the cone of power. If it's an aggressive or intense working, I'll put on my old favorite Led Zeppelin. If it's something more serene like healing or centering work, I'll choose something more mellow. What's most important is that the music you choose adds to the working and doesn't distract from it.

When Working Alone You Can Sometimes Do a Little Less Buildup. My personal rituals tend to be less formal and structured than the things I do with my coven, and this applies to the times when I'm working with the solo cone of power. I'll sometimes skip calling the quarters, and I almost never use my sword to cast the circle. If I'm working at home with one of my well-used altars, there's usually not much need for cleansing or preparation.

If you are passionate about a particular working, it can also be done faster. Instead of allowing the energy to slowly build, like I would with a coven, sometimes it just all gets built up and released quite quickly. While working on a "leave me alone" spell at the ocean during the writing of this book, I poured just about everything that was inside of me out in only a couple minutes. What would have taken a lot of time with the coven was nearly done right after I started. Our energies work differently when we are on our own sometimes, and if you find that things move a lot faster when you are on your own, that's pretty normal. (Sometimes they might take longer, too. Things take as long as they take, not any more and not any less.)

THE INVERSE CONE OF POWER

The inverse cone of power is a magick technique that was created by my wife, Ari. Operationally it's very similar to the traditional cone of power, but instead of sending energy up and out, energy is sent downward, where it's sent directly to whoever or whatever it's being raised for. Unlike the traditional cone of power, the inverse version requires a couple of tools to channel the magickal energy being created. We've found this operation to be incredibly powerful, and it's especially effective if you are raising energy for a specific person and need it to arrive as quickly as possible.

For the inverse cone of power, you'll need a charged and activated pentacle, a focal point for the energy you'll raise, and something to connect the rite to the person you are raising energy for. The pentacle is often referred to as a "tool of earth," but it's much more than that. [82] Pentacles are traditionally gateways from which spirits, demons, and deities emerge. For the inverse cone, we will be utilizing the pentacle's unique properties as a window into other worlds and spaces.

Nearly anything can be used as a focal point, but we tend to produce better results when using a natural object. Our favorite is something akin to the traditional crystal ball, though much smaller. We have a small sphere-shaped crystal that we use for this rite, though any old piece of crystal will work just fine. Depending on the purpose of our energy raising, we occasionally use other stones to take advantage of their natural properties.

We use our crystal ball as a focal point for the energy we are raising, but we also use it as a link to the person we are raising energy for. Traditionally crystal balls were used for scrying, and they also served as a way to "check up" on certain individuals. We use the crystal's natural tendency to find people as a link to the person we are doing the work for.

Just in case our crystal ball doesn't provide a strong enough link to the intended recipient, we also like to use an item that connects us to the individual. This could be something as simple as a picture or perhaps one of their personal items. If none of those things are available, simply writing their name down on a piece of paper works well enough.

Before creating the inverse cone of power, the pentacle is placed on the center of the altar, with the crystal ball in the center of it. Also placed on the pentacle is the object or picture of the individual the work is centered around. The more connections you have to the focus of your ritual the better, so use all of them. Add-ons can be placed on the pentacle too, specifically rocks, herbs, or any other items whose natural energies might enhance the work. (If it's a healing ritual, you'll want to use stones associated with healing, for example.)

The inverse cone of power relies on traditional ways of energy raising to work. In most cases we use a combination of toning or chanting,

---

82. A pentacle is a round disc generally inscribed with a five-pointed star. It can be made from wood, ceramic material, wax, or nearly any other thing you can think of. In my book *The Witch's Altar* (co-written with Laura Tempest Zakroff), I spend a lot of time talking about this often overlooked tool.

along with the projection of energy from our hands. We activate our collective wills along with the natural energies of sound and then push those out of our bodies, through our voices and our extremities. Instead of raising our arms upward, we slowly move them outward and then down toward the pentacle.

Generally we work to get as close to the pentacle as possible, drawing in close to one another and lowering our hands until they are just a few inches from the crystal ball atop the pentacle. The goal with the inverse cone of power is to push the energy being projected downward and into the crystal ball, where it will then go through the pentacle. Instead of letting the energy go out and move around the circle, the energy is forced downward—and this is not how energy wants to behave. Part of the reason for keeping our hands close to the pentacle during this process is to make sure none of the energy being raised goes upward.

The energy being raised is focused on the crystal ball, and from there that energy goes downward into the pentacle and comes out on the other side where you want it to be. By using an object to connect your rite to a certain person (or place), the energy raised in the inverse cone of power comes out at that point. None of it is wasted, and it goes directly from your ritual circle, through the pentacle, and to the other side.

When finished with the inverse cone of power, remove all the items used during its conjuring from the pentacle. After that is done you'll want to sever the connection between the pentacle and the person you raised energy for. This can be easily accomplished by drawing a banishing pentagram on the pentacle and proclaiming that the work is now done and all will be as it once was. The inverse cone of power is most certainly not a traditional way to raise and send energy out into the world, but it works!

CHAPTER SIX

Operation Cone of Power

Old Dorothy called up "covens right and left; although by Witch Law
they should not be known to each other". And this was the start of
"Operation Cone of Power", when the witches, as they claim, sent up a
force against Hitler's mind.
— From chapter 13 of *Gerald Gardner: Witch*
(attributed to Jack Bracelin)

Operation Cone of Power is one of the most legendary Witchcraft rituals in modern history, yet we know very little about it. It's so shrouded
in mystery that we can't say with absolute certainty whether or not it
actually happened in the way described by Gerald Gardner. Operation
Cone of Power was first written about in September of 1952 in the English magazine *Illustrated* and was included in a feature on Witchcraft and
Gerald Gardner. Allen Andrews, the author of the article, describes the
rite: "The coven proceeded to conduct rites intended to raise the first
colossal 'cone of power' they had ever produced—and direct it against
Hitler."[83]

Gardner alluded to Operation Cone of Power in all three of the
nonfiction books on Witchcraft he had a hand in creating (*The Meaning*

---

83. Heselton, *Witchfather: A Life of Gerald Gardner, Vol. 1*, 239. Heselton's book has an
entire chapter on Operation Cone of Power.

of Witchcraft, Witchcraft Today, and his biography *Gerald Gardner: Witch)* and he spoke of it with people such as Doreen Valiente and Patricia Crowther, another of his early High Priestesses. Whatever Operation Cone of Power was, it seemed especially important to Gardner, and along with his initiation, it's one of the few rites he mentions participating in with the New Forest Coven. Despite being such a central story in his experiences as a Witch, Gardner devotes only a few paragraphs to it in his books.

Operation Cone of Power took place in the early days of World War II, most likely after the fall of France (June 1940) but before Hitler began bombing Britain in September of that year. The most common date given for the ritual is Lammas Night, either July 31 or August 1 (the date of Lammas can vary depending on the individual Witch), but it might have occurred over several days. In *Gerald Gardner: Witch,* Gardner is quoted as saying that the "ritual was repeated four times," though it's not specified whether or not the ritual was done four times in one night, on four completely different dates, or over four consecutive nights.

Though Lammas is the date most associated with Operation Cone of Power, there are some who think it may have occurred in May of that year. Gardner seemed to allude to a May date in 1954, though he also told both of his later High Priestesses (Patricia Crowther and Doreen Valiente) that it happened on Lammas.[84] If the rite took place over four different days, it's possible that the first operation took place at the end of May. We'll never know for sure.

What we can be sure of is just how imminent a land invasion of Great Britain must have felt from May of 1940 through the following autumn. As patriotic English folk, Gardner and his fellow Witches no doubt would have felt the call to do *something,* and magick is an especially big something. The threat of invasion would have been felt more urgently in the New Forest area of England too, as it is directly across the English Channel from France.

It's unlikely that very many Witches participated in Operation Cone of Power, despite Gardner claiming that Dorothy Clutterbuck called

---

84. Heselton, *Witchfather: A Life of Gerald Gardner,* Vol. 1, 240–241.

up "covens left and right, although by Witch Law they should have not known each other." He later stated that the ritual (or rituals) involved only seventeen other people, and it's possible that not all seventeen participants were Witches.[85] Faced with the possibility of an invasion by the Nazi war machine, I'm guessing that anyone even the slightest bit sympathetic to Witchcraft might have been willing to participate.

From Gardner's recollections, there are a few things that can be determined about the ritual itself. Light would have been in short supply, not just because the rituals likely occurred at night on the seashore but because blackout rules were in effect. Any illumination was likely limited to a very small fire and perhaps a candle. Doreen Valiente wrote that Gardner told her that the candle was a lantern and that the fire was placed in the southeast, which was thought to be the most likely spot for the invasion.[86] In the 1952 *Illustrated* magazine article, Gardner mentions the Witches all carrying dim, ceremonial firebrands, which possibly played a role in the rite.[87]

According to what Gardner told Doreen Valiente, the cone of power was built through dancing and chant, and she gives a pretty thorough account of how it was possibly done:

> The circle was marked out and people stationed to whip up the dancers....Then all danced round until they felt they had raised enough power. If the rite was to banish, they started deosil and finished widdershins, so many rounds of each. Then they formed a line with linked hands and rushed towards the fire shouting what they wanted. They kept it up until they were exhausted or until someone fell in a faint, when they were said to have taken the spell to its destination.[88]

The description given here by Valiente suggests that three different things happened during the building of this cone of power. The first was a rather standard cone of power rite, with the movement beginning

---

85. Ibid., 243.

86. Valiente, *The Rebirth of Witchcraft*, 45–46.

87. Heselton, *Witchfather: A Life of Gerald Gardner, Vol. 1*, 246.

88. Valiente, *The Rebirth of Witchcraft*, 45.

in a clockwise direction. This was followed by the circle suddenly moving counterclockwise. While widdershins is an effective way of raising energy for banishing spells, I think it may have been done to confuse the minds of Hitler and his generals. Moving energy around like that would have had a rather disorienting effect on the intended target. Chaos in the ranks of the German High Command would have helped Gardner and his fellow Witches to achieve their goal of keeping Hitler and his Nazis out of their country.

The third part of the rite involved both a chant and a rush toward the small fire placed in the southeast corner of the circle. Valiente says that they "formed a line," which suggests they got out of the circle formation used for the earlier dancing. This is a bit unusual but could have been done to direct the energy toward that area. Though we usually think of the cone of power as releasing through the top of the circle-sphere, there's nothing that says it can't leave from a different point. In *Gerald Gardner: Witch*, Gardner says that the cone of power "was raised and slowly directed in the general direction of Hitler," which in July/ August of 1940 would have been Berlin. (If Operation Cone of Power had been performed earlier in the year, it could have been Paris.)

In Valiente's account, she writes that Gardner told her the chant used was this: "Can't cross the sea! Can't cross the sea! Not able to come! Not able to come!"[89] In *Gerald Gardner: Witch*, Gardner states that this was the chant: "You cannot cross the Sea. You cannot cross the Sea. YOU CANNOT COME. YOU CANNOT COME." In *Witchcraft Today*, Gardner writes that the chant was this: "You cannot cross the sea," "You cannot cross the sea," "Not able to come," "Not able to come."[90] All three versions of the chant are simple and convey the same message. Since Gardner was writing and reminiscing about these events twelve years or more after they happened, some variation is probably to be expected.

Operation Cone of Power wasn't performed to erect a barrier around Great Britain or cause Hitler's death. Its focus was limited and specific. The cone of power was built to place the idea in the minds

---

89. Valiente, *The Rebirth of Witchcraft*, 46.
90. Gardner, *Witchcraft Today*, 104.

of Hitler and his military commanders that an invasion of the United Kingdom was impossible. "Not able to come, cannot cross the sea" is a simple directive and an outstanding use of magickal energy to achieve a specific result. Operation Cone of Power was directed at only a few individuals and had but one goal: no invasion. Simple magick is often the most effective magick.

There are a few more interesting tidbits in Gardner's recollections of Operation Cone of Power from *Gerald Gardner: Witch*, the first of which is that the cone "may not be done except in great emergency."[91] In this context it's difficult to ascertain if he's saying that the cone of power cannot be built except in an emergency or if building a "great circle" (a circle larger than nine feet across and with more than thirteen Witches) is what's prohibited. He could also simply be alluding to how much energy was poured into the circle. Gardner said that his asthma returned after the rite and that some coven members died.[92] Certainly Gardner suffered from asthma during the last twenty-five years of his life, but we'll never know for sure if anyone died during Operation Cone of Power.

Though no one else involved in Operation Cone of Power ever wrote about it, it's possible that a few folks who were there might have at least said something about it. Fantasy author Katherine Kurtz's 1983 novel *Lammas Night* is a fictional account of how England's many esoteric and occult orders might have worked together to stop Hitler's impending invasion. The novel includes cameo appearances by Dion Fortune, Aleister Crowley, and Gerald Gardner himself, and some have speculated that a New Forest Witch might have assisted Kurtz in writing her book.

The Reverend Selena Fox, founder of Circle Sanctuary and one of the most important contemporary Witches in the US, told me that in

---

91. Bracelin, *Gerald Gardner: Witch*. The account of Operation Cone of Power occurs in Chapter 13, "Into the Witch Cult."

92. In his book *Wiccan Roots*, Heselton speculates not only on who might have participated in Operation Cone of Power but also on who might have died as a result of it. I've chosen to leave such information out of this book due to how speculative it all is—and possibly because I want you to buy everything Heselton has ever written.

the late 1980s she met an Englishwoman in New York City who claimed to have been at Operation Cone of Power. As I write this though, it seems likely that anyone involved in the operation would have already passed on to the Summerlands by that time. Most of the people thought to be in the New Forest Coven were on the plus side of fifty when the ritual was performed and most likely took their secrets to the grave.

While we'll never know for sure if Operation Cone of Power truly happened, I feel that it's likely. England's occult community was certainly engaged in the Magickal Battle for Britain, which is attested to in the letters of Dion Fortune to her Fraternity of the Inner Light. Even if Gardner was not a Witchcraft initiate in 1940, he still could have done some sort of ritual either with the Rosicrucian Fellowship or with just Edith Woodford-Grimes, or even on his own. Because the story of Operation Cone of Power was such an important one to him, I'm guessing that it occurred in some fashion and probably happened like he said it did.

Gardner also claimed in his books that Operation Cone of Power wasn't the first cone of power raised by English Witches for the preservation of their country. He says similar rites were performed when the Spanish Armada attempted an invasion by sea in 1588, and again in 1803 when Napoleon threatened Great Britain. While I find it unlikely that people identifying as Witches participated in such rites, it's certainly possible that some magickal folks did and that legends of such rites circulated among magick practitioners. (Alternatively, Gardner might have simply made up these other events to provide a more ancient pedigree for his Witch religion.)

It's hard to say what sort of an effect Operation Cone of Power ultimately had on World War II, but it most certainly set a precedent. As I write this, many Witches are engaged in a mass binding spell against President Donald Trump. Time will tell if such efforts prove to be effective, but there is a long tradition of Witches standing up for their rights and in defense of their values, as evidenced by what happened on Lammas Night in 1940.

Part Three

Dedications, Initiations, and Elevations

CHAPTER SEVEN

Initiations, Today and Yesterday

I've been "initiated" into two different faith traditions in this lifetime. The first initiation occurred at my then United Methodist Church in the small town of Wytheville, Virginia. On the Palm Sunday of my sixth grade year, I was baptized and "confirmed" in the church. The ceremonial act of baptism acted as an official acceptance of Christianity, and my confirmation made me a member of the Methodist Church.

I doubt most Christians think of confirmation as an initiation ceremony, but it most certainly is one. It's meant to be a person's official *chosen* entry into a Christian tradition. Infant baptisms and christening ceremonies are performed without the consent of the person being baptized or christened. As a twelve-year-old, I was mostly making my own decisions and at the very least was conscious of what was happening.

I remember very little about my confirmation ceremony. I was given a cross, our minister said a few words, and then I went back to the pew containing my family. When I got home I put my cross in a closet, and today it's either inhabiting a long forgotten box or in a landfill. I have no idea where it's gone.

My second initiation ceremony happened in my early thirties and marked my admittance into Gardnerian Wicca. Because of secrecy oaths I can't tell you very much about that ritual. I can reveal that I remember it, though my recollection of it is not completely accurate. For me it was a night truly spent between the worlds and was one of the most magickal moments of my entire life. If I had any doubts about the power of initiatory Wicca, they were quickly extinguished that evening.

I can say a little about that night in this book but only in the broadest strokes. The people present at my initiation represented nearly fifteen years of my life as a Pagan/Witch up to that point. Many of the people I started this journey with were there to witness my initiation and participate as I became one of the Wica. My wife was also initiated that evening and did it before me, making her a Gardnerian Witch for slightly longer. (Because my ceremony happened after midnight, she "has a day" on me!)

There were some secrets shared with us that night, and the gifts I received immediately after my initiation are still a part of my magickal life. There were statues and necklaces, and unlike my cross from the sixth grade, I know *exactly* where all these items reside. My initiation ceremony was everything I wanted it to be and more, and my wife felt exactly the same way about hers. About a week after our initiations, she and I went on an evening stroll through our Michigan neighborhood. It was late March, a liminal time between winter and spring. There was life in the air but not quite yet on the ground or in the trees. The world still looked rather bleak and gray, and yet everything was much brighter than it had ever been before.

During a pause in our walk, my wife turned to me and said, "Does everything look different to you after our initiation? Like it was all in black and white before and now it's all in color?" I thought it was an odd thing to say, but I also agreed that she was absolutely right. The world *did* look different, and would never look quite the same to either of us ever again.

Like all good initiation rituals, our Gardnerian initiation changed how we see the world. This doesn't happen at every initiation ritual, but it happens at a lot of them. When talking to my friends who have also been through initiation rituals, I'm struck by how similar their stories are to my own. Ari and I aren't the only ones to be changed by an initiation rite, and we won't be the last.

By writing that my own initiation was life-changing, I think I'm creating an awfully high standard for such rites, but don't we as Witches set high standards for ourselves? If you are the one doing the initiating, then planning to change someone's life is probably a little much, but you most certainly should strive to create the most magickal environment possible. And for those being initiated, you need to be open to the experience for it to have any power.

WHAT ARE DEDICATIONS, INITIATIONS, AND ELEVATIONS?

Elevations, initiations, and dedications are markers on one's individual journey as a Witch. Not every Witch will seek out such ceremonies (nor should they), but for those who celebrate with a coven or a circle, group rites indicating the individual Witch's progress are a nice public statement on how far they've come in their studies. One thing about Modern Witchcraft is that we are always trying to further our understanding of things. We continually look to deepen our magicks, sharpen our skills, and grow closer to our gods. Rites of passage help us do that.

A dedication ritual can be performed individually or with a group. It's often a very simple rite and might be nothing more than a statement to the gods and nature that the individual doing the ritual now identifies as a Witch. Most people choose to be a little more elaborate than that, but a dedication ritual is essentially a simple declaration of faith or identity. Saying "I am a Witch" or "I practice Witchcraft" will do the trick.

An initiation is something very different from a dedication. Initiations generally require the involvement of a group or at least another individual. Within Witchcraft, initiation is something given by one Witch to another. You don't need to be initiated to be a Witch, but you can't initiate yourself into a Witchcraft tradition. Some of the best Witches I know have never been initiated into anything, and that's perfectly okay. It's an experience that's not for everyone, and no one should ever be forced or pressured into receiving an initiation.

The issue of initiation is a contentious one in our community. There are many who believe that self-initiation is possible or that initiation on the astral plane or during communion with the gods is equivalent to initiation with a coven. I don't completely disagree with such thoughts. Initiation will always be a chicken-or-the-egg situation since the first person to perform a Witch initiation couldn't have been an initiate. Initiation means different things to different people. For the purposes of this book, initiation means acceptance and admittance into a Witch coven, either new or established.

My eclectic coven met for several years before I devised an initiation ritual for it. When an initiation rite was finally offered, we had some coven members reject the invitation. They just didn't want to be initiated into anything under any circumstances, and since they had been with us from the coven's beginning, no one had a problem with it. Oddly, because my wife and I were the ones performing the initiations, we've never been initiated into the eclectic coven that we helped to create!

An elevation ritual is reserved for those who have been initiated into a coven and have met certain requirements of that specific tradition or coven. The earliest Modern Witch covens had three *degrees*, which are akin to a coven rank or at least a level of achievement. The third degree was reserved for those preparing to run their own coven (High Priestess/High Priest), the second degree for those capable of performing most coven duties, and the first degree for those just starting out. Elevations serve as public acknowledgments of a particular Witch's competence and progress in the Craft.

Dedication rituals, initiations, and elevations are not new things and have been around since people began putting together religious and spiritual rites thousands of years ago. Most religions today offer some sort of welcoming/initiation ritual, though many of those have been stripped of their spiritual power. Over the last five hundred years initiation rituals have also become essential parts of many fraternal orders (like the Freemasons), and those orders have had a large impact on the initiation rites of today's Witchcraft.

THE GREEK MYSTERIES:
INITIATION IN THE ANCIENT WORLD

Initiation rituals are probably one of the oldest forms of religious ritual among humans and could go back tens of thousands of years. In contemporary hunter-gatherer societies, initiations continue to play a large role in community life and often involve painful procedures such as the removal of teeth, circumcision, scarification, and blood letting.[93] Understandably, such forms of initiation are not common today in the Western world and have had little (if any) influence on modern Pagan practices. Much more influential have been the Greek mysteries, especially those that took place at Eleusis, a city just outside of Athens.

The Eleusinian Mysteries were the most famous set of initiation rites in the ancient world, and though it's likely that hundreds of thousands of people participated in them over the course of nearly a thousand years, we know very little about them. Initiates were sworn to secrecy, and only rarely were those vows broken—and generally by Christians who turned their backs on their vows. But thanks to those oath breakers, as well as ancient art (especially pottery) that depicted the Mysteries, excavations from Eleusis itself, and a few poems and letters, it's possible to at least intelligently speculate on what happened at Eleusis all those centuries ago.

Because of their secrecy, the Eleusinian Mysteries haven't been as influential as some might wish them to be, but every time we celebrate a mystery we are, in a way, celebrating Eleusis. The modern word *mystery* comes directly from the ancient Greek *mysterion*, which means "secret rite or doctrine," and mysterion itself derives from *mystes*, which means "one who has been initiated." [94] Just saying the word mystery links us to some of the most celebrated of all ancient Pagan rites!

The mysteries of Greek and Roman antiquity were not limited to those at Eleusis. Deities such as Dionysus, Orpheus, Magna Mater, and Mithras all had their own mysteries, and unlike the Eleusinian Mysteries, those cults were portable. (The Eleusinian Mysteries could be performed only at Eleusis.) However, we know less about those rites, probably because they weren't centrally located and were more likely to vary from location to location.

The Eleusinian Mysteries were dedicated to the grain and harvest goddess Demeter, along with her daughter, Persephone, who was known

---

93. Hayden, *Shamans, Sorcerers, and Saints*, 103–104.
94. Online Etymology Dictionary, https://www.etymonline.com/word/mystery.

at Eleusis as *Kore*, which translates as "the Girl."[95] Other deities were invoked at the Mysteries (including a form of Dionysus), but the rites revolved around Demeter and her daughter. The most famous tale of Demeter and Persephone involves the abduction of the latter by Hades, the Greek god of the underworld. In that tale, Demeter is distraught over the loss of her daughter, and her depression robs the world of its fertility. Eventually Persephone is returned to her mother, but not before eating four to six pomegranate seeds (depending on which version of the story you read). Because Persephone eats the food of the dead, she is obligated to return to that world for four (or six) months of the year. This story serves as a metaphor for the change of seasons.

It's unknown just how large a role that story played in the Mysteries at Eleusis, but it must have been at least a small one. While Demeter was distraught over the loss of her daughter, she worked for a time as a wet nurse for the king in Eleusis, promising to establish the Mysteries there after her daughter's return. Perhaps even more importantly, the Mysteries took place at the end of September/beginning of October.

Those of us living in the United States and Great Britain often interpret that period as a time when Persephone might be traveling to the underworld. However, in ancient Greece near Athens, crops were planted in the late fall because the summer was too hot for agriculture.[96] In other words, Persephone actually returns to her mother in the fall, and the Mysteries most likely celebrated that reunion.

One of the more intriguing bits of information about the Mysteries comes from the Christian Clement of Alexandria (150–215). In his *Exhortation to the Greeks,* he writes of a *synthema,* a word or object that brings one closer to deity and may even grant access to their power: "I fasted, I drank from the *kykeon,* I took out of the *kiste* [box], worked, placed back in the basket (*kalathos*) and from the basket into the *kiste.*"[97] Not surprisingly, Clement doesn't offer much insight into what this all

---

95. Burkert, *Greek Religion,* 159. Other books sometimes translate Kore as "the Maiden."

96. Bowden, *Mystery Cults of the Ancient World,* 28.

97. Burkert, *Greek Religion,* 286.

means, but it's likely that the "work" alluded to refers to a mortar and pestle.

The mortar and pestle might have also been important in the creation of the *kykeon,* a barley drink associated with the Mysteries.[98] Over the last hundred years it has become fashionable to try to link kykeon with hallucinogenic substances such as ergot, a fungus that grows on grain. The problem with this is that thousands of people participated in the Mysteries every year for a thousand years, and the amount of ergot needed for such an undertaking would have been quite large. Ergot is also very unpleasant, and it's likely the physical effects would have been commented on by writers and participants.[99]

The two biggest secrets at Eleusis likely had something to do with death and the afterlife, along with the civilizing power of agriculture. The famous orator Cicero (106–43 BCE) once wrote that the Mysteries teach "how to live in joy, and how to die with better hopes."[100] Officiants who presided over the Mysteries had epitaphs on their headstones with statements such as "death is not only not an evil, but good."[101] The rites themselves might have concluded with the showing of an ear of grain, the meaning of which might be related to wealth, the cycle of death and rebirth, a child, or the civilizing nature of agriculture. (This type of speculation comes from pottery, which often shows the ancient king of Eleusis holding an ear of grain while standing between Demeter and Persephone.)

Though we don't know exactly how the Greeks interpreted the Mysteries of Demeter, it is possible to construct an outline of how they were probably enacted. Unlike most of our more modern initiation ceremonies, initiation into the Mysteries took place over several days and involved a great deal of walking. The Mysteries began in Athens, where prospective initiates had to walk through the city with a baby pig and then take that piglet down to the sea to be washed and sacrificed. This served as a method of purification for initiates and was probably a major Athe-

---

98. Ibid., 286.

99. Burkert, *Ancient Mystery Cults,* 108.

100. Ibid., 21.

101. Ibid.

nian spectacle. Just imagine several thousand people walking around with pigs in their arms![102]

A few days after the piglet sacrifice, two processions departed from Athens to Eleusis, fourteen miles down the road. The initiation process at Eleusis was two-tiered, and the first procession was limited to past initiates seeking a greater understanding of the Mysteries. A day after their departure, the would-be initiates were allowed to walk to Eleusis. After a long walk they danced in honor of the goddesses and were finally admitted into the sanctuary. Upon admission they probably fasted, with their fast lasting until the revelation of the Mysteries the following evening.

Several different activities made up the bulk of the Mysteries, including a probable torchlit search for Persephone and an enactment of her reunion with Demeter. It's likely that initiates were blindfolded during the search for Persephone and forced to walk what must have felt like dangerous pathways. To aid them in their search for Persephone, those returning to the Mysteries were given torches, which they most likely waved near the heads of the new initiates. While the search was under way, a priest banged a gong in the sanctuary, summoning Kore to return to the world of the living.

Eventually Persephone returned and was reunited with her mother, a spectacle that could only be witnessed by those who had returned to experience the Mysteries a second time. The reunited Persephone and Demeter, along with the second-timers, then entered Eleusis's main sanctuary. Once in place the new initiates were free to remove their blindfolds and enter the sanctuary, which would have been awash in a sea of light from the thousands of burning torches.

After gazing upon the two goddesses (and likely a few other deities), the new initiates were ushered out of the sanctuary and the returnees were then shown an ear of grain. After the rites had ended there was probably feasting, merry making, and perhaps a few consensual orgies.

---

102. This entire summary of what happened at the Mysteries comes from Hugh Bowden's *Mystery Cults of the Ancient World*, pages 32–42. Bowden's account is extremely readable, a quality that can be challenging to find when mucking around in ancient history.

Due to the madcap energy present at the Mysteries, it's likely that every initiation experience differed from person to person. The blindfolds, the exhaustion, the fear from the fires—all of this must have had a transformative effect on the psyches of those involved. I'm sure the priests who led the Mysteries had their own interpretations of the meaning of everything, but the meanings that mattered most were those gleaned by the participants—and that's a truth that still applies to the mysteries of initiation today.

Masons and Other Fraternal Orders

Several years ago I was lucky enough to present a massive Samhain ritual at a Masonic hall in Santa Cruz, California. Though rather nondescript on the outside, the building hosted a lodge room (the Masons' name for a meeting space) that looked to me like a ballroom in a medieval castle. Even more impressive was how that room simmered with energy. It wasn't witchy energy, but it was close, and that's most likely because Modern Witchcraft has borrowed and adapted a whole host of things from the Masons.

A great deal of the terminology we use today comes straight from Freemasonry. Phrases such as "So mote it be" and "Merry meet, and merry part, and merry meet again" were used in Masonic lodges long before they were uttered in a magick circle.[103] Even "the Craft" as a synonym for Witchcraft and Wicca comes from the Masons.[104] Masonry has influenced more than Modern Witchcraft; it has influenced dozens of occult orders since the 1700s. If imitation is the sincerest form of flattery, then groups ranging from the Mormon Church to the Hermetic Order of the Golden Dawn owe the Masons a large debt.

It's not an exaggeration to suggest that Freemasonry has played a role in the initiation rituals of every occult and esoteric group of the last 350 years. Even groups that weren't directly influenced by the Masons most likely picked up something from them secondhand. Masonry has been

---

103. Nabarz, *The Square and the Circle: The Influences of Freemasonry on Wicca and Paganism*, 80–81.

104. Ibid., 70.

influential not just because of its longevity but also because its rituals (especially those pertaining to initiation and elevation) are effective.

To many people the Masons are an esoteric and occult order par excellence, and to others they are simply a harmless fraternal organization. The truth of the matter probably lies between the two extremes. Esoteric knowledge can be found in Freemasonry if one is looking for it, and if someone isn't seeking such things, the order can be experienced without those elements. The level of mystery to be found in Masonry is up to each individual member. Much like Witchcraft, Masonry provides a place to experience many mysteries, but how those mysteries are interpreted and received will vary from person to person.

Much of the intrigue that's attached to the Masons today comes from the rather speculative origins of the order. Depending on who one talks to, the Masons have either existed since biblical times or were formed a little more than 300 years ago when four Masonic groups in London got together in 1717 and formed a Grand Lodge. That first Grand Lodge then claimed authority over all the other Masonic groups in England.[105] While Freemasonry doesn't date back to biblical times, it certainly predates the eighteenth century and most likely emerged during the medieval period, slowly transforming from a guild of Scottish stonemasons into a strictly fraternal order.[106]

Evidence of Masonry's roots in the medieval guilds can be seen in tools such as the square and the compass, which would have been used by stonemasons to build churches and castles. Further evidence comes from a series of texts known as the *Old Charges*, which date from 1380 and provide structure and guidance as to the behavior of stonemasons, along with instructions on how to run meetings.[107] Beginning around 1600, a new series of rules were applied to masonic guilds, regulating their structure and assembly, and this eventually lead to *non-operative masons*, the term applied to people who joined the guild but were not actual stonemasons. Once people outside the actual profession of ma-

---

105. Ridley, *The Freemasons: A History of the World's Most Powerful Secret Society*, 33.
    Despite its rather grandiose title, this is a rather sober book on Masonic history.

106. Bogdan, *Western Esotericism and Rituals of Initiation*, 69.

107. Ibid., 68–69.

sonry were allowed in, the medieval guild became a fraternal organization instead of a business group.

Skilled trade groups in the medieval period had a three-tiered system of advancement (apprentice, journeyman, master), and it seems likely that this system had some sort of influence on the Masonic degree system. Today, first-degree Masons are known as Entered Apprentices and third-degree Masons are called Master Masons. The exception is the second degree, which is known as Fellowcraft in Masonry. It stands to reason that apprentices, journeymen, and masters all might have had their own initiation and elevation rites, which were absorbed into Freemasonry when it transitioned from medieval guild to fraternal order.

Masonic initiation and elevation rites have become so influential over the last several centuries because they are designed to be transformative. Not only do they reveal knowledge generally reserved for Masons,[108] but they also offer previously hidden wisdom and often employ frightening and disorienting techniques that lead to an overly emotional state. As we move later in this chapter into the ideas and practices found in many Witchcraft rites pertaining to initiation and elevation, we'll see many of the same techniques and concepts used by the Masons.

Written accounts of Masonic ritual include stories of being blindfolded, walking curious paths, and other uncomfortable moments. In his book *Turning the Hiram Key*, Robert Lomas states that during his initiation into Masonry he "had been blindfolded and walked around an unseen obstacle course…[and then] cramped into a distorted foetal position for another quarter of an hour."[109] In Lomas's account he mentions repeatedly how walking in what seemed to him at the time nonsensical paths while

---

108. Many of Masonry's secrets have been hiding in plain sight for over a hundred years now. In 1866, Malcolm Duncan published what has come to be known as *Duncan's Masonic Ritual and Monitor*, a guidebook of Masonic ritual. I don't think modern Masonic ritual coincides completely with *Duncan's*, but many of the ideas and practices are the same. All of my quotations of Masonic ritual are from this text.

109. Lomas, *Turning the Hiram Key*, 59–60. Lomas's book goes into Masonic ritual in great detail and is for sale at the United Grand Lodge in London, so the order must not have much of a problem with it.

blindfolded created a heightened sense of vulnerability, emotion, and excitement, with all the sensory deprivation softening him up.[110]

In addition to blindfolding initiates and leading them around by a rope called a "cable tow," the initiation and elevation rites also included physical threats. A swordsman oversaw the initiation rite's beginning, and at one point a knife was held to the bare breast of the initiate. In the third-degree rite, the elevating Mason was thrown backward, only to land on a piece of taut canvas that kept him from hitting the floor. (This is according to *Duncan's Monitor*; I'm sure something else is used in this day and age.) At the end of the initiation rite, the Masonic seeker was warned that "terrible and violent" retribution would come to anyone who shared the secrets of Freemasonry.[111] (No one can say with certainty whether such threats were ever carried out; it all depends on what history of the Masons one is reading.)

Along with the disorientation and physical threats, Masonic rites also reveal hidden truths. In the Entered Apprentice rite, the initiate is said to have begun his journey "long been in darkness, and now seeks to be brought to light."[112] Later in the ritual, the seeker is brought up to the lodge's main altar, where the blindfold is removed and the initiate is greeted by a loud "clap" by those attending the rite, along with a bright, blinding light (especially hard on the eyes after being blindfolded).[113] There the initiating Mason's chosen holy book (referred to as the *Volume of Sacred Law*) is revealed, along with the compass and the square.[114]

The symbolism and truths of the Masonic third degree are even more startling. There the Mason seeking the degree of Master is again blindfolded and made to reenact the murder of Hiram, the alleged builder of Solomon's Temple (the first temple of Jewish tradition). Over the course of the drama, the elevating Mason is pushed downward to enact their symbolic death before being raised up in an embrace called

---

110. Lomas, *Turning the Hiram Key*, 45–49.

111. Stavish, *Freemasonry*, 53.

112. This is from the "Seventh Order of Business" section of the Entered Apprentice rite in *Duncan's Masonic Ritual and Monitor*.

113. Lomas, *Turning the Hiram Key*, 48.

114. Stavish, *Freemasonry*, 52.

the "five points of fellowship": foot to foot, knee to knee, breast to breast, hand to back, and cheek to cheek (mouth to ear). According to legend, Hiram's body was somehow raised from the earth by an individual who touched his corpse at these five points. (That doesn't seem like a very effective way to pick up a corpse, but at least it's poetic.)

Following Hiram's symbolic death and raising, the soon-to-be Master Mason is taught the final secrets of Masonry, including handshakes, passwords, and a Masonic word, which had to be recreated after Hiram's death (the original having been lost). Because Masonic rites were meant to be kept secret, I'm uncomfortable writing about them too much in this book, but the major points outlined here were an inspiration for many Witches, though our rites have generally taken on a uniqueness of their own.

THE HORSEMAN'S WORD

By the end of the nineteenth century, fraternal orders were at their peak, with up to 20 percent of American and British males belonging to such groups.[115] Many of those groups had elements that would feel very "Pagan" to us today. There were fraternal Druid organizations, and groups such as the Grange (the National Grange of the Order of Patrons of Husbandry) utilized ideas taken from Greek and Roman mythology. The most interesting of the groups inspired by the Masons might be the Horseman's Word, a secret society whose rituals most likely inspired many Modern Witches for reasons that will become apparent when we look at their initiation rites.

The Horseman's Word was (and still is, in some parts of Scotland) a fraternal order open to any male over the age of eighteen who worked with horses in some capacity, folks such as blacksmiths, ploughmen, and harness makers.[116] The Horseman's Word is perhaps most famous for being a society for "horse whisperers," individuals said to be able to calm and train a horse with just one word (hence the name). The Horseman's Word was established in the early nineteenth century when

---

115. Hutton, *The Triumph of the Moon*, 64.
116. Howard, *Children of Cain*, 138.

the horse became the primary animal used to pull Scottish plows.[117] (Groups with *word* in their name were borrowing the idea of "the Mason's Word," a word thought to give a person power over certain forces.)

As its popularity spread, the Horseman's Word quickly became both a working guild and a fraternal order, eventually developing a rather unique and sometimes notorious initiation rite. Instead of borrowing their ritual directly from Freemasonry, the Horseman's Word instead adapted rites then being used by the Miller's Word. Unlike Masonic ritual, with its focus on the Volume of Sacred Law, the Millers introduced blasphemous elements into their initiation ritual, including a handshake with the Devil. Their initiation ritual was influenced by stories from the witch trials of the early modern period, and group members were said to receive magickal powers by reading the Bible backward three times over the course of three years.[118]

I think there's a tendency to look at the rituals of groups like the Millers and Horsemen and think, "Aha! Witchcraft." Certainly some of the rituals and ideas found within such groups are compatible with Modern Witchcraft, but initiates of such groups certainly didn't think of themselves as Witches and most likely didn't take the occult elements in them all that seriously. Blasphemous elements in rites were good for a laugh, and terrifying potential initiates with such a display made for memorable and effective initiation rites. In addition, hinting at occult and magickal powers (not to mention invoking a little fear) made negotiations over financial compensation easier for members of the organizations. (If your potential boss thinks you might curse him, he's probably not going to haggle too much over what you want to charge.) The Horsemen and the Millers used their meetings as an excuse for heavy drinking and lewd jokes, the kind of things we associate today with a "boys' night out."

The rites of the Millers and the Horsemen contain many direct borrowings from Freemasonry, making the possibility of either group predating the Masons unlikely. The idea that the Horsemen are truly an-

---

117. Hutton, *The Triumph of the Moon*, 62.

118. Ibid.

cient certainly has some appeal,[119] but it requires a belief in the Bible's book of Genesis being factually accurate. The Horsemen claim that Cain, a son of Adam and Eve, was the first Horsemen, which is a great piece of storytelling but not an accurate picture of history.

The initiation rite used by the Horseman's Word bears many similarities to that of the Masons. There are oaths, challenges, and uncomfortable moments, but there are also several unique elements, and many of them feel very witchy. Prior to initiation, future Horsemen receive an envelope containing a horsehair and some instructions letting them know that they have been identified as potential members. A letter included with the horsehair instructs them to meet at a certain spot at a certain time and to bring with them a bottle of whisky and a loaf of bread (often with jam).

Once at the designated meeting spot, the initiate is blindfolded and forced to walk a "crooked path" containing many twists and turns before arriving at the farm hosting the initiation rite. Upon arrival, the blindfold is removed and the initiate is shown a large bucket of what appears to be horse piss (cheekily referred to as *hospice*). The initiate is then taken outside and stripped of all but his pants, which are then filled with hay. The blindfold is reapplied and the initiate's hands and feet are bound, and he's forced to pull a plough behind him. Before moving on, he's whipped on his buttocks by "Brother Lucifer" (though the hay softens any pain from the whipping).

The initiate is then made to walk around the farm clockwise, and at every stop he is offered "cold pee." Thinking this is the bucket of horse urine seen earlier, the initiate refuses it at every stop, even when physically coerced into drinking it. The initiate is then brought into the center of the ritual space and is instructed to shake the hand of Lucifer, or "Auld Nick." The initiate though doesn't grasp a hand, but a cloven hoof instead! (The figure playing Lucifer is obviously holding a hoof on

---

119. And it's an idea promoted by writers such as Michael Howard (see *Children of Cain*) and others who write in that genre. I believe that the Horsemen's Word impacted Modern Witchcraft but that its rites influenced us, and not the other way around.

a stick.) In addition to the hoof, some Lucifers wear an antlered head-dress, looking very much like a version of the Horned God!

The initiate then takes the society's oath on a Bible and is given a prayer, a password, and the legendary origins of the order. After a few celebratory drinks of whisky, the initiate is made to stand trial for refus-ing the hospitality of his brothers earlier in the night. The horse urine hinted at near the start of the ritual is revealed to actually be beer. The new initiate is then told that the penalty for not trusting a fellow Horse-man is death.

Next the new initiate is bound, taken up into a hayloft, shown a trap-door and a noose, and again blindfolded. Once the blindfold is reapplied, a fake noose is put around the initiate's neck, the trap door is opened, and the initiate falls harmlessly into a pile of hay. (Though the shock and hor-ror of such a trick usually results in the initiate shitting his pants, thank-fully the hay stuffed into his pants earlier makes a good diaper.) After this faux-execution, the initiate is welcomed as a full member of the order.

During the course of the ritual, the initiate is introduced to several figures from Greek and Hebrew mythology, along with Lucifer. Be-cause the initiation rites of the Horseman's Word were not supposed to be written down, they did vary from location to location, and in cer-tain locations the Lucifer figure was instead called Hercules. In some versions of the rite, one of the figures introduced to the new initiate is Tubal Cain, which makes me wonder if the Horseman's Word was an influence on Witches such as Robert Cochrane.[120]

THE GOLDEN DAWN

An acquaintance of mine once told me that "Wicca is the Golden Dawn for the masses," and it's not a point I'd ever argue.[121] The Golden Dawn was an esoteric and occult order founded in London, England, near the end of the nineteenth century, and even though it lasted in its original

---

120. Society of Esoteric Endeavour, *The Society of the Horseman's Word*, 89–97. My rough outline of the society's ritual was taken from this terrific book. Early editions came with a strand of horsehair, though my copy sadly did not.

121. That quote came from Sam Webster, author of the book *Tantric Thelema* and founder of the Open Source Order of the Golden Dawn in Oakland, California. I visited this group in May of 2016, and this is when I believe I first heard this anecdote.

form for only about twelve years (from 1888 to 1900), it's had a lasting impact on the occult world. After its demise, various offshoots of the order arose, and have been arising every since. The Golden Dawn has a lot in common with today's Witchcraft and was likely an indirect influence on Gerald Gardner and others. (If Rosamund Sabine, at one time a member of an offshoot of the Golden Dawn, was a member of the New Forest Coven, then the links between Witchcraft and the Golden Dawn are even more direct.)

The Golden Dawn used many of the same elements found in Masonic initiations and elevations (such as oaths, challenges, and revelation of knowledge) but firmly rooted them in occultism.

The Masons *implied* links to esoteric knowledge and experience, whereas the Golden Dawn was far more explicit. The order was *about* magick, and about magick in a variety of forms. The most influential magickal tradition embraced by the Golden Dawn was the Kabbalah, or Tree of Life, which was originally a form of Jewish mysticism. The Golden Dawn linked the Kabbalah to a variety of other magickal systems (including the tarot) and sometimes even to pagan deities of antiquity.

The Kabbalah consists of ten spheres, or *sephiroth*, through which the divine expresses itself. The influence of the Kabbalah is so important to the Golden Dawn that ten of its eleven (or twelve) grades, or degrees, are expressed through its spheres:

Order Title	Sphere from the Kabbalah
Ipsissimus	Kether
Magus	Chokmah
Magister Templi	Binah
Adeptus Exemptus	Chesed
Adeptus Major	Geburah
Adeptus Minor	Tiphareth
Philosophus	Netzach
Practicus	Hod
Theoricus	Yesod
Zelator	Malkuth
Neophyte*	
*Bogdan, *Western Esotericism and Rituals of Initiation*, 122.	

The various grades in the order represent each member's journey up the Tree of Life, starting with the spheres that represent the four elements and then moving upward toward more spiritual pursuits.

On the outside, while it appears that there are eleven degrees in the Golden Dawn, it's probably best to refer to them as grades. First-degree members of the order are individuals who possess the grades Neophyte through Philosphus, and members of this first degree made up most of the order's membership. An inner order was set up for the most accomplished members of the Golden Dawn, which spans the grades Adeptus Minor through Adeptus Exemptus; this is the third degree of the order. Between the first and third degrees is the grade of Portal, which functions as a second degree and a sort of probationary station for those looking to become a part of the Ruby Rose and Cross of Gold, the organization's inner court. The order's final three grades are thought to be unobtainable by mortal human beings.[122]

The initiation and elevation rituals of the Golden Dawn were all focused primarily on the attainment of "Light." For many in the order, a life lived without magick meant a life spent in darkness. The Golden Dawn's Neophyte ritual illuminates this clearly: "Child of Earth, long has thou dwelt in darkness. Quit the Night and seek the Day."[123]

One of the things that made the Golden Dawn unique for its era was the use of pagan gods for ritual and symbolic purposes. Ritual officers in the Neophyte initiation were symbolic of Egyptian gods such as Osiris, Horus, and Anubis.[124] The elevation ritual for the grade of Philosophus utilizes the goddess Isis and characterizes her as "water, pure and limpid."[125] The Horned God even shows up in the Portal ceremony:

> The symbolic figure of Pan, the Greek god of nature. He stands
> upon the cube of the universe, holding in his right hand the pas-

---

122. The breakdown of the Golden Dawn's "degrees" came from Chic and Sandra Tabatha Cicero's *The Essential Golden Dawn*. I took my information about the grades from pages 115, 134, and 143.

123. Regardie, *What You Should Know About the Golden Dawn*, 87.

124. Bogdan, *Western Esotericism and Rituals of Initiation*, 139.

125. Regardie, *The Golden Dawn*, 232.

toral staff of rural authority, and in his left the seven-reeded pipe symbolic of the planetary spheres. [126]

While the Golden Dawn's system of magick has become the foundation for much of the modern occult world, the order itself was always too complicated for the average seeker. The Neophyte ritual alone requires at least seven people, not counting the initiate. Taking a cue from the Masons, the amount of space needed for a traditional Golden Dawn ritual was also prohibitive. A Witch coven can make due with a small living room, while the Golden Dawn requires the use of two large pillars in its rituals.

To the credit of the Golden Dawn, the order was open to everyone and counted many accomplished women among its ranks. That might be one of the order's most enduring triumphs, along with the magick. Even today there are many Witches who are a part of modern interpretations of the order, and while its rites are often complicated, they are powerful and are destined to be a part of the occult world for generations to come.

---

126. Ibid., 276.

CHAPTER EIGHT

Dedications and Degree Systems

Most initiatory forms of Witchcraft utilize a system containing three degrees, but not all do. If you are entering an established tradition, you'll pretty much be stuck with how that tradition operates (that's what makes it a tradition after all). But if you are creating initiation and elevation rites for your own coven, you can utilize or create whatever system you want. Certain traditions have a fivefold system, while others have just a single initiation. There's no right or wrong, but only what works for the particular tradition and its adherents.

The Anderson Feri tradition (and its many offshoots) typically requires only one initiation. Those interested in becoming Feri initiates generally study for a period of years. I don't think I've met a Feri initiate who wasn't a student for at least three years, and for most initiates the process is much longer. Because there are no further elevations, when a person is initiated into Feri they are thought to be ready to run their own coven and train potential new initiates.

On the other side of the spectrum are traditions such as Blue Star Wicca, which have five different levels of rank. Blue Star Witches start their journey as dedicants, which signifies the student's interest in the tradition and a level of dedication to it. Before being elevated to the first degree they can then reach neophyte status, a level that implies a high degree of familiarity with the tradition and its rituals. After obtaining the rank of neophyte, future elevations are to the traditional first, second, and third degrees.

Even covens whose traditions utilize the typical three-degree system will sometimes add a pre-first-degree step. Most initiation-only covens contain what is known as an outer court, which acts as an introductory setting to a tradition's rituals that doesn't break any secrecy oaths. Before admitting a student into an outer court, the coven might perform a public dedication ritual for that Witch or an adoption rite signifying that the coven has pledged to train that individual. Outer courts often function very much like initiatory covens, with a high level of love and trust among participants. A rite into such a fellowship, with the whispered promise of something else down the road, can have a profound effect on the dedicated Witch.

I've also known Witches who are completely comfortable in the outer court setting, with no desire to ever become a first degree. Such situations are rare, but they do show just how powerful an outer court can be. An adoption into such a group seems appropriate in such instances.

In some three-degree systems a fourth rank has been added. People who achieve this are usually referred to as Witch Queens (accompanying Witch Kings are rare to nonexistent). The title Witch Queen is most often reserved for a High Priestess who has had three or more third-degree High Priestesses hive off and form their own covens. There are many High Priestesses who actively bristle at titles such as Witch Queen, while others are only too happy to be referred to in such a manner. I think that for many High Priestesses Witch Queen ceremonies serve as "letting go" rites that make separation from a very much loved former student easier to bear.

The five-degree system utilized by the Blue Star tradition has the most steps or levels among popular Witchcraft traditions, but groups with even more levels are not out of the question. In the Scottish Rite of Freemasonry, there are thirty-three degrees in addition to the regular three degrees available to other rank-and-file Masons. Certainly there's nothing stopping a Witch tradition from adopting such a system, though I have trouble imagining a coven coming up with thirty-three powerful elevation rites.

Common Degree Systems in Modern Witchcraft

No Initiation: There's nothing wrong with a tradition that requires no sort of initiation. For years my eclectic coven functioned quite comfortably with no initiation rites, and many of the other groups I've been a part of over the years have also lacked such things.

Advantages: With no initiation ritual, no one feels left out, and everyone in the coven is most likely on very even footing. For groups just starting out, the pressure of coming up with an effective initiation ritual can be a little overwhelming.

Disadvantages: It's hard to establish a tradition that doesn't have a clear beginning. Rites of passage are important mile markers for many Witches. Many Witches want to hear their peers actively acknowledge how they self-identify.

One Initiation: Formal induction into the tradition takes place over a period of years and sometimes even a decade. Anyone who receives an initiation is thought to be ready to train new students and begin their own coven.

Advantages: Slow training means that only the most dedicated get through to the other side. The initiator only has to write one initiation ritual (though it had better be good!). Many of the best Witches I know are from the Anderson Feri tradition, which speaks well of this system.

Disadvantages: Discourages some seekers due to the long wait time before being inducted into the tradition. (I'm sure some will see this as a positive.)

Initiation, One Elevation: Though I'm not familiar with any covens that utilize a system of one initiation and one elevation, there are many groups that come close to using this model. In some parts of the world the third degree is not routinely given, and second-degree

Witches run covens, teach, and initiate new Witches. More than one level of rank means that Witches who use such systems have to show patience and dedication, which many believe are two hallmarks of the Craft.

Advantages: I don't usually see a big difference between second- and third-degree Witches, so eliminating the middle step is in some ways a more honest accounting of where a Witch is. Everyone in the coven, minus its leaders at the top, are equal with one another. This structure eliminates a person receiving the third degree just to be privy to a couple of secrets when they have no desire to run a coven or teach the Craft.

Disadvantages: For Witches who want to lead ritual yet not teach, the elimination of a middle step could be seen as a stumbling block.

Three Degrees: This is the most popular system in Modern Witchcraft and was the first to be used. This is the structure utilized by most covens, though there are some groups that may also have an optional rite at the end or beginning for certain Witches.

Advantages: Because the three-degree system is the most common in Wiccan-Witchcraft circles, most Witches understand what each degree signifies. Lots of books have published rituals for the three degrees.

Disadvantages: Keeps away certain individuals who might like to participate in a tradition but are uncomfortable with oaths. People who have misconceptions about certain traditions are not given a space to get over their misunderstandings. (I know a few people who I think would make great Gardnerians, but I can't share ritual with them and they are wary of traditions.) Many Witches would say that what I see as disadvantages are positive things.

Four or Five Degrees: Making an individual Witch's dedication ritual a part of coven practice has a certain appeal and most likely affirms the individual Witch's dedication to the Craft. Many groups and individuals already use a system with four or five levels, even if they don't realize it. (My own self-dedication was a powerful prelude to my initiation into Gardnerian Wicca.)

Advantages: Systems with an extra degree at the beginning can bring people into a coven on a temporary or trial basis more easily. Sometimes the people we click with socially do not make good covenmates, something that can't always be known until coven activity begins.

Disadvantages: Degrees have to be earned, even early ones such as dedicant or neophyte. An introductory level has the potential to be abused or overused. Many Witches don't understand levels of rank before the first degree.

LINEAGE AND FAMILY

When discussing initiations and elevations, one word that comes up with frequency is *lineage*. An initiated Witch's lineage is their Witch family tree. The initiates that one is descended from are a Witch's *upline*. The initiates of a Witch (and eventually the initiates of an initiate) are a person's *downline*. Most initiated Witches can trace their lineage back to the founder of their traditions and can easily recite every step along the way.

Though Modern Witchcraft has existed for at least seventy years, the uplines of most Witches are not usually all that long. Most Witches being initiated today are less than twelve steps away from the person who founded their tradition, and most fewer than that. As I write this book, two of Gardner's original High Priestesses are still active in the Craft! [127] Anyone they initiated today would have an upline of only two people.

Many Witchcraft traditions are matrilineal, and when I'm asked about my lineage I trace it through my High Priestess, her High Priestess, etc., until I arrive at the source of the tradition. As a Gardnerian Witch, I can trace my lineage back to Gerald Gardner. Alexandrian Witches trace their lineage back to Alex Sanders, and Witches of the Cabot line trace their lineage back to Laurie Cabot.

---

127. In the course of writing this book, one of those High Priestesses, Lois Bourne, passed near the Winter Solstice in December of 2017.

Many Witches claim a family lineage, meaning that magick was practiced within the family and then passed down through the generations. Family traditions often lack the more formal initiations and elevations of other traditions but are no less meaningful because of it. The lineage of a family tradition might skip a generation or two as well; not everyone is cut out for the life of a Witch, even in a historically magickal family.

Because many of today's Witchcraft traditions have initiates in the thousands and all over the world, it's become more and more common to hear about extended Witchcraft tradition *families*. When I visit Europe or the United Kingdom, I always meet up with other initiates I've met online for drinks or dinner. Closer to home in the United States and Canada, I can't go to a Pagan festival without running into another initiate. Becoming an initiate in a lineaged tradition is much like inheriting an entire second family, and one that's usually bigger than the family you were born into.

Many traditions play well together too. Most Witches deeply respect the work that goes along with being a second- or third-degree Witch, and they apply that respect to traditions outside of their own. I'm not an Alexandrian or a Feri initiate, but I recognize what goes into the degrees conferred by those traditions. A tradition doesn't have to be old to be respected either. There are lots of traditions that have emerged only in the last twenty years (or less) that are highly respected in nearly every Witchcraft circle. Most of us recognize that every tradition has to start somewhere!

DEDICATIONS

While an initiation requires at least one other Witch, anyone can dedicate themselves to the Craft, and it's a ceremony most often done alone. My own dedication rite took place a year after I discovered Modern Witchcraft. It was the early 1990s and I was out camping with my then roommates and several thousand Deadheads (the traveling followers of the rock band the Grateful Dead). I decided that after a year of falling in love with Witchcraft it was time to dedicate myself to the practice. Because I found Wiccan-Witchcraft compatible with a lot of the idealism of the hippie movement, that field full of Deadheads felt like the right place for a dedication.

On a July night, just before the sun dipped down below the horizon, I slipped into a nearby cornfield, took off all my clothes, and told the Goddess and God that I wanted to live as a Witch. I spoke to the moon as the Goddess and the sun as the God, and then poured them both a small libation of wine and left them some cakes. Though I was only a few yards away from several thousand people, I felt like I was worlds away from those individuals and inhabiting a space that contained only myself and the gods (along with hundreds of ears of corn). There wasn't much to my rite other than my small offerings and spoken words, but I felt different when I returned to camp. I felt as if I had made a choice, and that the deities and the Craft I loved had accepted that choice.

There's no real way to determine when someone is ready (or not) for a dedication rite; it's something we feel inside of ourselves. Many books and teachers suggest waiting for "a year and a day," with that marker of time also sometimes being extended to initiation and elevation rites. A year and a day is certainly traditional, but sometimes the Craft feels so much like home that you don't want to wait that long, and I don't think it's necessary anyway.

When your heart burns with passion for Witchcraft, magick, and the deities of modern Wicca, it's probably time for a dedication rite. Simply being attracted to the Craft is not enough. After all, the word *dedication* includes "committed" in its definition.[128] Dedications should not be done if the Craft is destined to be just a passing fancy or isn't taken seriously. While most dedication rites are between an individual Witch and the powers they serve, disappointing yourself can be just as painful as letting down a coven or a group of friends.

A dedication rite is a declaration to yourself, your gods, and sometimes your community that you've chosen to identify as a Witch (or as a Witch of a certain variety). It doesn't require any sort of elaborate buildup, and many of us who have done self-dedication rites have lacked the "essential" tools that most Witches have in their possession. The

---

128. Oxford Living Dictionary, https://en.oxforddictionaries.com/definition/dedication.

night I dedicated myself to the Craft, I had only myself and some small offerings, and that was more than enough.

It's time for a dedication rite when there's no question in your heart that you identify as a Witch, and Witchcraft has become something you love and respect. Part of that love and respect consists of identifying the earth as something sacred and worthy of our veneration and being comfortable with the gods of the Craft. A dedicated Witch knows that magick is real and accepts it as a part of their lives.

It's probably NOT time for a dedication rite if you are uncomfortable with the gods and have yet to try to facilitate a relationship with them, you question the reality of magick, and you see yourself as having dominion over the earth instead of simply being a part of it. If you have reservations about the word Witch or Wicca, it's probably best not to perform a dedication rite.

DEDICATION RITUAL: "I AM A WITCH"

Dedication rituals require little in the way of tools. All that's really necessary is a burning desire to be a Witch, though this ritual adds a few extra things. This ritual can be performed anyplace and at any time of day, but I suggest starting at least in the evening, though after sunset is preferable. I also suggest doing it on a night of a full moon. Witches traditionally celebrate esbats (full moons), and the energy of the full moon lends itself to rituals that are about creation and giving, both essential elements of this ritual.

While this ritual can be done nearly anywhere, that anywhere should have a modicum of privacy. This is a time for just you, your Craft, and the gods. It's not a good time for roommates or unsympathetic spouses or parents. Though most of my rituals these days take place indoors, I think the ideal space for a dedication ritual is outdoors. That outdoor setting doesn't have to be a forest or a secluded seashore; your own backyard or favorite spot in a local park is fine and possibly preferable. Those types of spaces will already contain a lot of your own energy and will amplify the intention you put into the rite.

Because I believe that our relationships with the gods are helped by the practice of reciprocity, I've included an offering in this rite. My favorite offerings are generally wine and some sort of bread or small cake, but what's most important about an offering is that it means something to you and the powers that are a part of your life. If you honor Hecate and she prefers apples, that's what you should bring. If you despise wine and prefer beer, you should bring beer. For an offering to be valuable it should mean something to you and your gods.

This ritual also requires a couple of candles. They don't have to be expensive or elaborate, and any sort of candle will work. If you want a long-lasting physical connection to your dedication ritual, I suggest long taper or pillar candles, but something as simple as a tealight is fine. What's most important is that you are comfortable with whatever you are using.

I don't think that solo dedication rituals require the creation of sacred space, but if you feel more comfortable operating in a circle and calling the quarters, by all means do so. You may want to burn some incense or light a candle for ambience, especially if you are indoors, but such things are not necessary.

Once you are comfortable, take a few moments to reflect on your surroundings. If you are outside, listen to the world around you. Take in all the insects, birds, and other creatures rustling around. Feel the breeze on your skin, and with your eyes closed, look up at the moon and try to sense its light. Connect with the world around you and feel and know that you are a part of it.

If you are indoors, open yourself up to the energies that are present with you. In my house I can often feel the energies of my ancestors, the deities I honor, my wife and cats, and all the energy we've created in our lives together. Let that energy wash over you, and absorb some of it into yourself if possible. Know that you are loved and cared for, and worthy of that love.

When you are all settled into your ritual space, think for a while about what being a Witch means to you and how you see Witchcraft changing your life. Most of us are never the same after embracing the word *Witch*, and it's best to reflect on the ramifications of just what identifying as a Witch might mean. Some people lose relationships with friends and family over Witchcraft. Are you prepared for that? It's possible to live in the broom closet, but in the age of social media it's becoming harder and harder to keep secrets such as Witchcraft.

Despite the problems that might come with embracing life as a Witch, most of us who have done so have benefited from it. In your mind's eye see yourself growing closer to the deities that are a part of your life, communicating with your ancestors and living in harmony with the earth. See the possibilities opening up before you that come with living a magickal life, and then feel that energy move from inside of yourself to outside. Revel in the tingle of magickal energy, and know that this is one aspect of a Witch's power.

When you feel comfortable with your choice to be a Witch, take one of your candles, place it in a candleholder, and light it. (Be sure you are lighting your candle safely and that you aren't in an area likely to start a fire.) As you light the candle, say:

Tonight I choose to live my life as a Witch. I choose to embrace the earth as my home and mother. I choose to embrace magick and create beneficial change for myself and the world around me. I am a Witch, and with love in my heart, I dedicate myself to this path. So mote it be!

Now take the second candle and prepare it as you did the first. When it's set up, light it and say:

Of my own free will I dedicate myself to the Goddess and God and their mysteries. Great Lady, tonight I become a Witch in your service and will strive to ever walk with you. Horned One, Lord of the Forest, tonight I become a Witch in your service and promise to honor you side by side with your Lady. Tonight I dedicate myself to the path of the Witch and the gods who are a part of that path. So mote it be!

Before finishing up your ritual, take out any offerings you've brought and pour/place them upon the ground (or if indoors into a libation bowl to be taken outside later) while saying:

As a Witch, I know that the gods will ever share their bounty with me. As the gods share with me, I choose to also share with the gods. Lord and Lady, accept this humble offering that I may ever grow closer to you. So mote it be!

After this rite you may choose to stay outside for a little while reflecting on the commitments you've just made. When you are satisfied that the rite is done, extinguish the candles while saying *Always with me* as a reminder that the magick and the gods of a Witch are always around you. If you've cast a circle and called the quarters, let those energies go and leave the site of your ritual as you found it (or in better shape than before). The candles you take from this ritual can be lit anytime you feel disconnected from the Craft or need to be reminded of the energies that are a part of your life as a Witch.

Going Deeper: An Extra Rite with Blood

There are many Witches who are uncomfortable with blood magick, and for good reason. Blood should never be drawn unwillingly, and it must be treated with great care. Blood is the essence of who we are, and there's the potential that someone could use our own blood against us or that we could receive, transmit, or contract a disease by improperly handling it. However, because of its great magickal potency, blood is a useful tool in ritual and can be used for a variety of magickal purposes.

For those interested in a dedication ritual with a little more gravity, I've included this little section as an add-on to the previous rite. It's certainly not anything that's required, and if you're uncomfortable with using blood for magickal purposes, just skip over this section. Also, because dedication and initiation rituals share many of the same elements, this little bit can be added to such rites if you or your coven desire.

If you choose to work with blood, you'll need a couple extra items: a lancet, an alcohol swab, and a bandage. Lancets are available at most drugstores and are guaranteed to be clean and sterile. If doing this ritual outside, make sure to keep your hands clean to ward off infection. If you choose to add this bit to your rite, I suggest slotting it in after lighting your dedication candles and before libations.

This rite requires only a few drops of blood and calls for pricking your finger. To do this somewhat easily, use your dominant hand to press below the tip of the index finger on your nondominant hand. With your dominant hand, prick the tip of that finger when you feel the blood pulsing in the tip. One good poke should do it, and when the blood begins to flow, stand up and say:

> With this blood I dedicate my life to the Craft. I will walk the path of the Witch and strive to ever preserve my Craft, my gods, and those I love. In the presence of the moon, the land, my ancestors, and the Lord and Lady, I make this solemn vow. May my blood nourish the earth, and may I ever walk the path of the Wise. I am a Witch. So mote it be!

While speaking these words, squeeze your finger until at least three drops of blood touch the ground (one drop for the Lady, one drop for the Lord, and one for the Craft). I think this is best done standing up in order to observe the blood leaving your finger. If you are inside, let the blood drip into your libation bowl to be poured out upon the earth later. When you are satisfied with this offering of yourself, disinfect your finger and place a bandage over the cut.

If pouring libations of wine, water, or any other liquid after this ceremony, pour that liquid over the drops of your blood to make sure your blood isn't taken or disturbed in any way. This should also help it sink into the earth much faster than it might on its own. Again, blood magick is not for everyone, and it's certainly not for the squeamish, but it's an effective addition to many rites if done safely and properly.

DEDICATION RITUAL WITH A GROUP: KNOT AND CORD MAGICK

Though most dedication rituals are done alone, they don't have to be. A Witch just coming into the Craft may choose to publicly embrace Witchcraft, and wish to do so in front of a circle of their peers. When I was younger I facilitated a dedication ritual for my peers in the college student group we were all involved in. Years later when I became an advisor to that group, we had members who would periodically ask for help in putting together a public dedication ritual.

Public dedication rituals can also be used when taking a member into a Wiccan outer court or as a way to introduce a new Witch to a coven that doesn't require an initiation. Sometimes people just want their friends to be a part of their first steps into Witchcraft, and that's something that should always be celebrated. Many Witches also choose to do both public and private dedication rituals. (I'm always in favor of more rituals that draw us closer to our gods and our communities!)

This ritual utilizes knot and cord magick. Though not practiced with a great deal of frequency today, knots have been used in magickal practices for thousands of years. The Greeks and Egyptians utilized knots for love spells, the Romans believed that they could cause impotency, and sailors tied and untied them to control the winds.[129] Knots are effective in magick because they store energy. When a Witch ties a knot and pours their intent into it, that knot becomes charged with magickal power.

Some Witches believe that the magick takes place when the knot is untied and the energy contained within it is then released out into the world. For this particular ritual we want the energy placed into each knot to stay in the cord so it can be utilized later by the dedicating Witch. The most effective cords for spells utilizing knots are ones made from natural fibers. Synthetic materials are okay if you've got no other option, but cords made of cotton or other natural fibers are easily acquired.

Some covens require the dedicating Witch (or the initiating Witch— this ritual can also be adapted and used in an initiation rite) to make their own cord. There's certainly a great deal of power that comes from making one's own cord, and the process of knitting is both therapeutic and meditative. However, making your own cord isn't a requirement unless you are entering a tradition mandating such things.

Cords are utilized in many traditions as an indication of rank. Dedicants, along with first-, second-, and third-degree Witches, might all wear different colors of cords depending on where they are in their practice. Other groups might confer a cord just once and then ask that it be worn by members at most rituals. Cords look especially cool around a robe and are useful for hanging an athame on. There are even some

---

129. Guiley, *The Encyclopedia of Witches & Witchcraft*, 188.

skyclad covens where members wear cords. Even if you aren't dedicating into a group that actively uses cords, a cord whose magick is dedicated to an individual can be a useful thing to have.

Everyone who participates in this rite will be asked to add a knot conferring some sort of energy and power into the dedicating Witch's cord. I wrote this ritual for nine Witches (including the dedicant), but that number can be added to or subtracted from. If the dedicating Witch has made their own cord, they should give that to the ritual's officiants before the rite begins.

Because this is a rite for a circle or coven, sacred space should be created by calling in the quarters and casting a magick circle. Whatever deities the circle or dedicant works with should be called in as well. Once all of the preliminaries are out of the way, the rite begins.

High Priestess: *It is my understanding that there is someone in this circle who wishes to dedicate their life to the Craft and live as a Witch. Who among us is that person?*

Dedicant: *I am (Name), and I wish to be a Witch.*

High Priestess: *Welcome, (Name of dedicant). Step forward and stand here in front of our altar.*

The dedicant stands in front of the altar and face to face with the High Priestess, who stands behind it.

High Priestess: *The life of the Witch is not for the faint of heart. There will be some who fear you for joining the Craft, and there will be others who despise you for not being one of their own. There have been Witches who have lost family, friends, romantic partners, and much more for identifying with Witchcraft. Are you ready to accept such losses if they may happen?*

Dedicant: *Yes, I am.*

High Priestess: *Good, and now take solace in this, for anyone you may lose due to choosing Witchcraft, know that they will be replaced threefold by your brothers and sisters of the Craft and those who would be your chosen family. To live as a Witch is to live a magickal life, but with that magick comes a responsibility. Magick is not a trifle or a parlor trick; it is a reality in our lives. Do you dedicate yourself to living a magickal life, to using your power, gifts, and knowledge for good and never evil?*

Dedicant: *Yes, I do.*

High Priestess: *To be a Witch is to worship the Old Gods and honor our Lady and Lord who ever walk with us. Will you share your path with them and dedicate your life as a Witch to knowing their mysteries?*

Dedicant: *Yes, I will.*

High Priestess: *As you have accepted the Goddess, now know that she has accepted you. Drink this wine and know that she stands ever beside her children in the Craft.*

The dedicant is handed a chalice of wine or other beverage and takes a drink.

High Priestess: *Side by side with the Lady stands the God, the Horned One. His sacrifice is what ripens the grain and turns the seasons. Eat of his bounty and know that he too stands beside you.*

The dedicant is given a small piece of bread or other food item to eat.

High Priestess: *The gods are with you, and you are with them, and now you must proclaim that you will live as a Witch. Place your hands upon the pentacle and draw in the power that flows out from it. As you draw in the power, repeat after me.* (Alternatively: *As you draw in the power, open up your heart and let us know that you wish to dedicate yourself to the Craft.*)

The High Priestess can slowly repeat this next part and have the dedicant repeat it back to her, or the dedicant can memorize it beforehand or simply say whatever they wish here.

Dedicant: *Tonight I choose to live as a Witch and to dedicate myself to Witchcraft. May I grow strong in the knowledge of magick, the gods, the earth, and the mysteries. May my love for the Craft sustain and nourish me in times of trouble, and may I provide strength to those who might have need of it. I forsake nothing to take this journey, and I take it willingly. Tonight let it be known to the gods, my peers, and to the world that I, (Name), am a Witch!*

High Priestess: *And as a Witch, you shall never be alone unless it is by choice. (Picks up cord from altar.) And now may this cord serve forever as a reminder of this night and the powers that now walk beside you.*

Everyone at the rite should tie a magickal knot into the cord, beginning with the High Priestess, though that can be changed as circumstances warrant. People should feel free to pour whatever magick they wish into the cord and their knot, or use one of the suggestions below. The knot should be pulled tight as the words *So mote it be* are said.

This knot is for the Great Lady. May you always walk with her love and her light. So mote it be!

This knot is for the Horned One. May you always be reminded of his sacrifice and know the joy of the wild spaces. So mote it be!

This knot is for your chosen family, those gathered here tonight already known to you, and those who are yet to come. So mote it be!

This knot is for your ancestors. May they guide you on your journey and always provide counsel when it is required. So mote it be!

This knot is for the Mighty Dead. May you know the wisdom of those in the Craft who came before you, and may their lessons always be heeded. So mote it be!

This knot is for the magick you will practice. May it always be strong, may it always be effective, and may you always know your true will. So mote it be!

This knot is for the earth and the turning of the wheel. May you always feel connected to the natural world and continue to receive its blessings. So mote it be!

This knot is for the Craft. May Witchcraft be a solace when you are hurting and a source of strength to overcome that hurt. So mote it be!

People may add more than one knot to the cord if they so desire, but everyone in attendance should add at least one.

High Priestess: *(Name of dedicant) has now truly dedicated herself/himself to the Craft and the life of the Witch! With our blessings we present you with your cord. May it help you upon the path you now walk for as long as your love of the Craft survives. So mote it be!*

Once the ritual is over, there should be feasting and celebrating to commemorate the new Witch dedicating their life to the Craft. Blessed be!

CHAPTER NINE

Creating Initiation and Elevation Rituals

Ideally, initiation and elevation rites are more than just markers on the individual Witch's journey. They are meant to be transformative events, and the truths and information they impart should deepen the experience of Witchcraft. To that end, most of these ceremonies share a few common traits. If you are interested in creating your own initiation and elevation rites, I'm of the opinion that they should all include some of the following components.

Witchcraft is essentially a mystery tradition, so it would make sense that any sort of induction ceremony include the *revelation of a mystery*. These mysteries might be small or large, and range from an often heard instruction (such as "An it harm none, do what you will" from the Wiccan Rede) to something far less familiar. Mysteries can be spoken, and they can also be physical objects. The point of revealing a mystery is to share another facet of a tradition's or coven's practice.

The path of the Witch is not for the faint of the heart, which is why many initiation and elevation rituals include some sort of *challenge*. That challenge could be asking a Witch to identify all the tools on the altar or to recite a few words learned in a previous ritual. An elevation rite especially might serve as a testing ground for a maturing Witch, requiring them to share all they have learned up to that point.

Many covens also share *gifts* either after or during elevation and initiation rites. If the gift giving occurs during the ritual, it's often something related to the coven or the degree being bestowed. Examples of this include being given a medallion unique to the coven or perhaps being awarded a Book of Shadows after initiation. (I'm speaking from experience here. Both of these gifts are included in my eclectic coven's initiation rite.) Gifts after ritual are also welcome, because an initiation is much like a birthday. It often marks a Witch's official induction into a chosen family.

Since most initiation rituals are oathbound and private, it's common for an initiating Witch to recite some sort of *oath* (one of the many things borrowed from the Masons over the years). Most oaths include a promise not to reveal any of the secrets gained in the tradition or to "out" a member without permission. Oaths often include a penalty, which might include a curse or other threat. Being asked to share in a tradition's secrets is a huge honor and one I think most Witches have taken seriously over the years. Oaths are generally used only during a first-degree initiation ritual.

Rituals designed for the giving of degrees are also meant to be something beyond the ordinary sabbat or esbat rite. Many covens use techniques borrowed from the Masons such as blindfolding to create a *heightened sense of awareness or disorientation*. In my coven we create a physical circle of oak leaves during initiations to make the rite a bit more unique.

In this section of the book I've included a whole host of mysteries, challenges, and gifts that can be used for initiation and elevation rituals. Because every coven and tradition has their own way of revealing the secrets of the Craft, I've not organized anything by degree (though you can see where I'd place at least some of them in the rituals located at the end of the chapter). Instead, individual groups and people can mix and match all the things listed here in whatever way works best for them. And I most certainly did forget several mysteries, most likely because I don't know about them or can't write about them. That's what makes them mysteries after all!

UNVEILING A MYSTERY

There are all sorts of mysteries that can be revealed during an initiation or elevation rite. Those mysteries can range from the revelation of magickal knowledge to things like handshakes or signs. The mystery revealed might also have something to do with the nature of the gods or perhaps the history of the coven and/or tradition. Because there are so many secrets that might be a part of a coven, there's no limit to what might be revealed. If your coven does something they don't want others to know about, it's a secret and can be revealed at an initiation.

Handshakes and Other Secret Signs

The Masons have several secret handshakes, and these vary by degree. This practice has been adopted by some Witch covens over the last seventy years and serves as both a greeting between Witches and a way to say "Yes, I'm part of the family." Similar in this respect are distinct hand signs used by some groups. An example of this is in the 1899 Ritual (see chapter 3), where the signs include the horns of Pan and a kiss blown to the goddess Diana.

Specific ritual postures might also be included as a mystery revelation. Though they aren't a secret in my coven, we have a set series of hand and arm movements that we use while calling the quarters. We hold our athames in our power hand (our dominant hand) and then cross our arms over our chest, with the athame on the outside. (This is called the *Osiris position.*) When we call to one of the four quarters, we then raise our athames up over our heads in salute, with our other arm to our side. After the quarter is called, we all say *Blessed be* and return our arms to the Osiris position. This is repeated three more times as the remaining quarters are called.

It's visually striking to see a coven or circle call the quarters in this way, but there's also a great deal of symbolism involved. If I were to add how we call the quarters to our coven's initiation ritual, I'd explain that mystery this way:

High Priestess: *In our circle we honor the elements of air, fire, water, and earth, the watchtowers of the east, south, west, and north. As Witches we know that without these four elements there is no life and there is no we.*

In the circle we honor the elements by beginning in the Osiris position. Osiris was dead and then resurrected by his love, Isis. Before being exposed to the powers of the elements, we too are dead—dead magickally, stuck in the world of the mundane and unable to change our circumstances.

But when we are touched by each of the four great powers of the world, we slip back into the world of magick and a time that is not a time and a place that is not a place. That is why we salute the elements, thanking them for their presence in our lives, for stirring up the magick that exists inside us, just waiting for a way out. As a sign of our love, we end each call to them with a kiss from our blade, showing that it is our true will to love and share in the powers of the world. So mote it be!

When it comes to handshakes, ritual postures, and other signs, there's really no end to what can be created and revealed. Often coven traditions start completely by accident, and only over time do people figure out that they are doing something that has evolved into a secret tradition. Building these types of mysteries into an initiation or elevation rite makes a coven even more special and secret.

As Above, So Below

"As above, so below" is a magickal formula adapted from the legendary Emerald Tablet. This text generally consists of fourteen lines (this can vary from translation to translation), the most famous of which is "That which is above is from that which is below, and that which is below is from that which is above, working the miracles of one." [130] This line is generally simplified into the phrase "As above, so below."

The Emerald Tablet's origins are the subject of some debate. There are some who believe its philosophy represents Christian ideals, and others who think it might have originated in China or perhaps pagan

---

130. Christopher Drysdale, "Every Trick in the Book: The Emerald Tablet," in Jason Mankey's *The Witch's Book of Shadows*, 85–88.

antiquity. The earliest source we have for the tablet dates from 800 CE and was written in Arabic, and a Latin translation followed three hundred years later.[131] The text is often attributed to the legendary figure Hermes Trismegistus, who originally was a merging of the gods Hermes (Greek) and Thoth (Egyptian), though some traditions see Trismegistus as an enlightened human being and not a deity.

"As above, so below" is a phrase used by a wide variety of magicians and occult seekers. Depending on who is using the phrase, it's meaning can change somewhat. In many traditions it's used to express the idea that the small reflects the large. Many people see the whole of the universe reflected in each individual person on Earth, which is representative of the small (a person) reflecting the large (the universe). To take this a step further, we can learn to understand the universe if we learn to understand ourselves.

The phrase has other meanings in Witchcraft and magick too. When a Witch raises energy in the magick circle (that sacred space between the worlds), they are sending their magickal power out of one world (the space where gods and mortals both tread) and into the physical world we inhabit on a daily basis. In order to make changes in our daily lives, we have to first make changes in magickal space, or perhaps even simply just inside of ourselves, before that change can manifest in the mundane world.

The phrase is sometimes linked to astrology as well, with the movements of the stars and planets (as above) bringing about changes on our planet and within ourselves (so below). In my own practice I use the phrase to describe the nature of the Lord and Lady. My deities are most certainly gods of the living, but they are also gods of the dead. They are with me in this life and will be with me in between lives. This idea is explored in the first-degree initiation ritual in chapter 10.

"As above, so below" is a handy little phrase that can be used as a greeting in circle and as a call-and-response piece. It makes an effective password that an elevating Witch might need to say to their High Priestess, and is

---

131. Ibid., 86.

a phrase that an initiating Witch might need to elaborate on when being challenged in the circle.

The Wiccan Rede

The Wiccan Rede is probably the most famous maxim in Modern Witchcraft circles. Gardner used a version of it in his 1959 book *The Meaning of Witchcraft*, writing that Witches

> are inclined to the morality of the legendary Good King Pausol, "Do what you like so long as you harm no one." But they believe a certain law to be important, "You must not use magic for anything which will cause harm to anyone, and if, to prevent a greater wrong being done, you must discommode someone, you must do it only in a way which will abate the harm." [132]

The Wiccan Rede was first articulated in its present form of "An it harm none, do what you will" in 1964 by Doreen Valiente at a dinner hosted by the Witchcraft Research Association (though it likely predates that event). [133]

There are many Witches today who actively despise the Wiccan Rede, believing that it limits their magick. What they forget is that the Wiccan Rede is not a law but is simply a suggestion. (The word *rede* means "advice or counsel." [134]) Witches are free to heed the advice of the Rede or ignore it all together. Besides, I think the actual meaning of the Wiccan Rede is lost on many of its loudest critics.

Wicca is not a belief system with a series of cosmic challenges and tests of spiritual purity. Witches are free to do whatever they wish, and since Witches are a people responsible for their own actions, they generally live up to the idea of "harm none." More importantly, every Witch has to figure out for themselves what actually constitutes "harm." Is us-

---

132. Gardner, *The Meaning of Witchcraft*, 93. For those who are curious, King Pausole (Gerald forgot the *e*) was not a legendary king at all but a twentieth-century French literary creation.

133. d'Este and Rankine, *Wicca: Magickal Beginnings*, 64.

134. Oxford English Dictionary, https://en.oxforddictionaries.com/definition/rede.

ing magick to bring a thief to justice a violation of the Rede? I don't think so; the harm would be in *not* utilizing our magick for such things.

The Wiccan Rede does not stop any Witch from using magick to take control of a situation. If someone is actively hurting others, they've forfeited their opportunity to be among the "none" in "An it harm none." Witchcraft is about personal responsibility and figuring things out for oneself, and part of that includes deciding how to define "harm" and just who or what constitutes "none."

In initiation and elevation rituals, the Wiccan Rede is most often used as a password. Since most Witches are very aware of the Rede, this is not an exceptionally difficult challenge, but it's such a part of our history that to ignore it feels short-sighted. Besides, its absence would probably be more noticeable than its inclusion.

The Witches' Pyramid

The Witches' Pyramid is a magickal philosophy that predates Modern Witchcraft and was first articulated by the French occultist and magician Éliphas Lévi (1810–1875) in his two-volume *Transcendental Magic: Its Doctrine and Ritual*, released in 1854 and 1856. In *Transcendental Magic* Lévi writes:

> To attain the SANCTUM REGNUM, in other words, the knowledge and power of the Magi, there are four indispensable conditions an intelligence illuminated by study, an intrepidity which nothing can check, a will which cannot be broken, and a prudence which nothing can corrupt and nothing intoxicate. TO KNOW, TO DARE, TO WILL, TO KEEP SILENCE such are the four words of the Magus, inscribed upon the four symbolical forms of the sphinx. [135]

For Lévi, the magi were the carriers of magickal tradition. Just before introducing his readers to what would become the Witches' Pyramid, he writes that "magic is the traditional science of the secrets of nature

---

135. Lévi, *Transcendental Magic*, 30.

which has been transmitted to us from the magi." [136] In Lévi's world, in order to become a successful magician one must be like the magi, and to be like the magi one must adhere to the four principles of "to know, to dare, to will, to keep silence."

Lévi is quite explicit in what these four principles mean. To be a magician, one must know one's craft and study, and be fearless in that study, afraid of nothing that it might reveal. This requires an iron constitution and a deep inner strength, along with a sense of judgment unhindered by outside forces. Because Lévi equates his four words of the magus with the legendary sphinx, his indispensable conditions are sometimes referred to as the Four Powers of the Sphinx. In ceremonial magick circles they are often called the Four Powers of the Magus (or Magician). The term *Witches' Pyramid* is used exclusively in Witchcraft and was most likely first used in the 1950s, seventy-five years after Lévi's death.

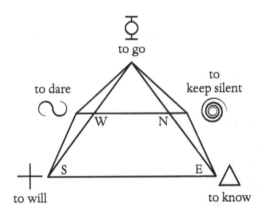

The Witches' Pyramid

Lévi was a tremendously influential magician and thinker, and his four powers were picked up by the Golden Dawn as well as Aleister Crowley (an initiate of the Golden Dawn), who incorporated them into his practice of Thelema. Crowley introduced a fifth idea into Lévi's powers, the power "to go." Crowley's addition would eventually make

---

136. Lévi, *Transcendental Magic*, 29.

it into some Witchcraft traditions where "to go" is equated with the element (or power) of spirit.

Modern Witchcraft has a long history of being influenced by ceremonial magick, so it's not surprising that many Witches picked up on the ideas of Lévi. The first book containing Modern Witch rituals, Paul Huson's *Mastering Witchcraft* (1970), mentions the Witches' Pyramid as an essential magickal first step. Instead of using the familiar "to know, to will, etc.," Huson writes about the four powers as "a virulent imagination, a will of fire, rock-hard faith and a flair for secrecy." [137] These ideas sync up nicely with Lévi's original vision and remove any ambiguity in the meaning of the Four Powers.

The first book to feature complete Witch rituals published by a major press was *Lady Sheba's Book of Shadows*, published in 1971. In that work Sheba begins with the Witches' Pyramid, which she calls the "foundation" of Witch power. Like Huson, she doesn't use Lévi's short-and-sweet phrasing but instead describes the four sides of the pyramid like this:

> The first side of the four so-called sides of the pyramid is your dynamic, controlled will; the second, your imagination or the ability to see your desire accomplished; third, unshakable and absolute faith in your ability to accomplish anything you desire; and fourth, secrecy—"power shared is power lost." …
>
> These four things, will power, imagination, faith, and secrecy are the basic rules and the absolute basic requirements for the working of Witchcraft. [138]

Huson's and Sheba's books have been wildly influential over the last forty-plus years and are worth mentioning here because they are the foundation of "do-it-yourself" Wicca outside of an established tradition. By writing about the Witches' Pyramid, they guaranteed that it

---

137. Huson, *Mastering Witchcraft*, 22. Originally published in 1970. My copy is the 1980 Perigree edition. Huson's book is the first to contain Witch ritual that resembles Modern Witch rituals.

138. Jessie Wicker Bell (Lady Sheba), *The Grimoire of Lady Sheba*, 1. I'm quoting from the Centennial Edition published on Llewellyn's 100th birthday.

would be a part of numerous Witch traditions and practices, and that its ideas would be shared, debated, practiced, and elaborated on long into the future.

As Witchcraft has grown over the last seventy years, the Witches' Pyramid has grown alongside it, with each of its four tenets being given additional meaning. As with most things pertaining to the Craft, there are several different interpretations of the Witches' Pyramid, and it's possible that other authors and Witches will disagree with my understanding of them. Traditionally the four sides of the pyramid are thought to build upon one another, which means that without knowing, there can be no daring, etc. With that being said, here are my thoughts on each of the four sides of the pyramid.

To Know: There are many different types of knowing, which makes the first lesson of the pyramid open to several different interpretations. As Witches we should obviously possess a degree of book knowledge and an understanding of how our practices work, but "knowing" is a continual process. We don't have all the answers once we are initiated or make our first contact with the Goddess. We must be dedicated to seeking wisdom and truth in our lives.

Knowing is also about what is inside of us. Answers exist both within ourselves and out in the greater world. A wise Witch knows not to give up on their dreams and desires. After all, it's often our dreams and wishes that fuel our magick and give us hope when things look bleak. Creative visualization—the ability to see what we want in our mind's eye—is one of magick's foundations. "To know" is often associated with the element of air.

To Dare: Magick is often uncomfortable. We might create the cone of power to the point of exhaustion, and for many of us, simply finding Witchcraft required a gigantic leap of faith. Even though Witches in the West don't face the level of discrimination they did just thirty years ago, this is still a path that sometimes comes with negative consequences. To be a Witch is to dare to be different, to live a life that's different from one spent in the throngs of mundania.

Though standing in sacred space is not often equated with bravery, I believe that it's a very brave act. To walk in the footsteps of goddesses and expose yourself to things greater than us humans takes courage, but Witches dare to do such things. As Witches we also explore the feelings and emotions that exist inside of us, and often these are things that we might find disturbing. But we do this as Witches because we want to explore our worlds both within and without.

The mantra "to dare" is often associated with the element of water, the element of death and initiation. Death and initiation are both journeys into the unknown, and such rites of passage require bravery and daring.

To Will: When I call upon my will during a magickal operation, I'm using all the collective energy and experience I have inside myself to create a new reality. Our will is what manifests change, and if we don't utilize our will we won't get the results we are looking for in our magickal work. Our will also applies to the tools we have at our disposal outside of ourselves; our will fuels the internal fire that gives us the desire to study and learn.

Our will is also about overcoming roadblocks and getting around obstacles and obstructions that stand in the way of our goals. In its purest form, the inner will is reflective of who we are as people, and most every Witch I've ever met is steadfast and determined. When circumstances are difficult, the Witch overcomes those challenges out of a sheer desire to succeed. "To will" doesn't mean that we will always be able to solve every problem thrown at us, but it does mean that we are capable of getting past them. The will has always been associated with the element of fire, and that's no different in the Witches' Pyramid.

To Keep Silent: Lévi originally called the last leg of the pyramid "To Keep Silence," but most Witches today use the better-sounding "to keep silent." Silence can refer to many things. It's about the power of listening and saying nothing when the time calls for it. It's about the still, small voice inside ourselves that often offers wisdom and guidance. Instead of offering excuses for our failures, it's often better just to be quiet and accept the truth of our failings so we can learn from them.

Silence also extends to other Witches. A Witch should not "out" another Witch unless they have permission to do so. (It's easy to understand why this was an extremely important principle fifty years ago.)

There's also power that comes with being silent about our magickal operations. If we broadcast what we are doing magickally, we risk the possibility that our magick might be countered or interfered with in some way. Most magickal operations are better off not being spoken about. "To keep silent" is often associated with the element of earth.

To Go: This is not traditionally a part of the Witches' Pyramid, but some groups use it for a variety of purposes. "To go" can be seen as the end result of using the four sides of the Witches' Pyramid, meaning once we figure out those pillars, we know how to go forward with our magick. Since "to go" is often associated with the element of spirit, the pyramid's four columns are seen as supporting that power.

The Witches' Pyramid is often pictured as a pentagram, with spirit as the top or defining power. (The right-side-up pentagram is often thought to represent the triumph of the spiritual over the material.)

I use the Witches' Pyramid as one of the essential pieces of knowledge shared in the second-degree elevation rite later in this book, though there are other uses for it when designing your own rituals. It can be used as a password, with every Witch being asked to go through the pyramid upon entering ritual space. It can also be used as a challenge during such rites, with prospective initiates asked to recite the Witches' Pyramid or explain its meaning.

The Eight Paths of Power

Many Witches believe that there are eight distinct paths that allow us to use magick effectively. These are known as the Eight Paths of Power and were first published in *Lady Sheba's Book of Shadows* in 1971.[139] Each path offers a different way to change the individual consciousness of the Witch and to gain power and/or knowledge that will help with magickal endeavors. In this book I have included a modified version of the eight paths that I find to be more practical. Those who are interested in the more historical version can find it in a variety of places. (Check the bibliography for more sources.)

---

139. Jessie Wicker Bell (Lady Sheba), *The Grimoire of Lady Sheba*, 5.

The Eight Paths of Power are a great addition to an initiation or elevation ritual, and since some of the techniques are rather advanced if fully explored, they're probably most appropriate for a second-degree elevation instead of an initiation. In addition, they might also make a powerful test if a High Priestess were to ask a potential second degree to recite them. Since every coven and tradition is different, it's possible for every group to have their own eight primary ways of working magick. Witchcraft is always adaptable, so use what works for you.

Much like the Witches' Pyramid, the Eight Paths of Power are meant to build on each other, with the more advanced (and sometimes dangerous) techniques reserved for the end. Entire books have been written about each of these eight paths. What I offer here is only a sketch of their potential use.

Creative Visualization: This is the building block of all magick. If we are able to picture the things we love, want, and desire, we will be able to manifest them.

The Astral: There are worlds outside of the physical one on which we reside that we can visit and explore. Exploring the astral plane allows us to make contact with beings and entities who might help us in our journey as Witches, and gives us access to powers and energies we might not otherwise be able to acquire.

The Natural World: Our physical world is full of magick, and we can utilize that magick if we know where to look. Stones, herbs, springs, and so many other things have natural properties that can add to our magick and manifest things all on their own.

The Written Word: Books are full of knowledge, but the power of the written word extends far beyond that. We can use alphabets such as the runes or Theban script not only for their magickal properties but also to divine the future and to safeguard our secrets.

Movement and Dance: The cone of power can be filled with the energy of our movements and then sent out into the universe to create change.

Sound: Toning can raise energy, but even just the words we say can have a magickal effect. Telling someone they are beautiful or that you are thankful for them is a wonderful way to transfer energy. Music can induce emotion and create an altered state of consciousness that can be used for magickal purposes.

Intoxication and Indulging the Senses: Wine, marijuana, or even something as simple as caffeine can create an altered state of consciousness that allows certain Witches to more easily find their way to the gods and indulge the spirit. Intoxication is not a path that should be abused or used all that often, but people have been using intoxicants for millennia in order to have mystical experiences. In addition, things like incense can create a change in consciousness. Try using only one type of incense (or a proprietary coven-only blend) during ritual for an extended period. Eventually just the scent of it will result in a subtle change of consciousness.

The Great Rite: Sex can be used for magickal purposes, and it can also be used to feel and experience the divine. Part 5 of this book is dedicated to it.

The Eight Paths of Power can be introduced during an elevation rite with a small explanation of each path, or something symbolic of each path could be given as a gift. Since that would end up being a lot of stuff, I think it makes more sense to present the paths as a revealed mystery. In a second-degree ritual, this might come after a challenge and include the promise that the coven will endeavor to teach these techniques now that the Witch being elevated is a second degree. Here is an example.

High Priestess: *Tonight you have proven that you are one of us and are worthy of elevation. As we raise you up, we now offer to you additional knowledge that will help to guide your path as a Witch.*

High Priest: *Harken to the Witches' Eight Paths of Power. Magick is a multifaceted manifestation, and there are many ways it can be wielded. When you step upon the eight paths, you will grow closer to our gods and this coven and develop a stronger understanding of yourself.*

High Priestess: *The first path is one that you have already walked, or you would not be here with us tonight. Magick begins inside of ourselves, and what we see there we can accomplish and make a part of our lives.*

High Priestess: *There are worlds beyond this one that can be traversed when the soul is separated from the body. The power to step out and away from this world resides within you. As Witches we travel between worlds.*

High Priest: *The Witch also knows what exists outside of themselves and what gifts the earth offers. There is the magickal both within and without, and the wise Witch takes advantage of those things while remembering to thank the Great Mother who provides us with all.*

High Priestess: *To you I present the Theban script, which hides and guards our deepest secrets.* (The High Priestess provides a parchment with the Theban script upon it, or allows the elevating Witch to copy it into their Book of Shadows.) *This is the language of the magician. Guard our secrets but ever search for your own. To be a Witch is to thirst for knowing, for knowledge is power.*

High Priest: *That the gods love us can be seen in the joy of the dance. There is magick in happiness, fellowship, movement, and rhythm. Your place is now secure in our circle and know that we shall ever hold your hand as we walk together with the gods.*

High Priestess: *From within our will we can project sound and energy to work our magicks, but know also that the words you utter both in and out of circle have the power to change worlds. A Witch is ever responsible for their actions, thoughts, and deeds. Heed the power of your own voice and use it for the betterment of the world and others.*

High Priest: *Drink deeply from the cup of life, taste the wine, and share the vine that you might grow closer to the Lord and Lady. Soften your analytical mind so that you might more easily walk between the worlds, but be ever mindful of your responsibilities and do not indulge too deeply. Extend your senses and partake of all that this coven offers. Breathe deep and smell the incense, and when you have need of us, light this that our power and presence might come to you.* (The Witch is given a small vial of coven incense.)

High Priestess: *And finally, the Great Rite. Sex is not a test or a challenge; it is a pleasurable act and also a way to raise power and be one with the gods. The Lord and Lady offer union for all who would walk in their ways.*

High Priest: *Heed the Eight Paths of Power, and use them to your advantage and never your detriment. Respect the gifts that been given to you and never abuse them, for the wrath of the gods will be your punishment if you do. Hail the Craft and hail (Craft name), newly made second-degree Witch!*

The Goddess and God

The first public Modern Witchcraft traditions kept the names of their deities a secret. Only initiates were allowed to know the specific names of the deities a coven honored in their rites. Of course a Witch can worship whatever gods they want or decide not to worship any gods at all, but many covens have primary deities that are called upon more often than others. Initiations often culminate with the names of the coven's primary goddess and god being revealed.

Originally the terms Lord and Lady were not meant to identify a specific, all-encompassing God and Goddess, but instead were meant to be used as titles for the deities whose names could not be shared in public. As Pagan-Witchcraft became less and less of a hidden tradition, people began doing ritual in public and in outer courts, and in order to not break their oaths they used "Lord" and "Lady" in place of more specific deities. Eventually people began using Lord and Lady as terms for the deities within certain Witchcraft traditions and not as placeholders.

Having a goddess and a god specific to a coven or tradition allows each covener to develop a powerful relationship with those deities. It also serves as a bonding mechanism for a coven or tradition. I honor several deities in my home and in my Witchcraft traditions, but two deities are generally reserved for my initiatory coven, which gives those rituals an extra degree of power. Those deities have also become whom I call upon when I have a particularly vexing or troubling issue to take care of. For lack of a better word, the exclusivity of their worship has made for a more intimate connection between them and myself.

In addition to naming a specific deity, initiation and elevation rituals are also excellent places to simply reveal information about a particular deity or perhaps a different understanding of a well-established goddess or god. For instance, we tend to think of the gods Apollo and Dionysus as existing in opposition to each other, but in Delphi (the home of Greece's famous oracle) the two not only shared a temple but also appear to have been worshipped as alter egos of each other.[140] That's the kind of information that makes for a dramatic reveal as to the nature of a particular deity.

In the first-degree ritual included in this book (chapter 10), the natures of the Horned God and the Great Mother are revealed, hopefully providing a different understanding of the gods and how we interact with them. A particular understanding of a deity shared by a coven doesn't mean that's the only way a covener might understand the mysteries of Dionysus and Apollo. The Greeks, for instance, worshipped several different versions of the same deity, understanding that different places and people all interpret the divine differently.

The Charge of the Goddess (see appendix 1) was partially written to explain the nature of the Goddess to newly initiated Witches. The word *charge* is a Masonic one and originally indicated a set of instructions. In the case of the Charge of the Goddess, it's thought of as a first-person (or first-Goddessperson) set of instructions for practicing Witchcraft. It's another way of revealing the nature of deity at the end of an initiation rite.

THE CHALLENGE

Witchcraft is not easy, and I don't think it's meant to be. Finding magick, finding the gods, finding a community, and finding a coven are all things that can take years to do. Many of us have endured a whole lot of slings and arrows just to arrive at the point we are at today. Initiation and elevation should be no different, and shouldn't simply be conferred upon a person without some sort of challenge.

---

140. Broad, *The Oracle: The Lost Secrets and Hidden Message of Ancient Delphi*, 41.

Those challenges can take several different forms. As in Masonic ritual, with its threats of swords and daggers, dangers are often a part of Witch rituals. There are also the challenges that come with proving a certain amount of knowledge and/or proficiency. If someone can't name all the tools upon the altar, they are probably not ready to be a High Priestess or High Priest. A degree is not just a reward for sticking with a coven or tradition for a number of years; it's an indication that a Witch *knows something* and that their knowledge is acknowledged by other people in their coven and tradition.

THE PHYSICAL CHALLENGE

No Witch has ever sliced off the ear of an initiate after threatening them with an athame or sword. There's no point in that, and that's not what such confrontations are about anyway. Confrontations are about conveying the gravity of the situation to the initiate. An initiation or elevation is meant to be a life-changing experience. Someone standing in front of you with a sword suggests such a truth.

A physical challenge with a sword during a degree rite is meant to be an obstacle that can be overcome. The swordsperson might ask for a password, and when that password is given they would then step aside. An example of this might be asking an initiate to recite the Wiccan Rede:

Swordsperson: *Before I allow you entry into this circle, you must recite the counsel that governs the magick of all the Wise.*

Initiate: *An it harm none, do what you will.*

Swordsperson: *If that is the code you live by, then I shall allow you to pass and experience the mysteries. Blessed be!*

Obstacles can be placed anywhere in an initiation or elevation ritual. The easiest place to station someone with a large sword is at the entrance to a ritual space, either immediately outside the circle or perhaps guarding a doorway into it. Many years ago a friend of ours asked us to write a dedication ritual for him outlining the things he had learned so far while in the Craft. We put several obstacles in his way as he moved through our backyard and then eventually into our house and our ritual space. He ended up facing three individuals before being allowed entry into ritual space and was forced to recite the Wiccan Rede, "Perfect love and perfect trust," and "As above, so below."

During the dedication ritual of our friend, not all of us were armed with pointy pieces of metal. Simply stepping in front of someone provides an obstacle, and having a teacher or mentor ask a question can be just as intimidating as someone waving a sword in front of you. Obstacles don't have to be stationary either. An initiate could find themselves "trapped" by several other Witches dancing around them. "Freedom" might come only by answering a question or perhaps joining in the dance itself.

As a ritual technique, a covener trapped by a group of dancers nearly writes itself:

> "And how do we know now that you are one of us?" asked the dancer coyly. "Because you have joined us in the dance of the Witches and done so with perfect love and perfect trust in your heart! Go forward now on your quest!"

Physical challenges don't have to involve only obstacles either. In my eclectic coven's initiation ritual, we bind the initiate's wrists together and then their feet and ankles (though loosely enough that they can still walk). Eventually the High Priestess cuts the cords around the initiate's wrists with her athame before presenting the initiate with their own athame and instructing them to free their feet so that they might "walk the path of the Witch with this coven." [141]

I know many covens that require initiates to taste a "bitter drink" symbolizing the difficulties of Witchcraft. Such drinks might contain a few crushed-up aspirins in order to make them bitter and unpleasant. Another alternative is pure lemon juice, which often leaves the mouth with an odd feeling. I've never heard of any coven that uses a test requiring an initiate

---

141. I love this ritual, but it's not in this book because I put it in *The Witch's Athame*, my 2016 book also published by Llewellyn. That quote is on page 219. Yes, I'm quoting myself again.

to drink something truly awful or that force someone to go against their dietary preferences.

Challenges might also involve the deprivation of the senses, such as making an initiate wear a blindfold (which we'll come back to later), as in the case of the Masons, or making an initiate walk a crooked path, in the tradition of the Horseman's Word (and doesn't that just sound witchy?). No challenge should ever seriously threaten a Witch, but there's nothing wrong with creating or utilizing something that gives a potential initiate pause. Besides, if it were all easy, wouldn't everyone be an initiate?

THE CHALLENGE OF KNOWING

Some challenges are easy and self-explanatory. Asking an initiate to recite the Witches' Pyramid while someone stands in front of them with a sword or an axe is rather obvious, but there are other tests of a Witch's skill and knowledge that require actual doing instead of just memorizing a couple lines. What follows are some tests of competency that work well in initiation and elevation rituals.

The Test of the Tools

Asking a Witch to name every tool on the altar is perhaps the most common test in these types of rites, coming either at the first or second degree. If a coven uses a pretty basic altar without a lot of extras, it works well at the first degree, but if a coven has specific names for certain candles and uses a lot of tools, it's probably best to use this at a second-degree elevation.

In our coven we keep thirteen tools on the altar, and initiates are expected to know each one and what they are generally used for. We use the chalice, wand, athame, sword, goddess statue, god statue, spirit candle, water, salt, incense, fire candle, white-handled knife, and libation bowl. Bonus points are awarded if someone calls the white-handled knife a *kerfan*, a traditional but mostly forgotten word for this knife that my wife says is never coming back. A greater challenge is to have the elevating Witch either describe or demonstrate how each tool is used in the circle.

Call the Quarters, Draw the Pentagrams, Know the Ritual

Many covens use invoking and banishing pentagrams when calling the quarters, casting the circle, and invoking the gods. In some covens just one pentagram is used for each operation, and in other covens there's a different banishing and invoking pentagram for every element! That makes for eight pentagrams in all, which can be a lot to know—which is why it makes for such an effective test.

Witches might be asked to simply draw the appropriate pentagrams in front of the altar or to draw them at the proper cardinal points in the circle. If a coven uses particular ritual forms (such as the Osiris position for calling the quarters), those can be incorporated into the drawing of the pentagrams. The point of such an exercise is never to set someone up to fail, but to allow them to demonstrate their competency. In the heat of the moment we all forget things, and I'll admit that I've whispered a hint to an initiate or three.

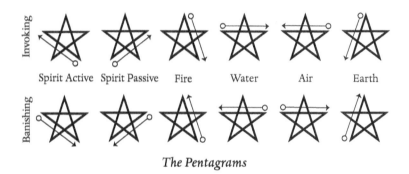

The Pentagrams

If a coven requires its members to memorize certain portions of the ritual, that can be used as a challenge. While I'm not of the opinion that everything has to be memorized, knowing the words used for circle casting, calling the quarters, and celebrating cakes and ale seems reasonable. In the case of casting the circle, this is a skill that can also be tested during an elevation rite.

Drawing Down the Moon

The rite of drawing down the moon (see part 4) is a fine challenge for a third-degree Witch. However, the act of drawing down hinges not just on the Witch being elevated but also on the deity being called to. If a coven is going to proceed with invoking deity as a test, there need to be some caveats. If deity chooses not to show up, is that the fault of the Witch doing the drawing down? Most often not.

More important than the rite being successful is that it is done properly. Are the words the coven uses for this ceremony being said correctly? Are the individual components of the ritual being followed? Because Witchcraft is a plea and a call to higher powers, there are some things that can't be judged as unsuccessful simply because they didn't proceed as we had hoped.

For many covens, drawing down the moon is one of Witchcraft's most important rites. Being able to draw down is a skill that I think every second- and third-degree Witch should possess, but it's also not a parlor trick or an ability that can be turned on or off depending on the circumstance. If this is a test you choose for your initiates, proceed with caution and with the knowledge that it doesn't always work as hoped for.

Test Before the Initiation or Elevation

Our rites of passage and accomplishment are earned, and in a sense much of what goes into them happens before the elevation and initiation ritual. Expecting certain conditions to be met before an initiation or elevation is not unrealistic. If a coven requires their initiates to hand-copy their Book of Shadows, then providing proof of that accomplishment before a second-degree elevation is certainly acceptable.

I have yet to meet a High Priestess who gives her initiates written exams, but I know many who require their students to pass certain tests before initiation or elevation. One of the most common tests is successfully running a ritual according to their coven or tradition's parameters. If a potential second-degree Witch forgets to cast a circle while setting up the working space, then they probably aren't ready to be elevated. Being able to lead a ritual requires more than rote memorization or reading from a book; it also requires specific skills such as reaching out to the gods and casting powerful circles.

Other assessments might involve testing the humility of a potential third degree. A third-degree Witch serves their coven and their community; they don't look for people to serve them. In many ways the months and years leading up to an elevation are their own sort of test. They test a Witch's mettle, their dedication to the Craft, and how they interact with those around them.

THE GIVING OF GIFTS

An initiation or elevation rite is cause for celebration, and many covens commemorate such milestones with the giving of gifts. Often the gift giving is done after the rite has ended, but gifts can also be presented during the ritual itself. Usually the gifts given during an initiation or elevation contain secrets of mysteries of the Craft and fit well alongside the other components of such ceremonies. As long as whatever is given away resonates with the spirit of the coven, it can be worked into the initiation or elevation, but some things work better than others.

Degree Symbols

The most common gift given during an initiation ritual is the degree symbol. Many traditions have specific symbols for the three degrees and require members of the coven to wear those symbols to the coven's rites. The traditional set of degree symbols has been in use since the 1950s and is still used by many covens today.

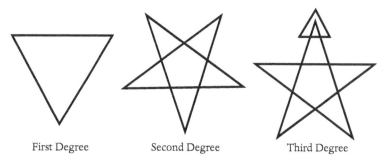

First Degree   Second Degree   Third Degree

Degree Symbols: Inverted Triangle,
Upside-Down Pentacle, Triangle and Star

In that particular system the first degree is symbolized by an inverted (single-point-down) triangle. The triangle in this position is seen by many traditions as representing the *yoni*, which in the original Sanskrit translates as "source" or "womb." [142] As such, it represents the Goddess, which is appropriate since she was the gateway to Witchcraft for so many of us.

The second-degree symbol is an upside-down pentagram, which means a single point is facing downward. The upside-down pentagram is often interpreted as the triumph of the physical over the spiritual, and for this reason it has been adopted by many Satanist groups. This has made some Witches wary of wearing this symbol, and I'll admit I'm not sure I've ever met a Wiccan-Witch who wears one. [143] In Witchcraft the upside-down pentagram can symbolize putting physical needs over spiritual ones, but it's most often seen as a symbol of the Horned God. The two points facing up are his horns and the point facing downward his goatee.

The third-degree symbol is a combination of the triangle and pentacle, but with both now facing up. The upward-pointing triangle is often used to symbolize fire, and in the case of Witchcraft it symbolizes our inner fire, our will. The pentacle with its point upward represents the triumph of the spiritual over the material, a symbolism that has always appealed to me as a Witch. Some also see it as representing the gods: the Goddess as Maiden, Mother, and Crone and the Horned God as Lord of Life and Death. Like most symbols, what matters most is how it's interpreted by the individual Witch.

Traditional symbols are not the only ones that can be used to represent degrees. There are literally thousands of options, as long as what's being used has meaning to the coven using them. Some options include using an acorn for the first degree, an oak leaf for the second, and the Tree of Life for the third. Another option is an empty circle for the first degree, a single star pointing upward for the second, and the full pentagram enclosed in a circle for the third.

Coven Symbols

Some groups who have only one degree or don't bother with degree symbols instead choose to hand out some sort of token representing

---

142. Oxford English Dictionary, https://en.oxforddictionaries.com/definition/yoni.

143. Zimmerman and Gleason, *The Complete Idiot's Guide to Wicca and Witchcraft*, 249–250.

the coven. My eclectic coven has only an initiation rite, and upon completing it, all of our coveners are given a medallion with the Tree of Life on it. The only way to receive that token is by becoming an initiate in the coven. (We chose a tree because our coven is named the Oak Court.)

A coven symbol can be a common Witch symbol or something less obvious. There's nothing wrong with simply handing out a pentacle or something representing the goddess honored by the coven. Less obvious symbols often make great tokens because they encourage knowing winks from everyone in the coven and will often confuse others who don't know how to interpret them. (When members of our Oak Court visit Pagan events with their coven symbol around their necks, they often get questioning looks from other Witches wondering just what it means and what group it belongs to.)

Simple tokens can contain a lot of meaning. The first-degree ritual in this book includes a key, which symbolizes admittance into the coven and a chosen family. It's the kind of symbol one can wear anywhere without attracting any sort of attention while taking pride in knowing what it means and symbolizes. Even covens that are a part of a well-established tradition will sometimes adopt their own symbol to highlight the individuality of their coven.

Book of Shadows and Magickal Names

Nothing implies trust in a coven member or new initiate more than giving them a Book of Shadows. It's one of the greatest honors one can give another Witch. With the exception of actual practice, a Book of Shadows is the clearest window into the beliefs and rituals of a coven or tradition. In our coven's initiation rituals we always conclude with the presentation of the Book of Shadows.

Covens with a well-defined degree system often withhold certain pieces of information for the second and third degrees, meaning that additional parts of the book can be built into second- and third-degree rites. In addition to presenting a Witch with a Book of Shadows, there are other uses for a Book of Shadows in an initiation or elevation rite. If a coven uses a shared book for their rites, they might invite a new initiate to sign their magickal name in the book, marking their entrance into the coven (see the Margaret Murray–inspired ritual back in chapter 3).

Many Witches use a magickal name both in daily life and in the circle. Some traditions require the use of a magickal name when doing ritual, and the announcement of an individual Witch's magickal name is often a part of initiation rituals. There's something magickal about announcing to your chosen family the name you most desire to be called, and to do so on one of the most important nights of your life as a Witch.

For many Witches the name they were given at birth is just not who they are. A magickal name allows a Witch to embrace and announce who they truly are to those they trust most. Knowing someone's true name is thought of as a source of power by many. Having a magickal name that we share only with other Witches takes that power away from our enemies. Magickal names are often reserved only for use in the circle, and it's considered a breach of trust to share someone's magickal name without their permission. (There are also many Witches who will happily share their magickal names. For instance, my magickal name is … On second thought …)

A Tool Used in the Ritual

Tools make great gifts for initiating or elevating Witches, especially if that tool is used in the ritual. An example of this might involve requiring an initiate to drink a bitter beverage and then giving them the cup or chalice. This is not a particularly common practice, but I think it has a nice symbolic quality to it, and doing something that most other covens don't will make your own individual rites more unique.

One of the most common tools to give away during an initiation or elevation rite are the candles used during that rite. The idea behind this is that the power generated during the initiation will be absorbed by the candles and can then be accessed anytime the Witch has need of it simply by lighting the candle. I think this is a beautiful tradition and is one of my favorites. I know there have been nights when I'm separated from my favorite Witches and it's nice to know that their energy is nearby if I need it. Similar to this is giving initiates any material that was used to create a physical boundary during the rite. After an initiation, our initiates always leave with a few oak leaves.

Some Other Symbol of Rank

Degree sigils or medallions aren't the only symbols of rank in a coven, and there are other gifts that can be given that symbolize where a Witch is in their journey. The third-degree rite in this book (chapter 10) includes giving a set of horns or a crown to a newly made third-degree High Priestess or High Priest. Covens that use different-colored cords with their robes might hand these out during an initiation or elevation. As with everything related to the Craft, ultimately it's about what matters to the individual Witch and their particular coven.

THE OATH

Most initiation rites end with an oath, which details what's expected of the newly made initiate. In the Masonic tradition, many of these oaths contain thinly veiled (and not so thinly veiled) threats. I don't know of any Witches who have ever been physically harmed for violating an oath (and there are several well-known oath breakers in Witch history), and most Witches believe that the reckoning that comes from violating an oath ends up between the violator and their gods.

I think oaths are important because they convey the solemnity of initiation. We should not take the trust given to us lightly, and oaths drive home just how much faith has been put in us by our initiators. Most oaths are variations on the "obligation" used by the Masons:

> I, [Initiate name], of my own free will and accord … do hereby and hereon most solemnly and sincerely promise and swear that I will always *hail*, ever conceal, and never reveal any of the arts, parts, or points of the hidden mysteries of Ancient Free Masonry, which may have been, or hereafter shall be, at this time, or any future period, communicated to me, as such, to any person or persons whomsoever, except it be to a true and lawful brother Mason … All this I most solemnly, sincerely promise and swear, with a firm and steadfast resolution to perform the

same, without any mental reservation or secret evasion of mind whatever, binding myself under no less penalty than that of having my throat cut across, my tongue torn out by its roots, and *my body buried in the rough sands of the sea*, at low-water mark, where the tide ebbs and flows twice in twenty-four hours, should I ever knowingly violate this, my Entered Apprentice obligation. So help me God, and keep me steadfast in the due performance of the same. [144]

The oaths used in Witchcraft are much like the one used in Masonry in that they simply ask the initiate not to reveal the mysteries given to them in the Craft. This doesn't mean an initiate can't acknowledge that they are a part of a tradition or coven, but only that the rites of that tradition or coven are not for outside consumption. Our covens and traditions give our lives as Witches meaning, and they can't simply be hidden away in a box except for sabbats and esbats, but the exact details of what we do during those sabbats and esbats is easily kept oathbound. No one has to know exactly how I call the quarters as a Gardnerian or what the names of my coven's deities are. Those are the types of secrets that are oathbound, not the fact that I cast a circle or celebrate cakes and ale.

If and when we leave a coven or tradition, we continue to respect our oaths. Oaths are often made to the gods, and who wants to disrespect them? They were here long before us and will be here long after. It's always best to stay on their good side.

DISORIENTATION

An initiation or elevation is designed to be memorable and transformative. Presenting challenges and obstacles creates a heightened sense of anticipation and emotion for the person going through the rite. Another way to do this is by disorienting a potential initiate. The Masons did this by using a blindfold and binding a cable tow to their initiates. (The symbolism of the cord was expressed by where it was tied to the initiating or elevating Mason.) Ritual works best when it transports us away from

---

144. From *Duncan's Masonic Ritual and Monitor.* Emphasis in the original, along with some editing for clarity by the writer of this book (me).

the mundane world, and one of the best ways to do this is to create experiences that just don't happen in our everyday, ordinary existence.

Changing how we interact with the world has another unique effect: it makes everyone's initiation or elevation different. Because we aren't relying on our usual senses, we will experience things in a manner unique to ourselves. I can't tell you what happened at my own initiation, but I can tell you that my recollection of it is not accurate. I remember it not how it happened but only how I experienced it. Months after it happened I was talking to my wife about it and she told me, "That part didn't happen," and she's most likely right, but it happened in my world, so it also did.

Blindfolds and cords are ways to create a disorienting experience, but there are others. Leaving an initiate in complete darkness for thirty minutes to an hour before initiation forces them to look inward before looking outward to the gods and their chosen family. It's a powerful way to get someone to face their fears and connect with their true will.

If you want to create a heightened sense of confusion and cause a Witch to wonder just where they are, spinning them around while wearing a blindfold will have that effect. Not only will they possibly be dizzy, but they won't know if they are coming or going. Initiation and elevation rituals should remove us from the usual, and not knowing where a ritual is taking place or how we arrived at that space is certainly unusual.

Sound can be extremely disorienting. Tones and bells sounded in odd places can be bewildering and help to create an otherworldly experience. Music has a great deal of power over our emotions. Playing something witchy or even ominous can heighten a person's emotional response and make them more receptive to the mysteries being shared. Scents are powerful too, and even just the right essential oil placed above the lip can be transformative.

In Masonic tradition the initiate is marched around the lodge room in what seems to be a random sequence, though that pattern is later revealed to have symbolic meaning.[145] In a similar fashion, an initiator

---

145. Lomas, *Turning the Hiram Key*, 63.

might make their charge walk an invoking pentagram to mark their entrance into the Craft.

Everything we do during an initiation or elevation ritual should have some sort of greater purpose. Simply throwing a blindfold over someone's eyes is pointless if it doesn't play a role in the ritual. The Masons would remove the blindfold before showing a new initiate the light of the Masonic craft, and similar symbolism works in Witchcraft. For most of our lives we are separated from both the Goddess and magick, so revealing those truths should be as powerful an experience as possible.

CHAPTER TEN

Rituals for the First, Second, and Third Degrees

Initiation and elevation rites should be unique events in the life of a coven and should not be piggybacked onto a sabbat ritual or a full moon rite. Because initiations are often complex things, they generally require a greater degree of prep time than the standard ritual. I'm of the opinion that because an initiation or elevation is a very special day in the life of a Witch (and their coven), it should be treated differently than the usual Witch ritual.

One of the easiest things to do to make an initiation ritual different is to change up your ritual space. This doesn't mean finding a new location, it just means doing a little extra setup before ritual begins. Most Witches don't make a physical circle, but using one adds greatly to the ambience of an elevation ritual. Leaves and flower petals are easy to set up as the perimeter of the circle and both look and smell lovely too. If this is an idea your coven adopts, you can get even more creative with it. Perhaps use fresh green leaves at an initiation, dried autumn leaves for the third degree, and a mixture of the two for the second degree. Similar things can be done with flower petals. Leaves and flower petals are among my favorites because they are inexpensive and make great ritual keepsakes for the initiate!

Rocks and stones make for great circle markers too, and the colors you use can be changed from initiation to initiation or degree to degree. Even the old-fashioned use of salt or flour would probably be surprising to an initiate simply because it's not done all that much anymore. Nearly anything you can set on a floor works here, though the more elaborate it is, the less likely it is to be given away to a new initiate.

Creating a physical circle is not the only way to change up ritual space. Another nice addition is to use new candles or candles that are a different color than what is normally used. Some groups use certain candle colors for specific rites. Combinations such as yellow at initiation, red at second degree, and blue at third are memorable ways to make the initiation or elevation experience unique, and, like rose petals or leaves, they can be given away at the end of ritual if the coven chooses.

Much like how many families have fine china that they use only for special occasions, many Witches and covens have their own "fine tools" that they don't wheel out all that often. For instance, we use my wife's oldest chalice only during certain rituals because of its age and condition, and when we do use it, everyone realizes that what we are doing that night is special. Designating a coven pentacle to be used only during initiation and elevation rituals is an easy way to make the altar different for one of these special events.

Many covens require a thorough cleansing of the initiate before the ritual begins. This is often something beyond the normal purification rites most covens use and might require the initiate to shower or take a bath. In such cases they might instruct the initiate to bathe with sea salt, lavender, yarrow, or something unique to that tradition.

My house is very small and requires an additional step before an initiation: a long musical playlist cued up and ready to be cranked at a very high volume. There are two reasons for this. The first is that a prospective initiate is not allowed to hear our ritual until they are initiated, so we don't want them overhearing any deity names or knowing how we set up the circle. (This makes their first post-initiation ritual extra special because half of it they've never experienced before.) We also tend to initiate in pairs, and we want to make sure the person being initiated last can't hear the first initiation. The house where my wife and I were initiated was three stories tall (it's not as impressive as it sounds—the third story was the attic), so this step was unnecessary, but in our little two-room house it's vital!

Initiations and elevations can be all-day affairs if there's attention paid to every detail. Be sure to give yourself and your coven enough time to get everything set up. Also make sure you are respecting the time of future initiates. I once went to an initiation that started four hours late on a weeknight. The complete lack of planning showed disrespect not only for what should be one of the most memorable rituals ever undertaken by a Witch but also for everyone who attended.

KNOWING WHEN SOMEONE IS READY FOR THE FIRST DEGREE

In the early days of Modern Witchcraft the only way to access Witch rituals and beliefs was by becoming an initiate. Back then, from the early 1950s through the late 1970s, it was very common for covens to initiate almost anyone with an interest in the Craft. It's rumored that all someone had to do to become an initiated Alexandrian back in the late 1960s was to walk by the London flat of Maxine and Alex Sanders! Such rumors are almost certainly an exaggeration, but Alex and Maxine did initiate a lot of Witches back in the day.

One of my favorite High Priestesses has shared stories with me about initiating several famous science-fiction writers back in the 1970s. Before there were Pagan gatherings, many Witches and like-minded souls gathered at sci-fi cons, and when someone there expressed an interest in the Craft they were whisked away to a hotel room and made an initiate. (And no, I don't have any names I can give you, but I have some suspicions.)

Today things are much different. Most people who join lineaged covens are already experienced and well-regarded Witches and have most likely been practicing for years or even decades. Candidates for initiation are expected to know something about Witchcraft these days, which is radically different from how things were forty years ago. This doesn't mean that people are no longer running outer courts or providing training prior to initiation—just the opposite. Because there are so many more outlets for Witch and Pagan rituals today, there's less urgency to initiate people. This allows covens to be more selective about who they choose to initiate.

My wife feels that it's up to the potential initiate to indicate that they are ready for a first-degree ritual. Certainly asking to be initiated shows courage and initiative, two qualities that are valued in the Craft. There are instances when such expectations lead to problems. For example, many initiates believe that *we'll ask them* when we think they are ready. In our practice, I'll sometimes talk to a potential initiate to see if they are interested in the experience and then instruct them to ask Ari, my wife, High Priestess, and the true leader of our coven (I'm just loud).

There are qualities that should be looked for in an initiate. Are they trustworthy? Will they keep the secrets of the coven and/or tradition? If there are any reservations about this, initiation should wait until they convince you otherwise. In addition, we tend to reserve initiation for only the most dedicated of Witches. If someone doesn't show much interest or curiosity about the Craft, initiation is probably not for them.

A coven is also a chosen family, so compatibility is extremely important. A coven full of deity-believing Witches whose central mystery is drawing down the moon probably shouldn't initiate a nonbelieving Witch. There are also other considerations, depending on how the coven practices. If the rites are skyclad, is the potential initiate aware of this and comfortable with it? Is their spouse or partner? There's nothing sexual about dancing around naked, but you don't want a knock on your door from a jealous partner who is ignorant of that fact.

There are timing issues to consider with initiations as well. Many Witches will initiate seekers only at certain times of the year. For the first degree that's generally thought of as the time when the earth is green, or at least soon to be. The period from Samhain to Imbolc is the darkest part of year and is not considered a good time to initiate. Even when we're sure someone would make a great initiate, that doesn't mean we can just run out and do it the next day. Many Witches also time initiations and elevations around astrological considerations and full moon cycles. This is already a long book, so adding such additional information would probably make it too long! Just be sure that whatever you do is comfortable for the initiator and the initiate.

I believe that if someone is hesitant about a potential initiate, the time for initiation is probably not nigh. However, we do play tricks on ourselves, and as Witches we have other means at our disposal for figuring out just what we should or shouldn't do. It's perfectly fine to consult the tarot or runes to decide upon a course of action. There are also the gods, and the question can be posed directly to the Lord and/or Lady if necessary. One of the great things about being a Witch is that our deities are always within reach, and they usually answer!

A person is ready for the first degree (initiation) when they

- have earned the trust of everyone in the coven.
- prove they are capable of keeping secrets and not violating a trust.
- have shown a sincere interest in the Craft.
- have a basic understanding of Witchcraft.
- have proven they are comfortable in a situation where they won't be in charge.

FIRST-DEGREE INITIATION RITUAL

This initiation ritual doesn't require any extra tools but does include the gifting of a skeleton key as an initiation gift/token, and the High Priest should be wearing some sort of horned/antlered headwear. The initiate should be kept out of ritual space until the circle is cast, the quarters are called, and the gods are invoked. Some covens perform a drawing down the moon rite before the initiation begins just to make sure the Goddess doesn't have any last-minute reservations regarding the new initiate. (Silence is considered a good sign if you choose to go this route.)

The initiate is brought into ritual space and is met at the perimeter of the magick circle by the High Priestess. Using her athame, the High Priestess cuts a doorway into the circle and then takes the initiate's hands into her own.

High Priestess: *Tonight many of the mysteries will be revealed to you, and you will leave this space a member of this coven and a true Witch, if the gods are agreeable. Before we proceed, there is one secret that you must know and keep deep within your heart during tonight's proceedings:*

> *We walk in perfect love and perfect trust.*
> *Faith in the coven is a total must.*
> *Chosen family is what you enter.*
> *Let this truth now ever be your center.*

The High Priestess pulls the initiate into the circle, and the doorway is sealed behind them by the High Priest. The initiate is then walked around the circle three times by the High Priestess as the High Priest narrates their journey.

High Priest: *Three trips around the magick circle: The first for the Goddess, our Lady full of beauty and grace, Mistress of the Moon, Queen of the Waters, and the Heart of Nature. The second for the Horned One, he who leads the Wild Hunt and is Lord of the Forest. The third for the crooked and winding path that all take on their way to the Craft.*

The initiate is left by the High Priestess facing the altar, but standing between the altar and the initiate is the High Priest, who brandishes a sword and wears a horned helm upon his head. He faces the candidate for initiation and points the sword at the initiate menacingly before asking them a question.

High Priest: *You know the password of perfect love and perfect trust, but what rule also guides the Witch upon their journey? Failure to reply properly will result in the end of this initiation, and your induction into the Craft of the Wise will be forced to wait until another night. What counsel was given to us by the Mighty Ones in regard to the use of magick?*

The initiate answers with the Wiccan Rede: *An it harm none, do what you will.* The High Priest lowers his sword and lets the initiate pass to stand before the altar, where they are instructed to kneel and rest their head upon the altar. The High Priest moves to stand next to the High Priestess, placing the cold metal of his sword upon the left shoulder of the initiate.

High Priestess: *Before our secrets can be revealed, the oath must be administered. Failure to speak the oath will remove you from the fraternity of this coven, and you will forever be denied the mysteries of the Craft. The iron upon your shoulder will then cast you out of our circle and away from us, but remember the first secret given to you tonight, for we are those who would be your chosen family. Do you, (Name of Witch), wish to proceed?*

The initiate should reply in the affirmative.

The High Priestess continues: *And now I ask that you repeat after me:*[146]

> *"I (Witch's name), of my own free will and accord and in the presence of the Lord, the Lady, and those who would be my chosen family, confirm that I have chosen to live my life as a Witch and as a part of this coven. I swear to ever lock away the secrets of this coven and to never reveal the mysteries that have been shared with me unless it be with a coven member. I swear to love my brothers and sisters in the Craft and to be there for them. I swear to honor the Goddess and God, the earth below my feet, and the sun, stars, and moon overhead. Because of love and respect I swear to share the mysteries of the Craft as I know them with my now chosen family. From this day forth I will live as a Witch and a member of (Name of coven). All of this I swear and promise with my whole heart, knowing that if I ever break this oath the retribution of the gods shall be terrible and that I shall be cast out, forced to ever wander alone. In perfect love and perfect trust, I make this oath and swear these things. In the names of the Lord and the Lady, so mote it be!"*

The High Priest should now remove his sword from the shoulder of the initiate and set it upon the altar or the ground. Then he tells the initiate to stand.

High Priest: *Now that you have promised to keep secret our mysteries and truly be a part of this coven, we shall reveal to you the second mystery: "As*

---

146. This is a lot of text, so whoever reads it should break it down into small sections. When I'm in a situation where I need a covener to repeat things after me, I break every sentence down into sections of not more than ten or twelve words.

above, so below." This phrase is one of the fundamentals of magick, for we cannot bring forth change without moving energy and will from one plane to another. But the truth of this law runs even deeper and is a part of all that this coven does.

High Priestess: *"As above, so below" is not a law limited to magick; it is a law that applies to both us and the gods. For within us are all the keys to the universe, and within the universe are all the keys needed to unlock our magick and potential.*

High Priest: *You have been told that the Lord we worship is nature's joy and Guardian of the Forest. This is true, for the Horned God is a part of the natural world and he walks upon it with us. But our God is also a Lord of Death, he is the Dread Lord of Shadows and the Lord of Death and Resurrection. His nature is dual. He is with us in life, and he will still be with us in death. He keeps one foot upon the path of the living and a second upon the road of the dead. To love and worship him means embracing not only life but also death. As above, so below! So mote it be!*

High Priestess: *They call her Maiden, Mother, and Crone, but our Lady is much more than those things. She is the huntress and warrior who seeks out those who would commit injustices upon others. She is the comforter and counselor who hears our cries and dries our tears. She is vengeance, but she is also love, for she only punishes the wicked, and finds joy in the happiness of those who follow her. She too is the Goddess of both the living and the dead, for to walk with her is to embrace both worlds. She is the mystery of the end and the wonder of beginnings, and holds the universe in her hands. As above, so below! So mote it be!*

High Priest: *And now you know another of the mysteries, and the truth of the Lady and Lord we love so much. They are the gods of the living and the gods of the dead, and to embrace them in this world is to embrace them in the next. This mystery extends to this coven, for as long as we share mutual love and trust, we will walk the world and be one chosen family.*

The High Priestess takes a key (preferably on a chain) and places it in the hand of the initiate or over their head and welcomes the initiate into the coven.

High Priestess: *As a sign that you are one with this coven, we present this key. It unlocks the door that leads to our family and our rites, but it also serves as a key that shall reveal the greater mysteries that you have yet to learn. When you wear this key, think of this night, this coven, the gods we serve, and the mysteries yet to be revealed. We now welcome you into our coven as a full member! Congratulations, newly made Witch of the (Name of coven). Blessed be!*

Everyone in attendance should now give the newly made first-degree Witch a hug and a welcome greeting. The circle should then be closed up, with presents and a celebration happening once the rite has ended.

WHAT A SECOND DEGREE SHOULD KNOW, AND KNOWING WHEN SOMEONE IS READY FOR THE SECOND DEGREE

I was probably not ready to be a second-degree Witch when I was elevated to that position. By that point in my life I had a very firm grasp on Witchcraft but not necessarily the Witchcraft practiced by my tradition. In the end it all worked out okay, and my initiators certainly knew what they were doing because my elevation helped me understand the things that had previously eluded me.

My wishy-washy feelings about my second-degree elevation dovetail nicely with how many people interpret this particular step on the Witch's path. Initiations are very straightforward in terms of their intention, as are third-degree rituals, where the end result is generally one's own coven or a place of leadership in their existing one. But the second-degree Witch exists between those two extremes, and knowing when someone is ready for the second degree is often a judgment call to be made by those running the coven.

For me, a second-degree Witch is someone capable of conducting ritual from start to finish. That doesn't mean that they have every bit of the coven's ritual memorized, but only that they are familiar with how their coven operates and understand the reasoning behind those operational decisions. A second-degree Witch is a Witch who truly understands their Craft and is capable of doing nearly all the heavy lifting required during ritual.

Many covens see second degree as a learning opportunity. It's a chance to both observe and practice ritual. It's also a place to learn leadership skills and prepare for the challenges and rewards that come with running a coven. Coven leadership is more than just directing ritual; it's about interacting with other Witches, scheduling sabbats, and figuring out just how to teach and train future Witches.

For many people the second degree is merely a layover on their greater journey, but it doesn't have to be. The idea that every Witch in a degree system has to obtain their third degree is an erroneous one. If someone has no desire to lead ritual or start a coven of their own, there's no need for a second- or third-degree elevation. As Witches we all have different skill sets, and some people are completely comfortable with just being a part of something and letting others run it.

There's a local coven leader in my area who expects all of her students to read at least thirty different books all dealing with various magickal and witchy topics before initiation or elevation. It's an inclination I understand, yet I know from experience that such requirements are not for everyone. My wife is one of the most highly skilled High Priestesses I've ever met, and the number of Witchcraft books she has read over the years is negligible. (I can write that in this volume because I'm rather sure she's not going to read this book.) Some people learn from books, and others are more intuitive.

If you are running a coven, there has to be some variance as to just what you should expect from an initiate or a candidate for elevation. Everyone learns differently, and certain people gravitate toward specific ideas and techniques while being ambivalent about other skill sets. I know great Witches who are poor ritualists and amazing magick practitioners. Determining just what someone should know for a second-degree elevation is a judgment call that requires evaluating the strengths and weaknesses of each individual candidate.

Witchcraft is about doing and experiencing. There is knowledge to be gained from reading and discussion, but that's not the only way to learn things. Someone preparing for the second degree has to be able to do more than recite the Wiccan Rede; they should be able to feel the magick that fills the circle when the cone of power is raised and feel some sort of connection with the coven's chosen gods.

A person is ready for the second degree when they

- can articulate the basic concepts of Modern Witchcraft.
- are familiar with all the tools of the Craft.
- are capable of effectively running a coven's rituals.
- are able to draw down deity.
- have a thorough understanding of the history of Witchcraft, their tradition, and their coven.
- are seen as capable and competent ritual leaders by the rest of the coven.
- have shown proficiency in the magickal arts.
- are respectful of Craft elders and understand why those individuals are important to our history.

I'm not of the opinion that a Witch needs to know *everything* (I'm part of a coven, so my friends can fill in the gaps, so to speak), but many covens require or encourage second-degree Witches to also have the following skills:

- Proficiency in at least one form of divination (tarot, runes, etc.)
- A basic understanding of astrology and/or the ability to cast a chart
- Knowledge of herbs, incense, and/or oils
- An affinity for natural things such as stones, types of wood, etc.

SECOND-DEGREE RITUAL: ASCENDING THE WITCHES' PYRAMID

This ritual does not require much in the way of tools, just a blindfold, a bell, a token representing the second degree, and an altar full of ritual tools. If you want to go a bit further down the Masonic rabbit hole, this ritual provides a perfect opportunity to lead the blindfolded Witch around with a cable tow. (A cable tow can be made out of anything. The Masons sometimes made them out of steel chains, but natural fibers are probably best.) As with the initiation ritual, it's generally best to make the second-degree elevation rite the center of the coven's work the night it is performed.

Unlike an initiation ceremony, a Witch being elevated to the second degree can participate in the building of circle, the calling of the quarters, and the invocation of the gods. If two or more Witches are being elevated, those going second or third should be cut out of the circle so they don't see the elevation rite before participating in it. It goes without saying that everyone involved in the elevation must have already obtained their second degree. Before beginning the rite, a drawing down can be done to determine if the Lady is agreeable with the elevations.

The rite begins after the gods are invoked or the drawing down is performed.

High Priestess: *There is one among us tonight who seeks to take the next step on their journey as a Witch. After many moons spent learning and perfecting their Craft, they have asked to be raised to the rank of second degree. We are here to grant that request, assuming they have the trust and skill needed to overcome the obstacles that stand in their way.*

The High Priest moves to stand in front of the altar, blocking the candidate's access to it. When he is in position, the High Priest speaks.

High Priest: *Would the candidate for the second degree, (Witch's name), please step forward toward the altar.*

As the candidate steps forward, the High Priest holds his position in front of the altar, blocking the candidate's access to it. When the candidate has stopped in front of him, the High Priest continues.

High Priest: *When I last blocked your way, I asked for a password that would allow you to continue. That password was "An it harm none, do what you will." You are here today because you have lived up to that rede. Tonight, before I can let you take the next step on your journey, I must ask you for the original password, the one that sums up our feelings for you and what we think are your feelings for us.*

Candidate: *In perfect love and perfect trust.*

High Priest: *As always, hold those words close to your heart as you go through this night. Blessed be!*

Candidate: *Blessed be!*

The High Priest then steps aside, allowing access to the altar for the soon-to-be second-degree Witch. The High Priestess then instructs the candidate to stand before the altar, facing her.

High Priestess: *Before we can proceed, we must know just how faithful and attentive you have been on your journey this far. Tell me, who are the gods we worship in circle?*

Candidate: *In this circle we honor the Goddess of both the living and the dead, and the Horned God who walks in two worlds.* (Names of individual coven deities can also be used here of course.)

High Priestess: *As beings who walk between the worlds, what rule do they follow, as do we?*

Candidate: *As above, so below.*

High Priestess: *So mote it be! A Witch should be familiar with not only their gods but also the tools of their art. Upon this altar lie the implements of the Witch. Before we proceed I must ask you to name them all and explain their use.*

The candidate should now identify and explain the use of all the tools on the altar. (The last step—"explain the use of"—can be dropped at the discretion of the coven, as it could take a while!) These are the main tools found on almost every altar, and their uses:

Athame: For directing energy and casting the magick circle

Sword: For casting the circle

White-Handled Knife: For physical cutting

Wand: For manipulation of energy

Chalice/Cup: Symbolic of the Goddess

Salt, Incense, Water, Fire Candle: Representations of the four elements: earth, air, water, and fire, respectively

Libation Bowl: For gifts and thanks to the gods

Pentacle: For summoning energy and blessing the elements

Many covens have other items on their primary altar, including deity statues, a cauldron, a mirror, cords, candles for the Goddess, the God, and spirit, and various other tools used in their respective traditions. Once the elevating Witch has identified everything on the altar, the rite proceeds.

High Priestess: *You have passed the first challenge, as we knew you would, and now the second phase begins.*

The High Priest slips a blindfold over the eyes of the candidate, making sure they cannot see. If a cable tow is being used, it is applied now. (In Masonic tradition, the cable tow is tied loosely around the neck for the first degree and is wrapped around the arm twice for the second degree and around the waist for the third degree. You should use whatever you think is most appropriate for your rite.[147]) The candidate is made to stand and is then spun around several times to disorient them so they have no idea which direction they are facing.

The High Priest then directs the candidate around the circle in a spiral, moving from the altar to the periphery of the circle and then around in a clockwise motion. The candidate will slowly climb the Witches' Pyramid as they stop in the east, west, south, and north, respectively. Before stopping at each cardinal point, the candidate should be made to walk at least one full lap around the circle. As the candidate and the High Priest walk around the circle, they should slowly inch toward the circle's center with every step. The High Priestess narrates the journey as they go around.

---

147. The positions of the cable tow come from *Duncan's Masonic Ritual & Monitor*.

High Priestess: *Tonight you will traverse the Witches' Pyramid, walking upward until you reach the ultimate truth at the pyramid's summit. Though blind, you walk in the light, because you walk in both love and trust. So mote it be!*

The candidate is made to stop in the east, the base of the pyramid. Before speaking, the High Priestess rings a bell, and when the bell's ringing has faded away, she speaks.

High Priestess: *"To know" is the base of our pyramid. Knowing is not just about what is written in books or given to you by way of instruction; true knowledge is the knowledge of the self. For we cannot progress as Witches if we do not know what we truly desire and just who we are as individuals. Listen again to the sound of the bell* [Rings the bell once, speaking again just before the sound of the bell fades away) *and follow that sound inward, knowing your true self.*

The High Priestess rings the bell one last time, allowing the candidate to journey inward to seek the knowledge of their true self. As the sound fades away, the candidate continues their walk up the pyramid, making at least one full circuit around the circle before coming to a stop in the west. When the candidate and the High Priest are situated, the High Priestess continues.

High Priestess: *To journey up the Witches' Pyramid is to dare. To stand here in this place, in a liminal space between the mundane world and the realms of the Mighty Ones, requires courage, conviction, and belief. The world is full of suffering and yet we continue to believe, and when we believe, the gods walk with us. You have been taught in this coven that the Goddess and God are a part of all things. Now you must seek them out, knowing that even in the darkness you will find them by continuing to walk the path you have already begun.*

The High Priestess moves out from behind the altar and speaks the Charge of the Goddess as found in Charles Leland's *Aradia*. She should stand in the south, near but behind the candidate. When she has finished reading the Charge, the High Priest should whisper "Seek our Lady" in the candidate's ear, with the candidate then moving deosil around the circle until they are finally embraced by the High Priestess. This is symbolic of finding the Goddess. If the candidate decides to "cheat" and walk widdershins to the Goddess, they should be reminded to search for her in harmony with the rising and setting sun (deosil). If the candidate does try to start walking backward, the High Priestess should take a step back and not allow herself to be caught.

High Priestess: *Whenever ye have need of anything, once in the month, and when the moon is full, ye shall assemble in some desert place, or in a forest all together join, to adore the potent spirit of your queen, I who am the Great Lady. You have fain would learn all sorcery yet have not won its deepest secrets; these I will teach you, and in truth all things as yet unknown. And ye shall be freed from slavery, and so ye shall be free in everything; and as the sign that ye are truly free, you shall be free to come unto me and embrace I who embrace you.* [148]

Once the candidate catches the High Priestess/Goddess, the High Priest should whisper in the candidate's ear.

High Priest (whispering): *And those who walk with my Lady and love her are also equally loved by me. Together we shall stand beside you for as long as your love for us shall last. Blessed be!*

The High Priestess lets go of the candidate and retreats once more into the center of the circle near the altar. The High Priest again guides the candidate around the circle before stopping in the south.

High Priestess: *To move forward and progress is to will. It is our will that provides the momentum on the path up the Witches' Pyramid. It is also our will that creates the reality we live in. As Witches we possess the power to change our circumstances, and we achieve that change through our will. Our will is the center deep inside of us that fuels our hopes and dreams and our magick. As you journey tonight, we require that you send your will out across the universe, from this magickal space into the mundane world.*

---

148. Slightly adapted from Leland's *Aradia*, originally published in 1899. Here I'm quoting from the 1998 Phoenix Publishing edition, pages 6–7.

Think about your path as a Witch, think of all you have learned and experienced, and think of what you have yet to accomplish. Now think of yourself doing those things, becoming the Witch and the person you have always dreamed of being. Let that power and energy burn deep inside of you. Visualize it, feel it, see it in your mind's eye and moving through you, and now project it out into the universe. Release your energy and your ambitions and put into the world that which you wish to still become. When you have released the energy generated from within, will it into existence with the words "So mote it be!"

All wait until the candidate releases the energy inside of them and lets out their hearty "So mote it be!" If the candidate has trouble accomplishing this, everyone in attendance should encourage the candidate to raise their personal energy and finish the spell. When the candidate has finished projecting their will, they are taken around the circle once more before stopping in the north.

High Priestess: *To keep silent. Many truths have been revealed to you as a Witch, but those who would be Wise Ones know also that there are times when it is best to say nothing. When asked about the gods of this coven, how should you respond?*

Candidate: *With silence.* (The candidate can also simply say nothing here.)

High Priestess: *When asking a question of our Lord and Lady, how is it best to receive their answer?*

Candidate: *With silence.* (Again, remaining silent is also acceptable.)

High Priestess: *Good, for the answers we seek often lie in the still, small voice inside ourselves, for it is written that "if that which you seek you find not within thee, you will never find it without." It is now nearly time for you to return to the light.*

The candidate is walked around the circle one final time before coming to stand next to the altar in the center of the circle. There the candidate's blindfold is removed and the High Priestess takes their hands into hers.

High Priestess: *"To know," "to dare," "to will," "to keep silent"—these are the four pillars of the Witches' Pyramid. Tonight you have journeyed from the east to the west to the south and finally to the north before making your way here into the center. Here the four columns of the pyramid hold up the final truth to be revealed to you this night: "to go." And as a sign that you have scaled our pyramid and reached the top, we give you this necklace as a sign of your rank.*

To know, to dare, to will, to keep silent, and now to go—for truly you will now go out into the world as a second-degree Witch and a High Priestess (Priest) of the Craft of the Wise. Congratulations, (Craft name of person just elevated), newly elevated Witch! So mote it be!

The circle is taken down as usual, and the newly elevated Witch is celebrated with gifts, feasting, and whatever else the coven deems appropriate when the ritual is over.

WHAT A THIRD DEGREE SHOULD KNOW, AND KNOWING WHEN SOMEONE IS READY FOR THE THIRD DEGREE

There's very little difference between second- and third-degree Witches. Both are capable of running a ritual effectively and both generally have a thorough understanding of the gods that are important to the coven. The difference between second- and third-degree Witches often has a lot to do with two things: leadership and ambition.

The third degree is for people who are ready to run their own coven or become part of an established coven's leadership structure. When my wife and I were elevated to the third degree, it was with the expectation that we would be starting our own coven, and we were elevated because our High Priestess and High Priest thought we were ready for such an undertaking. Not everyone wants to run a coven and not everyone wants to deal with the responsibilities of leadership, and that is okay.

There are some people who are born leaders, but most of us are not. It takes time and seasoning to make an effective High Priestess or High Priest. Real coven leadership is about more than knowing Witch ritual;

it's about managing egos, dealing with administrative details (someone has to schedule rituals), and making good decisions, because those decisions are going to affect everyone in circle.

In many covens it's the High Priestess who decides who will be initiated or who will even just be allowed to study with the coven. One bad apple and all the coven's secrets might end up on the internet in short order. A third-degree Witch is a caretaker of their tradition. They have the power to open and close the door to potential seekers, and it's a responsibility most of them take very seriously. (And sometimes the best decision a High Priestess might make is "no." For a variety of reasons, some people just don't make very good initiates. Luckily there are many kinds of Witchcraft and a multitude of traditions for those individuals.)

Third-degree Witches are most often teachers, and they are third degrees because someone saw within them the potential to train and nurture other Witches. Teaching is hard work. It's more than reciting text from a Book of Shadows and pondering where it came from or asking someone to remember all four elemental pentagrams. Real teaching is about opening up a window through which other Witches can experience the mysteries. Witchcraft is an experiential spirituality. Anyone can read a Witch ritual, but the power comes in the doing and understanding how it's done. That's the point that a good teacher gets across.

A third-degree Witch is someone who is motivated. Witches don't proselytize like Christians do (no one is going door to door asking people to join their coven), but they have to be available to potential seekers. Coven leaders put together rituals and get people motivated to experience those rituals. They find themselves excited about being in the circle even if they've had a bad day at work or are doing the same old coven Samhain ritual for the third year in a row. It can take years to find that motivation and to develop the skill set necessary to ensure the long-term survival and thriving of a coven.

Above all, the third degree is about service. It's about service to the coven and service to others. One who seeks the third degree in order to inflate their own ego is going to be a poor coven leader and shouldn't be elevated. A High Priestess is humble and realizes that she has just as much to learn from a new Witch as they do from her.

A person is ready for the third degree when

- they are capable of teaching the Craft to others.

- they possess the maturity and temperament needed to lead a coven.

- they are ready to live their life in service to Witchcraft and those who practice with them.

- they are in a position to start a coven or become a leader in their current one.

- they have the drive, desire, and ambition to form their own coven and keep it thriving.

- they have shown that they have sound judgment when it comes to identifying potential initiates.

THIRD-DEGREE RITUAL

Because the difference in the amount of knowledge possessed by a second- and a third-degree Witch is rather negligible, constructing a third-degree elevation rite is difficult. In some traditions third-degree rites are about partnership, since it's much easier for a coven to function with two people in positions of authority. In such cases the third-degree ritual is just as much about cementing the interconnectedness of the two working partners as it is about acknowledging the advancement of a particular Witch.

Third-degree rites suffer from another obstacle: the only people who can participate in them are third-degree Witches. Over the years I've met a lot of first- and second-degree Witches from various traditions, but only a select few ever make it to the third degree. As such, third-degree elevation rites generally involve only a handful of folks, as few as three to four people. Any sort of ritual created for the third degree has to be rather simple because there simply won't be a lot of people around to help.

This rite utilizes a couple different ideas. The first, sensory deprivation, is a technique used by some shamans.[149] This rite calls for absolute

---

149. Hayden, *Shamans, Sorcerers, and Saints,* 66–67.

darkness (or as close to it as the coven can get), and if absolute silence can also be achieved, all the better. The lack of light and/or sound often produces a trancelike or ecstatic state, the perfect setting for a third-degree rite. This rite also utilizes a variation on the Freemasons' five points of fellowship, as well as the penultimate line in Doreen Valiente's Charge of the Goddess:

> And thou who thinkest to seek for me, know thy seeking and yearning shall avail thee not, unless thou know this mystery: that if that which thou seekest thou findest not within thee, thou wilt never find it without thee.

That line to me has always implied that the divine resides both within and without us, harkening back to the idea of "As above, so below." This idea is expressed in the Pagan Church of All Worlds with their greeting "Thou art Goddess/God."

This ritual doesn't call for a lot of special tools, but it does presume that the coven uses candles at each of the four quarters and for the Goddess, God, and spirit. Harkening back to the first-degree ritual earlier in the chapter, the High Priest wears some type of horned headwear, while the High Priestess wears a circlet/crown. Both pieces of headgear are used here to convey status and are to be given to the person attaining the third degree.

The ritual begins as usual with the casting of the circle, calling of the quarters, invoking of the gods, etc. As before, one final drawing down can be done before the elevation rite just to make sure the Lord and Lady approve of what is about to happen. When that is completed, the ritual begins. This rite assumes that the only people in the circle are the High Priestess, the High Priest, and the soon-to-be third-degree Witch.

High Priestess: *There is one who stands before us this night who seeks Witchcraft's third degree. She (or He) is a worthy candidate, for we have watched her grow and progress in the Craft. She is a teacher, a mentor, a friend, and a trusted family member. She walks confidently in the Old Ways, and the Lord and Lady walk beside her.*

High Priest: *When she first came to us, we asked her to put her faith in this coven, and she has. We have circled together in perfect love and perfect trust, built the cone of power, celebrated the sabbats, and experienced the mysteries of the gods all together. But tonight we present her with a different sort of challenge.*

The High Priestess walks over to the candle in the east and blows it out. Then the High Priest speaks.

High Priest: *She has walked with us in perfect love and perfect trust, but tonight she walks alone.*

The High Priestess moves to the candle in the south and blows that out. Then the High Priest continues.

High Priest: *She has wielded her will with us and in accordance with the Wiccan Rede while performing magick in this space. Tonight she faces that truth alone.*

The High Priestess moves to the west and blows out the candle there, then the High Priest continues.

High Priest: *Together we have climbed the Witches' Pyramid, but this night she climbs alone.*

Before returning to the altar, the High Priestess blows out the candle in the north. Then the High Priest speaks.

High Priest: *An it harm none, do what you will, even when alone. Remember.*

The High Priest picks up the God candle and speaks.

High Priest: *During your time in this coven you have walked only in the world of the living. Tonight you shall walk in the space of the Dread Lord of Shadows.*

The High Priest blows out the God candle. Then the High Priestess picks up the Goddess candle and speaks.

High Priestess: *All she touches changes, and when that touch comes we move to the other side, and once there we are touched again and return to this* space. *Tonight you visit the land of the dead. In this sacred space, in the darkness, you journey alone through the cauldron to the other side. Reach out to her, touch him, know that the gods are with you, and that even in the time of the greatest darkness there is also the greatest light.*

The High Priestess picks up the center spirit candle from the altar, and the High Priest picks up his athame. Together they move toward the door of the ritual space, but before cutting themselves out of the darkness of the circle, the High Priestess, with the spirit candle in hand, speaks to the elevating Witch.

High Priestess: *And remember, "As above, so below." To be reborn we must die.*

The High Priestess and High Priest now leave the ritual space and retreat as far away from it as possible so the candidate for the third degree is left completely in the darkness (and perhaps silence, if possible). Ideally the darkness acts as a transformative force, allowing the elevating Witch to have a personal spiritual journey. After at least thirty minutes of darkness for the candidate (and probably not more than an hour), the High Priestess and High Priest return to the ritual space, cutting themselves back into the circle while carrying the still lit spirit candle.

The High Priest walks up to the elevating Witch and helps her to stand if she's sitting. Once the candidate stands, the High Priestess narrates the enactment of the five points of fellowship. At this point the spirit candle can be placed back on the altar or held by the High Priestess as she reads.

High Priestess: *The Great Goddess and the Horned One reach out to us in the darkness, and with their touch we are reborn. When preparing a soul for its return, they say: "I raise thee with thy feet that have walked in the land of death."*

The High Priest then faces the candidate and their toes touch. Ideally his toes lie just over the elevating Witch's toes.

High Priest: *I raise thee with my knees that have knelt at the Lady's cauldron.*

The High Priest and the elevating Witch's knees now touch (or close to it, depending on their heights).

High Priest: *I raise thee with my hands that have prepared the sacred doorway.*

The High Priest and the elevating Witch now grasp hands firmly.

High Priest: *I raise thee with my heart so that yours might beat again.*

The High Priest and the candidate are now chest to chest.

High Priest: *And finally I raise thee with my breath and speak the words all Wise Ones know.*

The High Priest and the candidate are now cheek to cheek, and he whispers in her ear.

High Priest (whispering): *What you seek you shall always find within and without you. For the final mystery is that "Thou too art Goddess" and she resides within you, in this world, and in the realms beyond. So mote it be!*

The candidate, the High Priest, and the High Priestess all now move toward the altar, and the candidate is given the horned helm or crown, signifying her rank now as a third-degree Witch. Turning to the elevating Witch, the High Priestess speaks to her.

High Priestess: *And now this circle is just as much your own as it is mine. As a High Priestess of the Great Goddess and the Horned One, I stand aside so that you may call them back to the circle, all while knowing they never left. So mote it be!*

The now third-degree Witch reinvokes the gods and calls upon the quarters once more, as the crown has been passed and a new third-degree Witch stands within the magick circle. After the ritual, there should be feasting and merriment to celebrate.

ADAPTING THE THIRD-DEGREE RITUAL FOR TWO PEOPLE AND OTHER NOTES

Because many third-degree initiation rites involve pairs, I've written this ritual so it can easily be adapted for two people. If elevating two people at once, the ritual is essentially the same, with "she" in the early text being replaced with "they." (For example, "When *they* first came to us, we asked *them* to put *their* faith in this coven, and *they* have.") The two elevating Witches are then left in the darkness together, where they are free to do whatever they wish. When the High Priestess and High Priest return, the elevating pair of Witches enact the five points of fellowship rite together, with the High Priestess and High Priest simply acting as narrators and directors. Finally, the rite ends with the pair calling the gods and bringing in the quarters.

As always, the terminology in this rite reflects the fact that my working partner is my wife, Ari. The High Priest certainly does not have to enact the five points of fellowship with an initiating female Witch, especially since we are reborn by the powers of both the Goddess and the God! Also, women can wear horns and men can wear crowns or circlets. The giving of the headwear is meant to imply status, and people should wear the headgear that resonates with them and best captures their experience with the gods.

Part Four

Drawing Down
the Moon

CHAPTER ELEVEN

Drawing Down Deity

My first few years as a Witch were a rather solitary affair. Occasionally I'd meet someone who was also interested in magickal things, but they were few and far between. After a few years of working on my own I joined a Pagan group at Michigan State University and started working with other Witches. For the most part we were *Witchlings* instead of honest-to-Gods Witches. We had only the slightest idea what we were doing, but what we lacked in knowledge we made up for in sheer exuberance.

In my second year with that group we all decided we should do a "big" Samhain ritual. To us "big" meant we would attempt to *draw down the moon.* Up until then we had always made a point of inviting deity to ritual, but we had never before asked a goddess to inhabit the body of one of our circle-mates. We looked at this endeavor as a chance to take our Witchcraft to the next level.

Looking back on that night many, many years later, it's obvious to me that we had no idea what we were really doing, but the power we had hoped for was most certainly present. The ritual began in the usual fashion: we called the quarters, cast the circle, and then invited the Horned God to join us for Samhain. After that, our acting High Priest stepped up and called the Great Goddess to inhabit the body of his wife, who was acting as our High Priestess that evening.

There was electricity in the air as he performed the fivefold kiss, moving up his wife's body from her feet to her lips, blessing and consecrating the vessel that would hold our Lady. Then he uttered the words "descend into this, the body of thy High Priestess and servant who stands here," and the eyes of our High Priestess opened and looked different than they had just moments before.

Generally, when a goddess is drawn down she interacts with the Witches who have gathered in front of her, or perhaps she reads the Charge of the Goddess. Since we had no idea what we were doing, we put a veil over the face of our High Priestess/Goddess and sent her off to sit in a corner. This was followed by my now wife (Ari) stepping forward to read the Charge of the Goddess, which we had just denied the Lady.

While Ari read the Charge, my gaze kept returning to the Goddess we had banished to the corner. To this day I swear that her skin was glowing in a rather alien way. It was like our High Priestess had swallowed several glow sticks and their light was radiating out from her. There was a power around her that I could feel, and it was that power that was making her literally glow in the dim light.

I felt unworthy looking at her, so my eyes and ears drifted back to Ari, and I was astounded by what I was hearing. I had heard Ari read the Charge before, but never like this. The cadence in which she spoke was different, and her voice was full and confident, as if she had suddenly transitioned from a girl of nineteen years to a full-grown woman. There was a power coming from her lips that she had never seemed to possess before. I was now awestruck in two directions.

As the ritual proceeded, my gaze drifted back toward our High Priestess in the corner. She was still glowing in the darkness, and I found myself both in awe and frightened of her. Just before I was able to look away, her gaze caught my own, and I felt like she was looking through me.

It was most likely just for an instant, but it felt like hours, and I expected her to jump up in front of everyone we were circling with, point at me, and yell "Fraud!" for all to hear. It felt as if she could feel every doubt I'd ever had about the Craft, and this made me feel ashamed. But instead of yelling at me, she just smiled, nodded her head, and broke our shared moment. I felt relief wash over me, but for the rest of the evening a little bit of that fear remained.

As the ritual ended, the High Priest removed the veil from our High Priestess, and his wife returned to who she had been before. Her skin no longer glowed and the power that she had contained just a few minutes earlier was now extinguished. Ari's voice also returned to what it had been, and suddenly we were all back in mundane space instead of between the worlds.

The next day over email we all shared our ritual experiences, and we all agreed that some sort of divine presence had visited us the previous evening. I remember making some comment about how we had seen "Ari grow up" that night, but it was far more than that. Years later I would find out that Ari too had drawn down the Goddess, which is why her voice and tone had been so different during the ritual. Looking back on it now almost twenty years later, that's painfully obvious to me, but that's only because we've shared many drawing down experiences together since that night.

That Samhain night back in 1998 was one of the most intense and spiritual experiences of my life. From that point on I knew that drawing down the moon and *standing in the very presence of the gods* wasn't just a hypothetical; it was one of the most awe-inspiring mysteries in all of the Craft. Not all of my drawing down experiences have had that sense of presence that I felt that October night, but many have to varying degrees.

A little less than a year later, with many of the same people who were a part of that Samhain rite, I drew down a god for the first time. Our ritual was focused on celebrating the Greek god Dionysus through the music of the band the Doors and at least a few libations. I had spent most of the days immediately before that ritual focused intently on "Big D," as we call him, but I didn't really expect him to show up, and I didn't learn that he had until the ritual was over.

I remember calling the quarters and reciting some poetry by Jim Morrison (the lead singer of the Doors), but the rest of the ritual remains pretty much a blank. An easy explanation for this is that I had consumed a few more drinks than I should have, but I know from experience that it's hard to drink too much when you are busy talking.

Drawing down a deity into yourself is a completely different experience than experiencing deity through another person. When I draw down a deity, it's like "checking out," and the people I've circled with have to fill me in on what happened during the ritual after it's over. That's what happened with Dionysus. When the lights came on, I was suddenly hearing stories about all of these things *I* had done, and I most certainly didn't remember doing them.

Apparently I was witty, clever, debonair, and had a lot of admirers (of both sexes) during our ritual. That was all Dionysus; it certainly wasn't me. I felt closer to Big D when the experience was all over, but not because I was conscious of what had happened in the ritual circle.

Since those early experiences of drawing down the moon, I've been in dozens of circles where the gods have been drawn down (or have been attempted to be drawn down anyway). Sometimes it's been as amazing as that Samhain evening, and other times it's been less than overwhelming. Much of my life as a Witch has been about experiencing another night like that first one. Being able to experience the gods in the flesh is truly transcendent and is one of Witchcraft's greatest mysteries.

What Exactly Is Drawing Down the Moon?

Depending on whom one talks to, drawing down the moon can be many different things. As a believer in deities (goddesses and gods), I think of it as I just described it—as a process and experience where a goddess or god inhabits the body of a human being. In my more clinical moments I like to describe it this way:

> Drawing down the moon is the opening up of oneself to deity so that deity speaks with your tongue, sees with your eyes, and experiences with your body. It's a willful surrendering of consciousness in order to become one with deity so that others around you may experience that deity.

To me what's most extraordinary about drawing down is that it's literally "a god made flesh." For a brief period of time, gods like Pan, Artemis, and Cernunnos inhabit a flesh-and-blood body, and we can touch

them, talk to them, and be seen by them. Perhaps even more importantly, drawing down is generally a willful surrendering of consciousness. This means that the gods aren't "taking over" our bodies; we are
allowing them to be at home within us.

Periodically I hear people use the term *possession* to describe the
drawing down experience, but I find that word troubling. Today, *possession* is generally used in a Christian context and in reference to evil
spirits or demons. Such entities are generally not willfully sought; they
come of their own accord and are hard to get rid of. In drawing down,
we *invite* the gods in, and they are certainly not unwelcome guests!

Not every Witch is a believer in deity, which means that drawing
down is sometimes interpreted in a different way by those whose beliefs
about the gods are different from my own. There are many Witches
who believe that deity is something that already exists within ourselves,
and that there are no gods or goddesses outside of our own consciousness. For folks with views such as this, drawing down is an awakening of
the divine that's already inside of us.

Beliefs such as this are backed up in some ways by Doreen Valiente's
Charge of the Goddess. As the end of the Charge, the Goddess states:

> And thou who thinkest to seek for me, know thy seeking and
> yearning shall avail thee not, unless thou know this mystery: that
> if that which thou seekest thou findest not within thee, thou wilt
> never find it without thee.
>
> For behold, I have been with thee from the beginning; and I
> am that which is attained at the end of desire.[150]

Perhaps the process of drawing down helps to activate the divine within
ourselves? It's not something I subscribe to myself, but I can understand
the reasoning.

---

150. While Doreen Valiente wrote the version of the Charge of the Goddess that is
most familiar to many Witches today, there are those of us who also believe that
her work was divinely inspired. So while Doreen's physical hand was pushing the
pen, it was being influenced by a higher power. For the text of Valiente's Charge,
see appendix 1. Doreen's work is hosted at http://www.doreenvaliente.com
/Doreen-Valiente-Doreen_Valiente_Poetry-11.php.

WHAT HAPPENS TO US
WHEN WE DRAW DOWN DEITY?

I believe that when we draw down deity we are bringing gods and goddesses into our own human bodies, but I expect science to be skeptical of such claims. My atheist friends who doubt the existence of something like drawing down the moon will often claim that it's a delusion we create inside of our own minds, or that perhaps we are engaging in personal hypnosis. My more negative friends have chalked it up to multiple personality disorder or some other sort of mental illness.

These suggestions are things I obviously disagree with, but I don't discount all of the theories of the skeptics. People who suggest that Witches who draw down are faking the experience are not always wrong. I have been in circles where I doubted the validity of the drawing down experience, and I'm not alone. Such experiences are heartbreaking, but most of the time I believe that the experience is being faked because the ritual leader feels pressured to create an extraordinary experience for their coven.

While no one has ever run a brain scan on a High Priestess engaged in drawing down the moon, there have been studies involving Pentecostal Christians speaking in tongues. While speaking in tongues is not a direct parallel to drawing down the moon, it is similar. An adherent who speaks in tongues believes that the Christian Holy Spirit is speaking through them, and it's a willful surrender much like our own practice.

A 2005 study found that the brain centers that control language were not in use while a person was speaking in tongues. However, the areas of the brain involved in maintaining everyday consciousness were active, which means the people speaking in tongues were not in a trance-like state. Speaking on the study, one of scientists remarked:

> "The amazing thing was how the images supported people's interpretation of what was happening," said Dr. Andrew B. Newberg, leader of the study team, which included Donna Morgan, Nancy Wintering, and Mark Waldman. "The way they describe

it, and what they believe, is that God is talking through them,"
he said." [151]

It's nice to see science backing up a person's individual experience with
the divine, but whether or not drawing down the moon (and related
practices) can be proven as "real" by researchers isn't of much importance to me. What I value above all else is the experience; I'm not really
all that interested in where it comes from, though it's fun to speculate.

INTERACTING WITH DEITY

Modern Witches interact with deity in a variety of different ways.
Drawing down the moon probably represents the pinnacle of that experience, but there are other levels. To fully understand drawing down the
moon as a mystery, it's important to look at our other forms of interaction with deity in our sacred spaces.

Calling to Deity

Almost every ritual I'm a part of involves a "call" to the Goddess and
God and/or calls to particular deities. A call is a simple invitation to deity asking it to show up in the circle. Since it's just an invitation, there
are times when deity declines that invitation. I've been to plenty of rituals where we've asked the gods to join us and it felt as if they passed on
that offer. There's nothing wrong with that. I'm sure gods have lots of
things to do.

Alternatively, I've been in circles where the gods have most obviously
shown up. Perhaps the energy level of the circle increased after they
were called to, or we felt their presence while engaging in a magickal
rite. Calls are the most common way to address deity, especially in public or eclectic Witch circles.

The Particular Energy of Deity Is an Active Part of the Circle

If a call to deity is especially successful, then the energy of that deity
can often be experienced during ritual. I was charged with putting together a Pan ritual at a local festival several years ago and was instructed

---

151. Carey, "A Neuroscientific Look at Speaking in Tongues."

to make sure it was rated PG. That was a real challenge with a god like Pan, but I did my best. When the ritual was over, a friend came up to me and said, "Jason, I felt a whole lot of Pan energy at tonight's ritual," and he was right!

After calling to the goat-footed one, all of us at the rite could feel some truly intense sexual and chaotic energy. No one acted on it during the ritual, but the next day I heard lots of stories from people about liaisons in stairwells and other things. The "goal" of the ritual was to make people feel sexy and confident, something I associate with Pan, and that's exactly what happened that night! When the energy of a god is a part of ritual, *that energy can change our consciousness and influence how we behave.*

When a Mother goddess is invited into ritual and truly shows up, our circle often feels like an intense hug or a warm bed on a lazy Sunday morning. Our temple space generally feels safe and inviting, but the presence of a Mother goddess magnifies that feeling, and I can't help but think it's her energy transforming our circle. When we invite a Maiden goddess like Eostre,[152] our circle becomes giggly, childlike, and deliriously happy.

A deity drawn down is the peak of all these experiences. Not only has a goddess or god been invited to circle, but their energy fills the ritual space, and we can talk to them! In such situations almost anything is possible, and emotions and feelings are likely to be strong and intense. When a drawn-down goddess feels grief, everyone in our coven feels it too, and when she feels joy, we experience that as well. Sometimes a drawing down experience can be especially intense, and other times a deity might want to visit for only a short period of time.

I tend to think of these ways of interacting with deity as overlapping ones. A simple call might lead to an intense visitation of energy by a particular deity, and sometimes deities show up inside of us humans

---

152. Eostre is generally seen as a Germanic fertility goddess and is where the holiday Easter gets its name. In the experience of our coven, Eostre generally comes across as "young," for lack of a better word. For more on the historical Eostre, check out this link: http://www.patheos.com/blogs/panmankey/2015/03/looking-for-eostre/.

even when they aren't formally called down. Deity can do anything from simply watching our activities to actually entering our circle—and I think that's when we truly begin to feel their energy in a transformative way. From there it's just a short hop into a willing Witch!

A friend of mine has always had a strong relationship with the Roman god Bacchus (the Roman version of Dionysus, though there are some differences). One night he planned a very long ritual in honor of his favorite wine god that involved visiting a grapevine and picking grapes before heading back to his apartment. As the evening wore on, a girl I was seeing at the time and I retreated into a more private corner of my friend's apartment.

Eventually my buddy came in to check on us, and as he left the room he flashed a grin that was knowing, devious, and a little bit sinister. As that smile unfolded, my lady friend and I felt an intense energy rush over us. Then the smile disappeared and my friend rejoined us, but without even trying he had drawn down Bacchus, and the Roman god of wine had made his presence known to at least my companion and me.

I know from my own experience that the gods I am particularly close to have no problem with "jumping in" to my coven's rituals now and then. To let them draw that close to me is something I embrace, which means our ritual circle often winds up with honored guests when we aren't expecting them. For most Witches, deities are very real entities, and when we invite them to our circles and to be drawn down, they often enjoy showing up. Just be prepared for the consequences that might result from a deity coming to visit.

Drawing down the moon isn't the only phrase associated with a person letting deity inhabit their body, but for a variety of reasons I prefer to use *drawing down* or *drawing down the moon* to the exclusion of the rest. Part of that is because drawing down the moon is a phrase that is explicitly associated with Witchcraft today, and part of it is simply to avoid confusion.

Invoke

Invoke is the most common "other" term for drawing down the moon and is used in a lot of the more common ceremonies to bring about a drawing down. One of the problems with the word invoke is that it's often used in a couple different contexts in Witchcraft circles. For many Witches *invoke* is synonymous with *drawing down*, but others use it more as an invitation to deity. A Google search for "Invoke the Goddess" provides results such as "11 Powerful Goddesses to Invoke Into Your Life." Obviously they aren't using it in a way that's equivalent to drawing down deity.

Dictionary definitions for *invoke* make the word even less clear. The Oxford English dictionary offers a couple definitions, including "Call on (a deity or spirit) in prayer, as a witness, or for inspiration" and "Cite or appeal to (someone or something) as an authority for an action or in support of an argument." [153] Neither of those definitions are anything like drawing down the moon. In my own coven we sometimes use the word invoke when preparing to call the Goddess and/or draw her down.

Similar to the term invoke is *evoke*. In fact, in the Oxford Dictionary the definition for evoke includes "Invoke (a spirit or deity)," along with "Bring or recall (a feeling, memory, or image) to the conscious mind." [154] I sometimes use the word evoke when commenting on the type of ritual environment I'm trying to create. Another word I've heard in relation to invoke and evoke is *envoke*, which, for the record, isn't even a real word.

Perhaps my least favorite analogue of drawing down the moon is *avatar*. In the Hindu religion an avatar is a deity who visits the earth in the flesh, and on occasion is an especially revered, enlightened, and highly respected guru. Because of this word's ties to the Hindu faith, I like to try to avoid it, as I think it might be confusing to those familiar with those traditions.

There are a few local groups near me who don't always specifically draw down deity but often appoint someone to act as a stand-in for a particular goddess and god. In their way of doing things, they often associate this "avatar" with an experience like drawing down the moon. Also, I can't hear the word today without thinking about James Cameron's 2009 movie of the same name.

---

153. Oxford English Dictionary, https://en.oxforddictionaries.com/definition/invoke.
154. Oxford English Dictionary, https://en.oxforddictionaries.com/definition/evoke.

One last term often associated with drawing down the moon is *aspecting*. Aspecting is used by some as a synonym for drawing down, while others use it to signify that a portion (an aspect) of a greater power is present. For instance, a person might "be in aspect" if they call upon the Great Goddess and the Lady shows up in the human vessel only as the Maiden. This word is also sometimes used to signify that only a piece of deity has arrived. Instead of completely drawing down a deity like the god Pan, the person in aspect picks up only the god's tendencies and his wisdom. The exact use of the term *aspect* can vary from place to place and community to community.

CHAPTER TWELVE

Possession in History and Literature

Modern Witches are not the first individuals to have face-to-face physical meetings with their gods. Experiences at least adjacent to drawing down the moon have been a part of history for thousands of years now and aren't exclusive to the paganisms of our ancient ancestors either. Many of the world's religious traditions have mechanisms in place that facilitate intense spiritual experiences similar to our own.

ANCIENT GREECE AND THE ORIGINS OF DRAWING DOWN THE MOON

The phrase *drawing down the moon* is an old one and actually dates back to ancient Greece. There it was most likely used in reference to eclipses and the proximity of the moon to the earth. Witches from the (Greek) region of Thessaly were often said to "draw down the moon" through spells in order to control the emotions and sexual passions of men.[155] Even today the moon seems to affect our emotions, so the idea of Witches drawing the moon closer to the earth to influence people (or

---

155. d'Este and Rankine, *Wicca*, 126.

using math to figure out when an eclipse is going to occur) makes pretty good sense.[156]

The Greeks used the term drawing down the moon in one other way: to describe the reflection of the moon in a bowl or jug of water. In the book *Satyricon* written by Gaius Petronius (27–66 CE), the process is described as "the image of the moon descending, brought down by my incantations."[157] The moon's reflection in a mirror might also have been described as drawing down the moon.

It's fitting that the Greeks used the term drawing down the moon because Gerald Gardner links the practice directly to them. In a sketch of an alleged Greek vase dating back to 200 BCE given to Doreen Valiente (see illustration), Gardner illustrates what he said was an ancient drawing down the moon ceremony.[158] Variations of that illustration have shown up in several Witchcraft and Pagan books over the years, including Margot Adler's seminal 1979 *Drawing Down the Moon*.[159]

The women in Gardner's drawing could be participating in a spiritual activity or something else entirely. If that's an athame in the hands of the woman on the left, then it's one of the largest athames ever used in ritual. The woman on the right is holding either a stick or a wand, items not often used in drawing down ceremonies. Whatever is happening here is ultimately up to the opinion of the observer. If someone wants to find an ancient Greek drawing down ceremony, they probably can; if one isn't looking for that, they'll see something else.

---

156. Mitchell, "Do Full Moons and Supermoons Really Influence People and Animals?" Yes, this is a weird source, but there are links to other things in the article.

157. d'Este and Rankine, *Wicca*, 130.

158. Valiente, *The Rebirth of Witchcraft*, image 15, immediately following page 128 in the text.

159. Adler, *Drawing Down the Moon*, ii.

KAΛH

ΘΙ ΠΟΤΝΙΑ ΣΕΛΗ

Drawing Down the Moon Vase

Even if drawing down the moon as we know it today wasn't practiced by the ancient Greeks, they did share the idea that deity can inhabit the body. The downside to this is that experience wasn't always a positive one. The Green word *entheos* translates as "within is a god" but was often marked by baffling movements and unintelligible language by the possessed individual.[160] Perhaps even worse is possession by the god Pan, *panolepsy*, which might have been used as a term for epileptic seizures and was sometimes marked by hysterical laughter.[161]

Perhaps even more shocking is *sparagmos*, a term that refers to the consumption of raw meat in honor of the god Dionysus. More of a literary invention than something practiced in actuality, sparagmos found the female followers of Dionysus (maenads) roaming the countryside

---

160. Burkert, *Greek Religion*, 109.

161. Borgeaud, *The Cult of Pan in Ancient Greece*, 107–108.

killing animals and eating their raw flesh. In their ecstasy and madness, the maenads were said to become one with Dionysus.

Much less shocking was the Oracle of Apollo at the sanctuary of Delphi. There young women would be consumed by the power of Apollo and share prophetic words, though their pronouncements were often difficult to understand. The prophecies given by the Pythia (the name of the human oracle at Delphi) were most often ambiguous and had to be interpreted. Oracles were also said to be possessed by a "divine madness" and often swayed and moved in strange ways while engaged in "rapturous union" with Apollo.[162] Even though hard to interpret, the Oracle had the power to depose Greek kings and determine the course of history.

All of the examples of possession in ancient Greece are radically different from that of drawing down the moon today. The visitations by deity in ancient Greece are brief and not very interactive. When the Goddess visits my circle, she is generally calm and self-possessed, and her presence is always welcome. She is often easy to understand, though not always so, which means she still possesses a bit of the Pythia found at Delphi.

Much more similar to drawing down the moon are the writings collectively known as the Greek Magical Papyri. The papyri are a hodgepodge of various pagan and sometimes monotheistic traditions dating from the second century BCE to the fifth century CE. Most of the papyri have been found in Egypt, but they are called the Greek Magical Papyri because they were written in Greek. The magickal formulas in the papyri vary, but for our purposes there are two things in them that are similar to today's rite of drawing down the moon.

The first is that some of the texts call for deity to be drawn directly into the body of a living person, most often a young boy. Deity would be summoned by the magician leading the operation, and once it had entered its human vessel the deity would either be asked questions or allowed to make pronouncements.[163] The young people involved in such

---

162. Broad, *The Oracle*, 11.

163. Hutton, *Witches, Druids, and King Arthur*, 114.

situations may not always have been willing participants, something unheard of in Witch circles.

Much more common in the Greek Magical Papyri are long invocations and formulas that find the magician stepping into the role of deity. But instead of the magician being inhabited physically by a goddess or god, it's probably more accurate to think of the magician in such rituals as "assuming the power" of the deity they are referencing. Many of these texts are written in the first person ("I, Horus, command you"), with the magician speaking with the power and authority of a specific deity. It has never seemed to me as if the deities being referenced were actually inhabiting the body of the magician.

POSSESSION IN OTHER RELIGIOUS TRADITIONS

I think there's a tendency among many Modern Witches and Pagans to just assume that experiences like drawing down the moon are common in a whole host of religious traditions, both ancient and modern. I don't think that's the case, but that doesn't mean practitioners of other traditions and faiths don't commune with the divine; they just do so differently. For believers in deity, reaching out to a god or gods is an essential part of spirituality.

Many Modern Witches come from monotheistic religious traditions such as Christianity, Judaism, or Islam. For many of us, those religions lacked an essential spiritual component of some sort. I found the Methodism of my youth rather boring and clinical, but not all Christianity is necessarily like that.

One of the closest parallels to drawing down the moon is the Christian practice of speaking in tongues. When someone speaks in tongues, they are literally possessed by the Christian Holy Spirit, which is in turn a part of the Trinity, meaning it's like being possessed by Yahweh or at least a part of him. What makes speaking in tongues markedly different from drawing down the moon is its brevity and its use of an angelic language that has to be translated.

While Greek gods are a common presence in my circle, they almost always speak English so that we are able to understand them. When someone speaks in tongues, they speak in an angelic language that must then be translated by someone else (and the person doing the translating is often said to be touched by the Holy Spirit too). Instances of speaking in tongues are also generally quick and might constitute just a sentence or two and be sandwiched between regular communication. My gods tend to show up for longer periods than what's observed when someone speaks in tongues, and the gods also tend to interact with the coven.

Though the Christian stigmata is not possession in the sense that a deity takes over a mortal's mental function, the deity (in this case Jesus) does force his bodily wounds upon his followers. Those who are blessed with (or suffer from?) stigmata generally replicate on their bodies the wounds that Jesus experienced while on the cross, meaning nail wounds on the palms (or sometimes wrists) and ankles, along with a spear wound in the abdomen. These wounds might then bleed continuously or heal miraculously. Many stigmatics feel closer to their god as a result of their wounds. (And if you were wondering, most cases of stigmata are fraudulent, but I'm sure the sincerity of some stigmatics is real at least.)

Most Islamic practices have never felt particularly ecstatic to me, with the exception of those practiced by Sufis. While Sufis engage in most of Islam's standard observances, their practice is also syncretic and often focused inward. Sufis don't just want to know their god; they are actively searching for unity with the divine.[164] While this is a bit removed from what most Witches do, it's still a direct communion with deity, though I don't think any Sufis are ever bodily possessed by Allah.

Sufism was at least indirectly influenced by shamanism,[165] just like the Norse traditions of Scandinavia were.[166] Modern-day practitioners of Heathen traditions (such as Asatru) often employ the magickal practice of *seiðr* in order to commune with the gods. (Seiðr can be spelled in a variety of ways, and often is. Other common spellings include sied,

---

164. Aslan, *No god but God*, 202.

165. Ibid., 199.

166. DuBois, *Nordic Religions in the Viking Age*, 131.

seidh, seidhr, seithr, and seidr.) Often this results in ceremonies similar to drawing down the moon.

The term seiðr is used in a variety of different ways in Norse literature but almost always comes back to magick, especially divinatory magick. Seiðr was seen as a way to change the fate of a person or persons, with the end result being a healing, control of the weather, or the assurance of an abundant food supply. It could also be used maliciously to curse someone, raise the dead, or ruin another's crops.[167]

Much like shamanism, seiðr served as a way of standing between the worlds of mortals and spirits. Practitioners were sometimes relaying knowledge directly from higher powers to their peers.[168] These messages weren't always necessarily from the gods, but they most certainly could have been.

Writing in the first century, the Roman historian Tacitus (56–120 CE) wrote that diviners were believed to have "something holy and provident about them," and an oracle from that time among the Germanic people was said to be treated "as nearly a goddess."[169] In another parallel to drawing down, those individuals who spoke with the spirits and practiced seiðr were nearly always women.

There are two nineteenth-century practices that might have had a direct influence on the practice of drawing down the moon. The first is Spiritualism, which was popular from 1850 until the early twentieth century. Spiritualists believed that the living could talk to the dead and have experiences with those who had passed on. Spiritualism was popularized by Kate and Maggie Fox, who began communicating with a "knocking sound" thought to be a spirit that their mother named Mr. Splitfoot in the winter of 1847–1848.

The rapping sounds soon became a phenomenon in rural Hydesville, New York, where the girls resided, and to escape the craziness that surrounded them they moved in with their sister Leah in nearby Rochester. It was Leah (several years older than her sisters) who is probably

---

167. Ferguson, *The Vikings*, 33–34.
168. DuBois, *Nordic Religions in the Viking Age*, 128.
169. Ibid., 134.

most important to our story. Sensing a money-making opportunity, she began to book public demonstrations of her sisters' abilities and eventually became the first trance medium of the modern age. While Leah was in a trance, the voices of the dead would speak through her, and people would pay big bucks to listen in. Eventually other mediums came forward and Spiritualism became a full-fledged phenomenon.

Spiritualism directly influenced the woman who has been called the "founder of the New Age movement," Russian psychic Helena Blavatsky (1831–1891). But instead of channeling spirits, Blavatsky channeled beings that she called her *Mahatmas*, or Secret Chiefs, who she claimed were enlightened humans who had moved beyond mortal existence. Most of her channelings were limited to spoken pronouncements and automatic writing, but Blavatsky, with the assistance of her Mahatmas, was said to be able to facilitate miraculous spiritual events. On several different occasions Blavatsky led individuals to seemingly undisturbed pieces of ground where wine glasses were found buried in the earth, the inference being that the wine glasses must have been buried using some sort of supernatural power.

Blavatsky's Secret Chiefs would inspire other occult and esoteric orders, and such figures were said to be around at the birth of the Golden Dawn. Blavatsky's teachings and beliefs led to the establishment of the Theosophical Society, a group that was directly responsible for injecting several "Eastern" religious ideas (such as reincarnation and karma) into the Western worldview. Neither the Theosophical Society nor those who practiced Spiritualism "drew down" higher powers in a way similar to Modern Witches, but their very existence was proof that such things were possible and might have served as a source of inspiration for those who eventually drew down the moon.

VOODOO AND THE LOA

The religious tradition with the most direct parallels to drawing down the moon is Vodou, or *Voodoo*, as it's more commonly known in the United States. Voodoo is a tradition with African origins, originally practiced by the Fon people of West Africa.[170] The words Vodou and Voodoo have their origin in the Fon word *Vodu* (or *Vodun*), which was used to describe the spirits honored by the Fon people.[171]

While I've always believed that Gerald Gardner was initiated into some sort of coven in 1939, it seems likely that the Witchcraft he shared with the world in the early 1950s was shaped to some degree by his own experiences. Voodoo was never widely practiced in Gardner's birth country, but he very well could have been exposed to it. In the winter of 1947–1948, Gerald and his wife, Donna, spent several months in Memphis, Tennessee, with Gerald's brother Douglas.

There's some confusion as to whether Gardner ever actually got to New Orleans during this trip, but Gardner was most certainly interested in Voodoo and would have sought it out in New Orleans or Memphis. Since he was in Memphis, a riverboat town also on the Mississippi River, Gardner wouldn't have even had to travel all the way to New Orleans to meet a Voodoo practitioner in 1947.

According to Gardner's biography *Gerald Gardner: Witch*, Gerald did make some contacts in the Voodoo world and was at least able to talk shop with a few practitioners (and perhaps witness a ritual). We'll never know just how much (or how little) exposure Gardner had to Voodoo during his brief trip to the US, but what we do know is that Voodoo's possession rites and the ritual of drawing down the moon are extremely similar.

To understand possession in Voodoo, it's first necessary to understand some of Voodoo's cosmology. Voodoo practitioners believe that there is one supreme unknowable deity who created the universe. Because that figure is beyond the reach of humans, they direct their prayers toward the *lwa* (sometimes spelled *loa*). The lwa are the "deities," or spirits, most of us associate with Voodoo today, figures such as Papa Lebat (or Legba), Baron Samedi, Maman Brigitte, Ogou, and

---

170. There are several different spellings of Vodou, and they generally vary by region. *Vodou* is a Haitian spelling, while most practitioners in New Orleans use the familiar *Voodoo*. I've chosen to go with the New Orleans spelling because the practitioners I know from that region use that spelling.

171. Tann, *Haitian Vodou*, 13.

countless others. And in Voodoo it's possible to go from human to lwa; many people today honor Marie Laveau herself as one of the lwa.

It's the lwa who inhabit the bodies of worshippers, and when I write *worshippers* that's exactly what I mean. Unlike in Wiccan-Witchcraft, where deity is generally directed into the body of a specific person, in a Voodoo ritual the lwa might possibly possess more than just the *mambo* (Voodoo Priestess) or the *houngan* (Voodoo Priest). A ritual participant who is possessed by the lwa is called a *horse*, because the lwa are said to be "riding" the person whose body they are inhabiting.

Being ridden by the lwa is often called *trance possession*, but I think that term is inadequate to describe the range of activities often engaged in by the lwa while riding a horse. The word *trance* has always sounded rather serene and sleepy to me, and those in trancelike states are often thought to be docile or inactive. Possession in Voodoo is something else entirely and is often a very physical experience.

Voodoo practitioners sometimes appear to be in great pain when they are being mounted by the lwa, and might fall down to the ground or convulse as the spirit takes over their body. The first stage of spirit possession is known as the *crisis*, and it's at this stage that the lwa begins to take over and the human soul is pushed out or shut down.[172] Once the lwa is firmly in control of the body of its horse, it may do things that we often associate with drawing down the moon: offer advice, lead ritual, diagnose a problem, or perform some sort of initiation.

But the lwa also engage in activity that I've yet to see replicated in a Wiccan circle. They might smoke a cigar or drink a large amount of rum (I have never seen a goddess inhabiting the body of a High Priestess who lights up a cigarette) or perhaps chastise a practitioner for not being attentive enough. Horses are often capable of extraordinary physical feats while being ridden, with mambos suddenly possessing enough power to hold a grown man up over their heads! The lwa also enjoy dancing and engaging in activities that are pleasurable in the flesh. Possession in Voodoo has always come across as more "physical" to me than possession in a Wiccan circle.

---

172. Tann, *Haitian Vodou*, 77.

But other than just how physical it is, possession in Voodoo is almost exactly the same as drawing down the moon. A horse who is being ridden *is the lwa*. They speak with the voice and authority of the lwa, just as a High Priestess speaks with the voice and authority of the Goddess during a drawing down. Voodoo practitioners who are ridden are doing it for the good of their community, not for personal glory, just like drawing down in Wicca.

There are a few other differences between Voodoo rituals and those of Witchcraft that are worth noting. Voodoo rituals are generally long affairs, often lasting from sunset to sunrise, and the lwa might ride a horse for much of the ritual. Drawing down the moon in a Witchcraft circle is usually something that lasts for only a handful of minutes instead of several hours. Possession in Voodoo can occur at any time during the ritual, and there's not a set rite for bringing it about, which is why anyone at a Voodoo rite might be ridden (but the lwa are generally nice: they usually only ride those who honor them). And then there are times when the lwa don't want to leave their horse and they have to be driven away by the mambo or houngan. (This is not common in Wicca, but I have been at a few rituals where Pan didn't quite want to leave.)

Despite some differences between the two traditions, possession in Voodoo and Witchcraft share a lot of similarities. I think it's the closest parallel to what we do in our circles, and having attended a few Voodoo rituals, I've generally felt at home during them because so much of what is happening is familiar. Hopefully the Voodoo and Witch communities will continue to grow closer over the coming years so we can explore this marvelous gift that exists in both of our communities.

GODFORM ASSUMPTION: THE GOLDEN DAWN AND ALEISTER CROWLEY

Another more contemporary influence on drawing down the moon can be found in the rituals of the Golden Dawn and the writings of English occultist Aleister Crowley. Though not quite drawing down as we understand it today, the process of *godform assumption* used in modern ceremonial magick is similar, and it's also a process that can be used by Witches.

The Golden Dawn originally paid (at least) lip service to the idea of monotheism. In its first official document, the society stated: "Belief in One God necessary." [173] Such prohibitions didn't limit the Golden Dawn to a conventional Judeo-Christian worldview though, and those within the order used the names of various Pagan deities in their rites and its members experienced and communicated with "spiritual and invisible things." [174]

When calling upon traditional deities, the Golden Dawn was generally referring to archetypes in the sense of Carl Jung. An archetypal godform is a thought pattern that "manifests through the collective unconsciousness of humanity." [175] For example the Egyptian god Thoth (he of the Ibis head) is the visual representation of humankind's desire to learn and gain knowledge. The godform has purpose but exists only because humans wish to learn and grow. Utilizing the image of Thoth, humans can tap into that universal current of knowledge that already exists within them. This is different from believing that the gods are real and independent beings, though many in the Golden Dawn (then and now) refer to deities in a way that implies actual belief in them.

I feel like I should point out that the Golden Dawn at the end of the nineteenth century most likely had members who believed that the various gods and goddesses worshipped throughout history were independent beings. There are also modern practitioners of Golden Dawn–style magick and ritual who are committed polytheists. Despite the order's origins and original ideas about the nature of deity and archetypes, it's certainly possible to use the godform assumption technique to commune with a particular goddess or god.

Modern-day Golden Dawn practitioners and authors Chic and Sandra Tabatha Cicero define godform assumption as

> a magical technique wherein the adept works with the energies of a particular deity by assuming its form. The archetypal image of the deity is created on the astral by focused visualization,

---

173. Drury, *Stealing Fire from Heaven: The Rise of Modern Western Magic*, 43.

174. Regardie, *What You Should Know About the Golden Dawn*, 112.

175. Chic and Sandra Tabatha Cicero, *The Essential Golden Dawn*, 261.

vibration of the deity's name, the tracing of its sigil, etc. The magician then steps into this astral image and wears it like a garment or mask, continuing to strengthen the image with focused concentration. This is performed in order to create a vehicle for that particular aspect of the divine that the magician is working with. The magician imitates but does not "channel" or identify him- or herself with the deity, although the adept may receive communication from the deity during the process.[176]

Godform assumption can be used for various purposes. It might be used by the individual magician to find a solution to a particularly vexing question or to harness the power and energy associated with a particular deity. If I was having trouble figuring out the answer to a question, I might "step into" the power of Thoth and use the energy that has accumulated around that archetype to find a solution. Godform assumption is sometimes used during the actual rites of the Golden Dawn as well, most likely to bring specific energies to the order's proceedings.[177]

In his work *Liber O* (originally published in the second volume of *The Equinox*),[178] Aleister Crowley gives specific instructions on how to perform a godform assumption.[179] Unlike most of Crowley's work, his instructions in *Liber O* are very straightforward and clear and can easily be adapted by Modern Witches.

Crowley's Ritual of Godform Assumption (Adapted from *Liber O*)

1. The magician should highly familiarize themselves with the image of the deity they wish to call upon. They should commit the image of this deity to memory and be able to call upon it easily.

---

176. Ibid., 270.
177. Ibid., 104. For the record the Ciceros don't say exactly why godform assumption is used during ritual, but only that those doing it don't "actively participate" in any physical duties during ritual.
178. *The Equinox* was the name of a journal published by A∴A∴, Crowley's magickal organization. It's second issue was printed in the fall of 1909.
179. The printing I have of *Liber O* is a 1976 edition by Samuel Weiser and is more pamphlet than book. Instructions for godform assumption are given on pages 19–20.

2. The magician should familiarize themselves with the posture of the deity desired. The magician should then practice assuming this posture until they've mastered it. Once the posture has been mastered, the magician should visualize the godform enveloping their physical body. When this has been achieved, the magician should feel the power and energy of the godform and be able to experience it.

3. The magician should next perform the Vibration of God-names. This requires saying the name of the godform being called to using a specific ritual process. Saying the god-name should help identify "the human consciousness with that pure portion of it which man calls by the name of some God." [180]

Sign of the Enterer (Horus)

4. (a) The magician should stand with arms outstretched.

(b) The magician should breathe deeply through the nose and not the mouth. As the magician breathes in, they should visualize the name of the deity desired coming into their body through their breath.

(c) The name of that deity should then descend through the body, moving from the lungs to the heart, the stomach, the abdomen, all the way down to the magician's feet.

---

180. Exact words from Crowley in *Liber O*.

(d) When the name of the deity touches the feet, the magician should step forward about twelve inches, led by the left foot. As they step, they should throw the rest of their body forward, pushing their arms and hands outward like an arrow (see illustration). Crowley called this the position of the god Horus. As the magician pushes their body forward, they should visualize and feel the name of the deity desired rushing up through their body while breathing that very same name outward through the nose. This should "be done with all the force of which you are capable."[181]

(e) The left foot should then be withdrawn and the right index finger placed upon the lips of the magician. Crowley called this the position of the god Harpocrates (see illustration).[182]

Sign of Silence (Harpocrates)

5. The Vibration of the God-names is performed correctly when it completely exhausts the magician physically. Crowley said correct

---

181. Ibid.

182. Harpocrates was the Greco-Egyptian god of silence.

application of the technique will cause the body to grow warm and/or perspire violently. It might also make standing difficult.

6. Correct performance of this technique will also be confirmed if the magician hears the name of the desired godform loudly spoken at the end of the conjuration. The voice announcing the name of the godform should be heard from outside the body and should not be an inner voice. Crowley said it will roar forth loudly like "ten thousand thunders."

This technique should be committed to memory, and when it is performed, all thoughts not pertaining to the godform should be extinguished. If the operation is a success, normal consciousness should be replaced by something greater. The longer normal consciousness takes to return, the more successful the ritual (at least according to Crowley).

The Priest as the Divine Incarnate: Margaret Murray

Much of the focus in Margaret Murray's works on Witchcraft is on the Horned God. (For more on Murray, head back to "A Ritual from Margaret Murray and the Witch-Cult" in chapter 3.) In Murray's estimation, the Witches of the early modern period worshipped a corrupted version of a very ancient horned deity who had become mixed up with the Christian Devil. When Murray writes of "Devil worship," she's actually writing about worship of the Horned God, with the terms *Horned God* and the *Devil* acting like synonyms.

One of the more fascinating things about Murray's Witches was that they interacted with the Devil much like Modern Witches interact with a High Priestess who has drawn down the moon. Murray's "Devil" was not just an abstract figure worshipped by Witches, but a deity who physically interacted with his charges. Murray writes that "the so-called Devil was a human being, generally a man, occasionally a woman."[183]

---

183. Murray, *The Witch-Cult in Western Europe*. Originally published by Oxford University Press in 1921, here I'm quoting from the Barnes and Noble edition published in 1996, page 31.

The High Priests of Murray's Witch-cult were powerful figures and adored by their charges.

Murray states that "this so-called Devil was God, manifest and incarnate; they adored him on their knees, they addressed their prayers to him, they offered thanks to him as the giver of food and the necessities of life, they dedicated their children to him, and there are indications, that, like many another god, he was sacrificed for the good of his people."[184] What's difficult about Murray is that she doesn't really offer any explanation as to just how the Horned God/Devil came to reside in his priests, or if those priests even truly believed in his existence.

Quoting another scholar, Murray brings up the idea that her Witches "seem to have been undoubtedly the victims of unscrupulous and designing knaves, who personated Satan."[185] Even if Murray did see the priests of the Witch-cult as hucksters, she saw the adoration given to him by Witches as a very central part of the cult.

Referencing an incident in France, Murray writes: "The mother took her young child to one of the great quarterly Sabbaths, and kneeling before the Incarnate God she said, 'Great Lord, whom I worship, I bring thee a new servant who will be thy slave for ever.' At a sign from the god she moved forward on her knees and laid the infant in the divine arms."[186] While no Witches I know today would bring their child in front of the Goddess and proclaim that the child was a slave to the Lady, the rest of that passage is similar to what goes on in some circles.

When looking at the historical precedents of drawing down the moon, the works of Margaret Murray have to be included. Not only did she write the introduction to Gardner's first book, but her own works have been mined by Witches for ideas and inspiration since they were originally published. If Murray thought that the leader of a Witch's coven was sometimes worshipped as the divine incarnate, it makes sense that the earliest Modern Witches would have included such a figure.

---

184. Ibid., 28.

185. Ibid., 33.

186. Murray, *The God of the Witches*, page 75, NuVision edition.

Dion Fortune and *The Sea Priestess*

Dion Fortune (birth name Violet Mary Firth, 1890–1946) is one of the most important figures in Witchcraft's rebirth during the twentieth century. Though she did not identify as a Witch (or even a Pagan), many of her ideas would become a part of Wiccan-Witchcraft, and her 1938 novel *The Sea Priestess* articulated Witch ritual long before it would be made public. A highly trained occult practitioner, Fortune was a member of the Alpha et Omega order, an offshoot of the original Golden Dawn. She would also go on to found the esoteric order the Fraternity of Inner Light, which has continued into the present day and is now known as the Society of the Inner Light.

For the most part, *The Sea Priestess* is a rather bland novel, complete with casual racism and several other uncomfortable bits. But its occult passages shine, and Fortune's descriptions of ritual in her novel are nearly hypnotic. If I had to name just one source for the modern ritual of drawing down the moon, I would pick *The Sea Priestess* because it so perfectly captures the essence of just what a drawing down rite feels like.

Fortune's ideas about invoking deity are based around the idea of male/female polarity. In Fortune's mind, drawing down required two polar opposites, female and male. It's easiest to think of this like a battery, with a positive and a negative side. In a battery the sparks between these two polarities conduct energy. Creating great magick and invoking the gods required something similar: friction between female and male energies. One of the great things about *The Sea Priestess* is that its magickal formulas are shared in long bits of exposition by the character Vivien Le Fay Morgan:

> Do you not know that at the dawn of manifestation the gods wove the web of creation between the poles of the pairs of opposites, active and passive, positive and negative, and that all things are these two things in different ways and upon different levels, even priests and priestesses.[187]

---

187. Fortune, *The Sea Priestess*, 172. *The Sea Priestess* entered the public domain in 2017.

The idea of male/female pairings in magick is a rather old concept and predates Modern Witchcraft (and Fortune's occult work) by several centuries. During the early modern period, magickal *charmers* (individuals who practiced magick with a specific item or spoken charm) believed that their power could be passed on only when exchanged with a member of the opposite sex.[188] To become a Witch in the American Ozarks required sexual initiation by a member of the opposite sex, at least according to popular tradition.[189] The idea of male/female polarity to create a magickal current was a common one in Fortune's time, and would later become an important idea in early Modern Witchcraft.

Fortune's drawing down rite unfolds almost as if it were an initiation and offers further insight into the nature of opposites and their power in magick and the workings of the universe:

> Learn now the mystery of the ebbing and flowing tides. That which is dynamic in the outer is latent in the inner, for that which is above is as that which is below, but after another manner.
>
> Isis of Nature awaiteth the coming of her Lord the Sun. She calls him. She draws him from the place of the dead.[190]

In *The Sea Priestess* it's readily apparent that Fortune's Vivien Le Fay Morgan becomes someone (or perhaps something) else when channeling the goddess Isis. In one particularly striking passage, the book's narrator and main protagonist remarks:

> **Then a voice spoke that was not Morgan's voice, curiously inhuman and metallic.**
>
> "I am the Veiled Isis of the sanctuary. I am she that moveth as a shadow behind the tides of death and birth. I am she that cometh forth by night, and no man seeth my face. I am older than time and forgotten of the gods." [191]

---

188. Davies, *Popular Magic*, 83. Pretty much anything by Owen Davies is a must-read for people interested in magickal history.

189. Randolph, *Ozark Magic and Folklore*, 267.

190. Fortune, *The Sea Priestess*, 219.

191. Ibid., 220–221. Emphasis Mankey.

As Fortune's invocation ritual continues, Vivien Le Fay Morgan's character begins to share bits of otherworldly poetry, with many of them sounding like an alternative version of the Charge of the Goddess (see appendix 2):

> I am the soundless bitter sea;
> All things in the end shall come to me.
> Mine is the kingdom of Persephone,
> The inner earth, where lead the pathways three.
> Who drinks the waters of the hidden well,
> Shall see things whereof he dare not tell
> Shall tread the shadowy path that leads to me
> Diana of the Ways and Hecate,
> Selene of the Moon, Persephone. [192]

Passages such as this one also reveal another lasting legacy of Dion Fortune's work: the idea that "all the gods are one god, and all the goddesses are one goddess, and there is one initiator." [193] The idea of an all-encompassing Goddess whose various facets are reflected in all the goddesses of pagan antiquity is still a common one in many Witchcraft circles, and it's an idea beautifully expressed by Fortune. By weaving together the ancient paganisms of Greece, Egypt, Mesopotamia, and Celtic Britain, she articulates a big and grand Paganism that can be drawn upon by magick practitioners.

Fortune's ideas about invocation and the nature of deity were not limited to just the divine feminine either. She wrote about the god Pan in her book *The Goat-Foot God* (1936) and referred to his resurgence in the nineteenth and twentieth centuries as the return of "vitamin P." [194] She believed that the male aspect of deity could be invoked just as powerfully as the feminine one, though she never articulated those rites with the poetic grace found in *The Sea Priestess*.

---

192. Fortune, *The Sea Priestess*, 221–222.

193. Ibid., 172.

194. Hutton, *The Triumph of the Moon*, 185.

It's unknown if Fortune ever crossed paths with the likes of Gerald Gardner or Doreen Valiente, but as esoteric circles in England were rather small, it's possible. In the end though, it probably doesn't matter. The power of her invocation rite most likely inspired similar rites among Witches, and rare indeed is the well-read Witch who doesn't own a book by Dion Fortune.

CHAPTER THIRTEEN

The Ritual of Drawing Down the Moon

One of the most frequent questions posed to me while discussing the contents of this book with friends was "Will it teach me how to draw down the moon?" My answer generally disappointed them because I'm not sure that drawing down is a skill that can be taught. One can be taught how to run a successful ritual, but drawing down the moon is another thing entirely; it's something that either happens or doesn't happen.

One of the biggest stumbling blocks when it comes to a drawing down, and the one that's most overlooked, is that it's not a one-person operation. Deity is not obligated to act on our whims. Goddesses and gods can choose to enter our bodies or not. There's nothing out there mandating that they participate with us when we try to draw them down. They might feel as if the circumstances aren't right to facilitate their revival, they could be busy, or they might not like the person calling them down. (No one said deity had to like us, and they most certainly play favorites.)

HOW DOES ONE DRAW DOWN THE MOON?

While drawing down the moon is a skill set that can't really be taught in a conventional sense, there are several things that I believe can assist in making it happen. None of these are guaranteed to create a drawing down experience, but I think they can help the aspiring Witch get there.

Letting Go

This is probably the most important part when it comes to drawing down the moon. In order for a god to come in and take control of our body, we have to be willing to let it happen. That means the person doing the drawing down has to open themselves up to the infinite possibilities that come with a belief in deity, and truly believe that the gods are real and that they can inhabit the body of a mortal being.

There's something very scary about turning off one's mind and allowing the body to be operated by another entity. There's a level of trust there that's often made light of. I think the gods generally have our best interests in mind, but ancient mythology often tells another story. Gods aren't all good, and they certainly aren't evil, but when a Pan or a Dionysus comes a calling they might want to partake in large quantities of alcohol or engage in flirtatious or sexual activity that's not appropriate for every circle.

If I have doubts about letting Pan into myself during a large public ritual because I'm worried about how he might behave, he's probably not going to show up. I say "probably" because he may see my reluctance as a challenge and demand to be around, with me rejecting that insistence and fighting him for control of myself.

For a deity to truly and clearly be present within a human vessel, it has to be embraced and welcomed. If a person has any reservations, it's likely that the drawing down won't work. I have also seen situations where the end result of a drawing down is something between a deity being in control and the human vessel ceding control. In one instance I remember a High Priestess addressing herself as "we." Apparently the High Priestess wasn't quite ready to give up control to the goddess she was invoking, but the goddess showed up anyway. After a couple of minutes the High Priestess returned to her normal self, the goddess leaving after realizing she wasn't as welcome as she thought she would be.

Clear Your Mind

When I begin a drawing down, I tend to try to do two things. The first is to completely clear my mind of anything mundane or petty. I let go of work, writing, thinking, and anything else rattling around in my brain. This is always the best way to operate in a Witch circle, but during ritual I generally find myself getting drawn back to at least "How is the ritual going?" During a drawing down I attempt to put it all away, out of sight and out of mind.

When my brain is finally clear, I try to focus on whatever god I'm reaching out to, and I hold an image of them in my mind. Generally that image is something that comes from mythology or art, but it's often influenced by my own experiences with the gods over the years. Cernunnos is a deity with no mythology and only a limited number of depictions in ancient art, so focusing on just how I understand him is equally important as anything else.

Know the Deity You Are Calling To

This sounds so obvious and simple, but I've met people who think drawing down a particular god will impress those around them, so they blunder into a drawing down without knowing the entity they are reaching out to. I always tell my students, "Would you call a person you don't know on the phone? Then why would you call to a god you don't know?" It's important to know just who (or what) you are calling to and build a relationship with that deity before trying to call it down.

There are many ways to build a relationship with a deity. The easiest way is to simply talk to whatever goddess or god you are trying to get to know. It doesn't have to be particularly focused, like a prayer; it can be informal and conversational. I usually do most of my talking to deity out in nature, but the various altars around my house are other good places to chat.

Deity doesn't respond quite like human beings do, but there are often signs that indicate they are listening. You might feel a powerful rush of energy overtake you or start to feel an emotion you weren't expecting. There are sometimes physical indications that they are listening, things such as a sudden shadow on the wall, a ray of sunshine, or a powerful breeze. What's important is talking to them and sharing exactly why you are seeking them out.

More advanced ways of reaching out might involve trying to get in touch with a deity through dreams or a guided meditation or on the astral plane. After establishing some sort of rapport with a deity, invite them into ritual space. If they show up, you should be able to feel their energy in the circle. Once a true relationship with deity has been established, a drawing down rite can be performed.

Knowing a deity is about more than just talking to them; it's about knowing their history. Mythologies are more than collections of stories; they are ancient insight into how deities act and behave. Reading those mythologies offers important insights into those deities, so take advantage of them. If you are looking to call Artemis, read every tale about her that you can! Peek into her history and learn how her cult spread and developed in ancient Greece.

Like Attracts Like

One of the oldest adages in magickal practice is the idea that like attracts like, and I apply this principle to drawing down. When reaching out to a particular deity, decorate your altar with the things that are sacred to them. When trying to draw down Aphrodite, my wife and I burn rose incense and decorate our altar with red and pink candles, seashells, and images of swans, all things we associate with Aphrodite and love.

I sometimes take this way of thinking even further. Before calling down Dionysus I'll eat a big steak dinner and drink a glass or two of wine. Dionysus is a meat eater, and his love of wine is well known. I want to make my body a place he'd like to visit, so I put his favorite things into it! I'll also play music that he seems to like and dress up in a way that I think will appeal to him. (In the case of Dionysus that's usually music by the Doors, along with leather pants. I think he's outgrown the toga most nights.)

I don't think these things are requirements, and as one's relationship with a particular deity grows and deepens over time, it becomes less and less necessary. But for someone just starting out and trying to call down a deity for the first time, every little extra step helps! It also shows deity that you are serious about drawing down.

Be Prepared for Doing a Drawing Down (The Obvious)

Though drawing down the moon is a magickal operation, there are a number of mundane factors that often determine whether or not it's successful. Some of these are rather obvious things, but they are often overlooked by many Witches.

Before doing a drawing down, make sure you are well rested. Drawing down can take an immense toll on the body, and your body has to be ready to deal with all the energy coming into it. If the body and the mind are tired, they are probably not going to be able to handle the strain. Deity has to be comfortable in our body too. If I only get three hours of sleep the night before the big ritual and "fatigue" is written on my face, I can't imagine a deity wanting to stop by.

Part of clearing the mind is about getting rid of stress, but stress is more than just a feeling in the brain. It's something that can affect us all physically. People who are under a great deal of stress are rarely successful at drawing down the moon. When my wife comes home from work after a particularly bad day at work, I know that ritual is not going to go as smoothly as I want it to that night, and my wife is one of the most capable Priestesses I know. It's not her fault either. Sometimes the mundane world simply takes a toll on us.

In addition to ensuring adequate rest and sleep, it's generally wise to eat before drawing down. While the god being called might give you a little bit of energy, you are also going to need your own! Get some sleep, be in a good frame of mind, and have a real meal before drawing down.

Drugs and Altered States

When it comes to drugs (including alcohol) and drawing down the moon, opinions can and do differ among Witches. Some people think drugs can help create a state of mind that encourages the drawing down experience. I don't entirely disagree. For those who have control issues, a glass or two of wine might be just what they need to let go and let deity take control. Others believe that the consciousness-expanding powers of hallucinogenics like LSD take the mind between the worlds, easing in the drawing down experience.

While there are many Witches who believe the use of mind-altering substances is completely acceptable, I am not generally among them. As a Witch, I believe that in ritual and magick it's important to keep my intent and my will sharp, and drugs inhibit this. To some degree I want to have control over what's going on in ritual, and as a High Priest I'm obligated to make sure the ritual space I've helped create is safe and accommodating for all of my coveners. I don't think those things can be done if a person is slurring their words or is unsure of just where they are. Moderation is probably the key here.

I have never needed any sort of mind-altering drug to draw down a god. I have had a drink or two before drawing down Pan or Dionysus, but I've also drawn them down while stone-cold sober. If a deity is associated with a mind-altering substance (and both Pan and Dionysus like wine), it might be worthwhile to experiment with it. If they aren't associated with any such substances, I'd keep those things far away from ritual. In the end it's really up to each individual (and the deity they are drawing down) as to whether or not drugs are an allowable accessory to drawing down and ritual.

The Ritual of Drawing Down the Moon

The ritual of drawing down the moon first appeared in print in 1972 in *The Grimoire of Lady Sheba*. Sheba's *Grimoire* (legal name Jessie Wicker Bell, 1920–2002) and her earlier *Book of Shadows* (1971) contained some of the earliest Witch rituals ever to be printed by a major publisher (in this case Llewellyn, the publisher of this book). Bell claimed to be a seventh-generation Kentucky Witch and that the rituals contained in her book had been passed down in her family for generations. In actuality, Bell's book was given to her by an English coven of Witches (led by Rosina

Bishop and Michael Howard) who were using a modified version of Gerald Gardner's original Book of Shadows.[195]

Bell's published version of the drawing down ritual is exceedingly short and lacking in any sort of context or instruction in just how to draw down a deity. Even though it's a rather limited account of the drawing down ritual, it does contain many of the words and phrases associated with the most common versions of the rite today. A more complete version of the ritual (with a bit of context) next shows up in Janet and Stewart Farrar's *Eight Sabbats for Witches* (first published in 1981 but likely more familiar to American readers as one half of *A Witches' Bible*, published in 1996). The Farrars' version of the rite is notable for including the fivefold kiss (which I sometimes refer to as the "blessed be's"), a frequent and I believe essential part of the ritual.

Most versions of the drawing down ritual are similar to what is described in the books of Bell and the Farrars, which is not surprising since both books use adapted versions of Gerald Gardner's original rites. Since neither Bell nor the Farrars were the original authors of the ritual in their respective books, I feel comfortable sharing some of their work in these pages, though like most Witches before me, I've adapted the material to some degree. The main point of this little section of the book is to explain what's going on when two people attempt to call down a goddess, and what the words primarily associated with that operation are trying to convey.

Despite how it looks on the outside, drawing down the moon is a two-person job. In our example here, there is the High Priestess: the willing vessel of the Goddess, the one that deity is being drawn into. Assisting her is the High Priest, whose job it is to verbalize the coven's intentions to the Goddess and to make sure that the deity being called upon lands in the right spot. I often joke with my wife that the person doing the assisting is kind of like a traffic cop, and she agrees.

Though the example I'm using here utilizes the terms High Priestess and High Priest, it's worth pointing out that two Priests or two Priestess

---

195. Howard, *Modern Wicca*, 223. Howard's book is a must-read for Wiccan history nerds like myself.

can also perform this rite. I also believe that men can draw down the Goddess and that women can draw down the God. I've chosen to word things here as I have since that's how it originally appeared in the books I just mentioned and because that's how my wife and I operate together in the circle. It is not meant to imply that the Craft is in any way heteronormative.

Most drawing down the moon rites have three components to them:

1. **The Fivefold Kiss.** The mini-ritual of the fivefold kiss is not exclusive to drawing down the moon, and is included in many versions of the rite. I think it serves some very important functions in the drawing down ceremony.

2. **The Invocation/The Invitation.** We cannot command things of the gods, which is why it's best to *invite* deity into the body of the High Priestess instead of commanding it. The invocation involves the High Priest communicating with the Goddess and making the intentions of the coven clear.

3. **The Adoration.** During the adoration, deity is making its way into the High Priestess, and the High Priestess begins to be addressed as the divine. This part also involves the High Priest acknowledging his status as a worshipper of the goddess being invoked.

The Fivefold Kiss/The Blessed Be's

The words that make up the fivefold kiss are among the most well known in all of Witchcraft. Because each stage of the fivefold kiss uses the phrase "blessed be," I often refer to this rite as the "blessed be's." The purpose of the blessed be's is to affirm the sacredness of the human body. No matter what a body looks like, it's sacred and holy, and the fivefold kiss serves as a way of reminding all involved in the ritual of that essential truth.

The way most Witches perform the fivefold kiss involves eight actual kisses spread over five regions of the body. The most common regions to kiss are the feet, knees, womb/phallus, breasts, and lips. Depending on the coven, the word *sex* is sometimes substituted for womb or phallus, while *heart* is sometimes substituted for breasts. On rare occasion I have seen groups that kiss the crown of the forehead instead of the lips.

The fivefold kiss was most likely adapted from a Masonic rite known as the five points of fellowship.[196] In the Masonic tradition, those "five points" involved the feet, knees, breast, a hand on the back, and brother Masons being cheek to cheek. There was no kissing involved, but the idea of proclaiming the body as something worthy of respect and admiration is similar to the ideas found in the fivefold kiss. (In this book, the five points of fellowship show up in the third-degree initiation ritual.)

The drawing down ceremony should start with the High Priestess in a comfortable position, either sitting or standing, as she sees fit. In many traditions it's customary for her to hold a ritual tool in each hand during the drawing down, but this is not necessary. What's important is that she's comfortable, in a safe spot, and free from distractions.

In my role as a High Priest, I begin my part in the drawing down process by looking into the face of my High Priestess. When I'm satisfied that we are both equally focused on the task at hand, I sink down to my knees and begin the fivefold kiss at my partner's feet, saying:

Blessed be thy feet that have brought thee to the Old Ways.

Then I kiss each of her feet, first the left foot and then the right.

As I move up to my High Priestess's knees, I stay focused on my task, thinking of the Goddess who will soon inhabit the body of my Priestess and feeling my own personal energy mingle and merge with that of my partner. Still on my own knees, I say:

Blessed be thy knees that shall kneel at the sacred altar.

Then I kiss her left knee and then her right.

Still on the ground, I raise my entire back, making my head level with the lower stomach (womb) of my High Priestess. The fivefold kiss is not a sexual kiss; it's simply meant to activate several divine parts of the body while affirming the sacredness of the flesh. The kiss at the

---

196. Hutton, *The Triumph of the Moon*, 230. Janet Farrar and Gavin Bone make the same observation in their book *The Inner Mysteries*.

womb is done on the lower stomach, above the waist. Before kissing this area, I say these words:

Blessed be thy womb, without which we would not be.

Often this part of the fivefold kiss is misunderstood. I am not praising the womb of my High Priestess here; I am praising the metaphorical womb of the Great Goddess, she who gives life to the world. The life that comes forth from her womb is created in a multitude of ways, and not always necessarily in a sexual way.

After kissing the womb, I rise onto my own feet and look down at the breasts of my partner, and say:

Blessed be thy breasts, formed in beauty (and in strength).

Then I kiss first her left breast and then the right. Again, this is not a sexual kiss, so the kisses involved here do not necessarily have to be on the nipple. Typically I kiss my wife here on her left and right bosoms, at the top of her breasts, well away from the nipples.

The most common version of the blessed be at the breasts involves only the phrase "formed in beauty," but many covens add the extra line "and in strength." This is due in large part to the popularity of kissing only the heart in some traditions, where the line is then changed to just "Blessed be thy heart, formed in strength." When I use both "beauty" and "strength" at the breasts in the fivefold kiss, I will sometimes kiss my wife's left breast after "formed in beauty" and then kiss the right one after saying "and in strength."

Now standing face to face with my lady, I end the fivefold kiss at the lips, saying:

Blessed be thy lips that shall utter the Sacred Names. [197]

The fivefold kiss then ends with a kiss upon the lips of the High Priestess before the High Priest again drops to the floor.

---

197. The blessed be's in this section are from *A Witches' Bible* by Janet and Stewart Farrar, pages 40–41, with some exceptions. "That have brought thee to the Old Ways" is a phrasing I prefer and is not in the Farrars' book, and they also omit the sometimes added "and in strength" at the breasts.

The Invocation

The second part of the drawing down ritual is the invocation. During this period, both the High Priestess and the High Priest are actively calling out to deity with their hearts and minds while the High Priestess opens herself up to the possibility that deity might soon reside within herself. The job of the High Priest is to articulate the goal of the rite and to flatter the Goddess herself in the hope that she will grace the coven with her presence. (Yes, even gods like to be flattered!)

Both early published versions of the invocation are alike in spirit, but there are slight differences in the phrasing of things. This is the version that appears in *The Grimoire of Lady Sheba*, with some slight formatting tweaks:

> *I invoke Thee and call upon Thee, O Mighty Mother of us all. Bringer of all Fruitfulness, by seed and by root. I invoke Thee, by stem and by bud. I invoke Thee, by life and by love and call upon Thee to descend into the body of this Thy Priestess and Servant. Hear with her ears, speak with her tongue, touch with her hands, kiss with her lips, that thy servants may be fulfilled.*[198]

During the invocation, the Farrars use this much more poetic line:

> *Bringer of all fruitfulness; by seed and root, by stem and bud, by leaf and flower and fruit, by life and love do I invoke thee to descend upon the body of this thy servant and priestess.*[199]

There are several important things happening in these invocations. The first is that the High Priest is asking a specific deity to join the coven in ritual. In this instance it's the "Mighty Mother of us all"; that is, the Goddess as an Earth Mother–type of figure and the power that provides the world with growth and regeneration. The phrasings "by seed and root" and "by stem and bud" are references to that regenerative power and the specific deity being called to. Many early Modern Witches saw

---

198. Lady Sheba, *The Grimoire of Lady Sheba*, 167.

199. Janet and Stewart Farrar, *A Witches' Bible*, 41.

the Goddess as a figure who literally helped turn the seasons. With that in mind, this call seems very fitting.

Having established the deity being called to, the High Priest then asks that deity to descend specifically into the body of the High Priestess. In some magickal traditions the human vessel is not signified, which means the deity being called to is free to "jump into" the body of whichever covener it chooses (see the section on Voodoo and the loa in chapter 12). This is not something you want to have happen! In magickal rites it's always best to be as specific as possible when voicing your intentions.

This specificity continues with the words "Hear with her ears, speak with her tongue, touch with her hands, kiss with her lips." This is the very essence of drawing down the moon and is exactly what we want to have happen in ritual. In essence the High Priestess gives up her ability to do such things because she's ceding control of her body to the Goddess she loves and adores.

I have been in circles where the High Priestess (or High Priest) suffered under the delusion that a drawing down the moon rite was about her, the Priestess. That is as far from the true purpose of this ritual as one can get. As the text states, "That thy servants may be fulfilled." Drawing down the moon is about the coven; it's not in any way about the officiant who is drawing the deity inside of themselves. In fact, if everything works out optimally, the High Priestess (or High Priest) probably won't even remember the time when the Goddess resided inside of her.

The Adoration

I'd like to tell you that Gerald Gardner and all the Witches who followed him were brilliant writers of ritual, full of original ideas and poetic thoughts. Sadly, that's not quite the case, and a lot of early Witch ritual was borrowed from other sources. One of the most popular of those sources was Aleister Crowley. The third part of the drawing down ceremony, what I refer to here as the *adoration*, comes almost word for word from Crowley.

Here is the adoration as it appears in the Farrars' *A Witches' Bible* (words would be spoken by the High Priest):

Hail, Aradia! From the Amalthean Horn
Pour forth thy store of love; I lowly bend
Before thee, I adore thee to the end,
With loving sacrifice thy shrine adorn.
Thy foot is to my lip [High Priest kisses right foot of High Priestess],
* my prayer upborne*
Upon the rising incense smoke; then spend
Thine ancient love, O Mighty One, descend
To aid me, who without thee am forlorn. [200]

By way of comparison, the majority of the invocation above first appeared in Crowley's poem "La Fortune," which was first published in the book *Rodin in Rime* in 1907. (Rodin in this case is Auguste Rodin, best known for his sculpture "The Thinker"). Crowley's poem reads as follows:

Hail, Tyche! From the Amalthean horn
Pour forth the store of love! I lowly bend
Before thee; I invoke thee at the end
When other gods are fallen and put to scorn.
Thy foot is to my lips; my signs unborn
Rise, touch and curl about thy heart; they spend
Pitiful love. Lovelier pity, descend
And bring me luck who am lonely and forlorn. [201]

The adoration section of the drawing down ritual is nearly a word-for-word borrowing from Crowley's poem! But I like to think this was done not because people were lazy, but because it so perfectly captures the essence of

---

200. Janet and Stewart Farrar, *A Witches' Bible*, 41. This passage does not appear in Lady Sheba's book.

201. Sorita d'Este, "Aleister Crowley, Wicca & the Amalthean Horn," *Adamantine Muse* (blog), July 6, 2016, http://www.patheos.com/blogs/adamantinemuse/2016/07/aleister-crowley-wicca-the-amalthean-horn/. For more information on the borrowings from Crowley and other sources in the drawing down the moon ritual, check out Sorita's book (with David Rankine) *Wicca: Magickal Beginnings*. Original text of "La Fortune" can be found at *Rodin in Rime* (Austin, TX: 100th Monkey Press, 2008), http://www.100thmonkeypress.com/biblio/acrowley/books/rodin_in_rime_1907/rodin_text.pdf.

a drawing down the moon ritual. In the case of the adoration, I think that's especially true.

This section of the ritual begins with a hearty "Hail, Aradia," in this case a greeting to a specific named goddess. Due to the influence and popularity of Leland's *Aradia*, the goddess of the same name was often called to in early Witch ritual. The reference to the Amalthean horn is an allusion to abundance. The Amalthean horn is a cornucopia full of fruits, vegetables, and other goodies.

The High Priest continues by asking the Goddess to share her love with the coven and then shows his devotion to her by bending before her, kissing her foot, and offering a sacrifice. In most cases today that "sacrifice" is time and libations (leftover cakes and wine); it's certainly not a living animal or wealth. Periodically my wife and I will offer the gods a bit of strong drink or a couple coins, generally left by the lemon tree in our backyard. It's a token of respect and not necessarily a burden. Though the word *sacrifice* is used in the ritual, any sort of major sacrifice is frowned upon by the Goddess herself. As she says in the Charge of the Goddess, "Nor do I demand sacrifice."

The rite ends with one final plea to the Goddess to descend into the High Priestess. Here the High Priest asks for aid and states that without the Goddess in his life he is "forlorn." For many Witches those precious few moments they get to spend with a deity such as the Great Mother or the Horned God in circle are truly momentous. While I would not quite say that I'm "forlorn" when the Goddess does not appear, a little embellishment never hurts.

In most instances this is the end of the drawing down ceremony, but the Farrars offer a bit of a coda. Instead of the Goddess moving to address the coven as she sees fit, the High Priestess/Goddess (for at this point they both inhabit the same body) is instructed to say the following words while drawing an invoking pentagram:

Of the Mother, darksome and divine,
Mine the scourge, and mine the kiss,
The five-point star of love and bliss—
Here I charge you, in this sign. [202]

---

202. Janet and Stewart Farrar, *A Witches' Bible*, 41.

In most other versions of the ritual that I've experienced over the years, it's the High Priest who speaks the final words and not the High Priestess. The reason for this is that the High Priestess should be "absent" from her body by this point in the ritual. If all has gone as it should, it's the Goddess who should be standing in circle at this point, and to instruct a goddess to read any specific thing is, in my opinion, the height of arrogance. We don't command the gods.

Both of the earliest published versions of drawing down the moon end with the Goddess/High Priestess reciting Doreen Valiente's Charge of the Goddess (the Farrars) or something similar (Lady Sheba). In reality, what happens next in ritual is up to the Goddess, and she might choose to address the coven, lead those gathered in some activity, or share some sort of gift or knowledge with them. Whatever she does, all in attendance should be respectful and humble toward her.

ENDING A DRAWING DOWN

Often a drawing down will end when the deity who is visiting decides it's time to leave. I've been in several circles where deity has said, "I think it's time for me to go." Usually this is followed by the person who has drawn down deity closing their eyes, and upon opening them again saying, "She's gone. It's just me again." But not every ending is that clean, and there are times when deity simply doesn't want to leave.

Instead of announcing their departure, deity sometimes just drifts away. In my own experience I have seen our coven's matron goddess slowly leave the body of my wife. In such instances the mannerisms of our goddess are slowly replaced by those of my wife until it's obvious that our Lady has left us and our High Priestess again stands in the circle. There are no dramatic cues in such instances, but only the dawning revelation that the experience has come to an end.

Even in situations such as these, where it seems deity has left willingly, it's best to check in with the person who has done the drawing down to make sure all is as it's supposed to be. When the drawing down has seemingly come to an end, I'll often ask the person who has held deity, "Have you returned to us, my High Priestess?" While waiting for their response, I'll pay attention to their facial expressions and mannerisms to make sure it really is my High Priestess standing there and not deity.

In my own experience, deity generally knows when it's time to leave and doesn't put up much of a fuss about it. But there are times when a drawing down seems to go on for far too long and it seems like the deity involved just doesn't want to leave. In such instances a question such as "Are you ready to return to us, my Priestess?" can help remedy the situation. The question serves as a reminder to deity that they can't inhabit a body indefinitely, and by addressing the human vessel as well, the question activates the reasoning of the person who has drawn down.

If that polite question doesn't have quite the effect I want it to, I usually ask again a bit more forcefully and use the name of the person who has done the drawing down. "Susan, it's time that you come back to us." If that's not enough, then it's time to announce that the rite is ending and it's time to go. It feels strange to chastise a goddess, but sometimes it's necessary. In such instances it's best to be firm but polite: "My Lady, our rite is now near its end and it's time for you to return to your lovely realm."

This usually does the trick, but if it doesn't, there are a few other ways to end a drawing down. One of them is through touch. My wife often likes to end a drawing down by holding my hands and using me to help ground and draw out the last of the divine energies within her. When deity doesn't seem to want to go, holding the hands or shoulders of the person who has done the drawing down can be helpful. Unexpected changes in the immediate environment can also get a deity to leave a human body. Simply turning on the lights suddenly in a dark room or surprising them with a loud, sharp clap will often have the desired result.

Deity leaving the human body is often not an all-or-nothing proposition. Sometimes the divine energy lingers, affecting the person's consciousness and influencing their decisions. If someone who has invoked deity is having trouble returning to their regular self, a pinch of salt on the tongue will often bring them back. If they won't willingly submit to a pinch of salt on the tongue, a few splashes of salt water will often accomplish the same thing. Food and drink are also great for grounding, so simply getting the possessed person to eat or drink something might also bring them back.

Most Witch ritual doesn't have a specific rite for ending a drawing down, but I personally find such exercises helpful, especially when working with a large group. I'm generally aware of when a working partner has returned to normal after a drawing down, but an acquaintance might not. A small rite indicating that the drawing down is truly over can be helpful to the person who has drawn down and those around them, vanquishing any fears or worries that deity is still around in a mortal vessel.

In such instances a physical object such as a horned helm or a circlet comes in handy. When starting the drawing down ritual, the circlet can be placed on the invoking officiant's head, indicating that they are now a vessel for the divine. When the time for the drawing down has ended, the return of the officiant who has drawn down should be formally requested:

> My Lady, our rite is now at its end, and we must ask that our High Priestess rejoin us.

Usually the deity who has been drawn down will nod and go willingly, but if that's not the case, hold on to the officiant's hands and ask again, speaking more forcefully:

> Our time together has ended, my Lady, and it is now time for you to return to the land beyond this mortal realm. We now ask that our High Priestess, (High Priestess's name), rejoin us once more in circle. So mote it be!

Once deity has left, remove the circlet from the head of the person who has done the drawing down and set it down upon the altar. After the circlet has been put away, take the person's hands and say:

> Thank you for your service tonight. All has been returned to how it once was, and you have now come back to us. Blessed be!

If the working partners are close to each other outside the circle, a hug or a kiss is appropriate after this exchange to serve as an additional grounding moment.

Personal Boundaries with Drawing Down the Moon

Even when we willingly share our bodies with the gods, those bodies are still ours, and we are ultimately responsible for what they do. Most deities are respectful; they are visiting us because they care about us and want us to know them. However, Pagan deities, while not human, do share some of our nature. The gods enjoy many of the same things we do, such as physical pleasure, food and drink, being silly, and all sorts of other things. Before drawing down a deity, it's best to let deity know ahead of time if you have any boundaries.

A whole host of deities in the ancient world were sexual. Is such behavior welcome in your circle, and will your partner be okay with it if something happens? There are many deities who enjoy kissing, flirting, and more. If that's not allowed in your present circumstances, it shouldn't happen. There are deities who like bloody meat, and a lot of Witches are vegetarians, so what happens when Dionysus wants to eat a steak?

It's always best to have a relationship with a deity before drawing them down, and that relationship will usually ensure that nothing unwelcome happens when they inhabit your body. But just to be sure, there's nothing wrong with making a list of what is and is not allowed and presenting it to deity in the days leading up to a drawing down. A deity in our body is a houseguest, and most of us have rules when people visit our homes.

If you have a shrine or altar where you interact with your gods, that's a great place to have a little heart-to-heart with them before drawing them down. For a little extra insurance, present them with a written list of dos and don'ts and make it clear that you are asking for your boundaries and limitations to be respected. Let them know how much you care, but also that you have to be true to yourself.

Since drawing down the moon is usually done in the presence of others, you should inform those you are doing ritual with what is allowed to be done with your body. If you are drawing down Aphrodite and she gets a little too flirtatious with someone and that's a line you can't cross, your friends should feel free to put a stop to it. "My lady Aphrodite, I appreciate your intentions, but this is the body of my friend Sarah, and you are doing something she would object to." If that doesn't work, it might be time to end the drawing down and ask for Sarah to return to the circle.

As your relationships with goddesses and gods grow over time, it's possible to "bargain" with them in order to retain some degree of control. A public ritual I put together called for drawing down Persephone, but because it was a public ritual, there were things we needed Persephone to help facilitate in order to get the people in the circle from point A to point B. In the days leading up to the ritual, my High Priestess worked with Persephone to guarantee that the ritual would mostly occur as written. The work wasn't taxing; it simply required speaking out loud to Persephone and asking for this particular favor.

In addition to asking for a deity's cooperation, presenting them with a gift can be helpful as well. It could be something as simple as pouring them a glass of wine and then sharing that wine with the earth. You could also make a donation to a charity that they might have a vested interest in, or burn some of their favorite incense. I don't recommend bargaining or asking for favors from an unfamiliar deity, but if it's a goddess or god you work with frequently, such requests are generally acceptable.

Deity should never put a circle member in a compromising or uncomfortable position. The goddesses and gods of today's Witches do not demand sex, money, or anything else from those who honor them. I want to be very clear about this: deity does not have the right to violate the free will of anyone. As Witches, we should be building a consent culture, and that culture has to extend to our deities as well.

CHAPTER FOURTEEN

Alternative Drawing Down Rituals

Instead of simply quoting the printed rites of others, I'm a proponent of creating my own individual rites. When calling to a specific deity, I try to tailor my drawing down ceremonies to that particular goddess or god. The more exact we are with our words and intentions in ritual, the more likely it is that the things we want will manifest in our rites. If you aren't calling a Mother goddess, there's no reason to say "Mighty Mother of us all." Rituals should make sense! Tweaking and adapting our rites is a way to do that.

In this section of the book there are four drawing down ceremonies, one specifically for Aphrodite, along with rites for three more "general" deities without specific names (in this case the Sun God, the Horned God, and the Corn Mother). I hope these rites will inspire you to write your own drawing down ceremonies for whatever deities are a part of your life.

Before beginning any drawing down ritual, the High Priestess and High Priest should determine which specific deity is being drawn down. Even when using a named deity such as Aphrodite, individual understandings of her may differ among folks, so discuss the particulars of how both partners visualize and interact with her. Since the previous chapter went over what should be happening to both ritual leaders internally, I have omitted those particulars from this section and instead will focus on sharing the rituals without a lot of exposition.

DRAWING DOWN APHRODITE

Aphrodite is generally known as the goddess of love and beauty, but she is far more complicated and layered than that. In addition to love, Aphrodite is a goddess of independence. She has always been free to take as many lovers as she desires, even when that was frowned upon by conventional Greek society. In this sense she is a goddess of freedom and personal empowerment.

Though sometimes seen as a trivial goddess due to her vanity, Aphrodite might actually be the strongest and most powerful of all the Olympians. As Helen (of Troy) says in Euripides's play *The Trojan Women,* "Zeus holds sway over all other divinities but is a slave to her." Such is the power of Aphrodite. If you do draw her down, proceed with caution.

When honoring Aphrodite in ritual, it's best to put things on your altar that she likes. In the case of Aphrodite, I suggest sweet-smelling incense, especially floral scents. Fresh flowers are also a good idea. Aphrodite likes beautiful things, so it's best to put your finest tools upon the altar.

The drawing down rite should begin with the High Priest standing in front of the High Priestess, both of them focused on the task at hand before beginning the blessed be's. Because Aphrodite is a goddess of sensuality, the kisses employed here can be more erotic than they normally would be (assuming the High Priestess and High Priest are both comfortable with it). When the rite is ready to begin, the High Priest should prostrate himself upon the floor and begin the fivefold kiss:

Blessed be thy feet that have brought thee to the temple of the gods.
Blessed be thy knees that shall kneel upon the earth.
Blessed be thy sex, source of pleasure and of life. [203]

---

203. Aphrodite is most certainly a goddess of love and pleasure, but she is also a goddess of childbirth, a fact not known by very many people. Though a goddess of childbirth, Aphrodite wasn't a Mother goddess and wasn't all that involved with children after their successful delivery.

Blessed be thy breasts, source of beauty and delight.
Blessed be thy lips that shall speak the ancient truths.

Now standing eye to eye with the High Priestess, the High Priest begins the invocation to Aphrodite:

I invoke thee and call upon thee, O Great Aphrodite, goddess of love, beauty, power, and sensuality. Come to us so that we might understand your mysteries. Rise up and fill the body of your servant and Priestess here, just as you once rose from the foam of the sea. Caress with her hands, walk with her feet, love with her heart, and speak beauty with her lips so that we may know and touch you, O loveliest of goddesses.

With Aphrodite invoked, the High Priest adores the Goddess:

Hail Great Aphrodite from Cypress fair,
Share your love with those that are gathered now.
It is you we adore with grace and care.
Come by leaf and bud, and by branch and bough.
I kneel before you [Kneel.] *and kiss your lips so sweet* [Kiss lips.]*,*
Our prayers and hopes fill this holy space.
Be with us tonight, make our rite complete.
You are the goddess we long to embrace!
Hail Aphrodite!

The ritual should now proceed as Aphrodite sees fit.

DRAWING DOWN THE CORN MOTHER

The Corn Mother is the Goddess of the Grain and the Lady of the Harvest. Her time of year begins in late July, when the cereal grains begin to ripen, and lasts through early October. This is the goddess my coven often honors at Lughnasadh (Lammas) and the Autumn Equinox. Specific Corn Mother goddesses include the Greek Demeter (whose Roman equivalent is Ceres), the Egyptian Isis, and the Cherokee Selu (and there are a multitude of other Native American goddesses related to maize, often known as Corn Mother or Corn Maiden).

Nearly any harvest goddess might be a part of the greater Corn Mother, and certainly corn isn't the only grain she blesses. Despite being used almost exclusively to indicate maize in North America, corn really refers to nearly any cereal grain, including rice, barley, maize, wheat, and many others.

When calling to a nonspecific deity, it's extremely important that the High Priestess and High Priest understand what force they are reaching out to. In our coven, when we call to the Grain Mother we envision her as a woman nearing the end of her childbearing years. Her skin is a deep brown and her hands have the appearance of someone who has been working in the fields. She is loving, she tends the fields, and she wants us to be well fed (and well behaved!), like most mothers do.

For this rite the High Priestess may choose to hold her boline[204] in one hand and an ear of corn or a sheaf of grain in the other hand. The altar should be decorated with the first fruits of the harvest, and bread should be kept nearby in case the Lady chooses to share some with the coven. The ritual begins in the usual way, with the fivefold kiss said by the High Priest:

Blessed be thy feet, which have walked the sacred earth.
Blessed be thy knees, which kneel to tend the fields.
Blessed be thy womb, from which all life grows.
Blessed be thy heart, which tends to your children.
Blessed be thy lips that share truth and knowledge.

With the High Priestess's body affirmed as sacred, the High Priest continues with the invocation:

I invoke thee and call upon thee, O Mighty Goddess of the Grain! Step
out of your fields and visit us with your powers of abundance and
growth. We ask that you descend into the body of your Priestess so that
we might come to know you better and partake of your gifts. Speak
with her lips, see with her eyes, hear with her ears, and touch us with

---

204. A boline is a curved knife used by many Witches to harvest plants in their garden. For more about the boline and other pointy tools, see my 2016 book *The Witch's Athame*, published by Llewellyn.

her hands. These things we most humbly ask she who gives us life and is beloved among those of this coven.

The Corn Mother, now invoked, is then adored by the High Priest:

Hail the Corn Mother from the ever-ripening fields! You are the source of all life and she that sustains the people. Come by the powers of maize and rye, and wheat and rice. By stem and stalk and berry and chaff we invoke thee. We honor your work and sacrifice [Kiss her feet at "work" and then kiss her hands after saying "sacrifice."] *for all the folk. Before you we are humble and thankful for your gifts and blessings. Hail the harvest! Hail the Corn Mother!*

The ritual is now in the caring and nurturing hands of the Corn Mother, who blesses us daily with her gifts. Be thankful for and appreciative of all that she has given us and will give to us in the future.

DRAWING DOWN THE SUN RITUALS

The phrase *drawing down the sun* is not quite as common as *drawing down the moon,* though the practice is essentially the same. In this book I use *drawing down the moon* over and over again because it's the phrasing I use the most in my own personal practice. In my coven, drawing down the God is just as important as spending time with our Lady. We just use the terminology exclusive to him with a lot less frequency (which is reflected in this book).

For this section of the book I chose to include drawing down rites featuring the God in his two most common guises: the Horned God and the Lord of the Sun. Both rites can easily be adapted for more specific deities such as Pan, Herne, Helios, or Belenus. When acting as the vessel in a drawing down rite, I find it helpful to hold a wand in my left hand and an athame in my right, but that's just my personal preference. What's always most important is to do the things that work for the people performing the ritual.

DRAWING DOWN THE HORNED GOD

The Horned God is a very complex deity. In many Witch circles he's seen as a combination of gods such as Pan, Cernunnos, Herne, the Green Man, Shiva, Dionysus, and many others. The complexity starts when one realizes just how little Pan and Cernunnos have in common. Pan is a wild, phallic deity with horns on top of his head. Cernunnos, by way of comparison, has antlers on top of his head (which are very different from horns), was probably a hunting god, and is never pictured with an erect phallus. They're entirely different gods, yet they've been drawn together into this larger figure.

This particular drawing down is a bit more focused on the Horned God in his Pan-like aspect. This call is to a god of fertility, lust, and the wilder parts of ourselves. I always counsel caution before drawing down the Horned God. He can be a bit aggressive sometimes, and most certainly horny. He's a deity everyone should be familiar with before the ritual, and they should be prepared for the occasional bit of bad behavior.

I used parts of Aleister Crowley's poem "Hymn to Pan" (from *The Equinox*, vol. 3, no. 1, 1919) in parts of the rite. Crowley's poetry wasn't always divinely inspired, but his ode to Arcadia's favorite goat god captures Pan in an extremely honest way. In addition, early Modern Witches happily used other sources when composing their rituals, so I think it's a nice homage to those pioneers who were influenced by Crowley too.

During the adoration of the Horned One, the final kiss from the High Priestess can be given to the Priest's/God's phallus or his right foot. (This is the kiss at the end of the rite, long after the fivefold kiss.) While I was writing this, it felt far more natural to kiss the phallus (most covens kiss above the actual organ) since the Horned God is a rather lusty fellow. However, if I were invoking the Horned One at an all-ages Beltane ritual, we'd definitely choose the right foot.

When calling the Horned One I like to include things on my altar that I know he likes. Natural items such as pine cones and acorns are always welcome. He also generally likes wine and other alcoholic beverages, so we always keep some in the altar's chalice in case he gets thirsty. Actual horns or antlers are other good decorative choices.

The ritual should start with the High Priest behind the altar. If he chooses to hold a tool during the drawing down, we've found that phallic ones tend to work best. Those include the athame, sword, wand, and broom. The High Priestess should look into the eyes of the High Priest before beginning the fivefold kiss.

> *Blessed be thy feet that walk the green fields.*
> *Blessed be thy knees that kneel upon the sacred earth.*
> *Blessed be thy phallus that brings forth pleasure and life.*
> *Blessed be thy heart that is filled with love.*
> *Blessed be thy lips that shall speak the truth of the Horned One.*

When the fivefold kiss is complete, the High Priestess should begin the invocation.

> *Thrill with lissome lust of the light,*
> *Come careening out of the night.*
> *Horned One, we invoke thee, descend!*
> *Into this vessel touch and transcend!*
> *Come and join your flock, with Priest's foot trod,*
> *Your power to his bone, your might to his rod.*
> *With hooves of steel you race on the rocks*
> *Through solstice stubborn to equinox.*
> *Everlasting god, wonder without end,*
> *Descend, descend, descend, descend!* [205]

With the god thus invoked into the body of the High Priest, the High Priestess then begins the adoration of the Horned God.

> *Hail the Horned God who has come over land and sea, from Sicily and from Arcady. Hail thee, Lord of the Wood, and make your desires understood! Come with flute and come with pipe, lead the coven ever ripe! Do as thou wilt as a great god can* [Kisses phallus or foot, according

---

205. Heavily adapted from Aleister Crowley's "Hymn to Pan."

to preference], *be here with your Priest and man! Hail the Horned One who has come this night! Great Lord, lead us in your rite.* [206]

The ritual is now in the hands and hooves of the Horned God. Be joyful—and wary.

Drawing Down the Lord of the Sun

After the Horned God, the Sun God is the most common male deity in Modern Witchcraft. In my coven he's a frequent visitor at Midsummer, Lammas, and Yule celebrations. Much like the Goddess mirrors the four seasons as Maiden, Mother, and Crone, the Sun God mirrors the growth of the sun each year. He begins the solar year as the Child of Promise at Yule, reaches the height of his powers near Midsummer, when the days are longest, and then ultimately "dies" at Samhain, only to be reborn a short time later.

This particular drawing down is directed at the Sun God who reigns during the summer months and beginning of fall. This is the Lord of the Sun who ripens the grain and allows for an abundant harvest. Since the sun "sees" everything on the earth, the Sun God is also a very wise deity and is generally aware of everyone's secrets. He's also the perfect complement to the Corn Mother, for they need each other in order to thrive. (His rays help the grain to grow, and he would not be reborn without the gifts of the Mother.)

When calling to solar deities I like to decorate the altar with a great deal of solar imagery and perhaps use a gold candle if I'm using a candle to represent the God on my altar. He enjoys the gifts of the garden and the fruit trees since that's where he can most easily see his handiwork. Ancient people used to invoke the sun to bear witness to oaths,[207] so his presence in ritual is especially welcome at initiation rituals.

Begin the ritual in the usual way, with the High Priestess facing the High Priest. If the High Priest chooses to hold an object or two while drawing down, I recommend using an athame (a tool of fire) and a *thyrsus*, which is a staff, spear, or wand-like tool with a pine cone or other

---

206. Also heavily adapted from Crowley's "Hymn to Pan."
207. West, *Indo-European Poetry and Myth*, 200.

natural item at the tip. The spear is sacred to the god Lugh, who is often interpreted as a solar deity, and the pine cone allows the Sun God to see his handiwork up close. Once the High Priestess and High Priest are focused on the task at hand, they should move on to the fivefold kiss to affirm the body.

Blessed be thy feet that shall gather the harvest.
Blessed be thy feet that shall kneel in our sacred fields.
Blessed be thy eros that allows us to be. [208]
Blessed be thy heart that beats for the Old Ways.
Blessed be thy lips that shall speak to us the truth of the gods.

Once the High Priestess has kissed her High Priest upon the lips, she should begin the invocation to the Sun God.

Lord of the Sun, radiant God of the Sky, we ask that you come and join us in our circle tonight. Descend this night into the body of thy High Priest so that we might know your mysteries and feel your magick. Bless us with presence as you have blessed us with the gift of the grain and the bounty of the earth. Let your power radiate from your servant here so that we may grow in the ways of the Witch. Now see with his eyes, touch with his hands, bless with his heart, and speak with his tongue. These things we ask of you, O Sun God that we adore!

With the Sun God now invoked and inhabiting the body of the High Priest, the High Priestess begins the adoration.

Hail the Lord of the Sun! It is your power that sustains the earth and allows us to live. Your gifts fall from the heavens and fill us, your servants, with both gratitude and joy. Shine this night in our circle and speak with those who adore you. So mote it be!

---

208. Many years ago my friend Dr. Christopher Chase suggested the term *eros* to replace *phallus* and *womb* in a large group ritual we were doing. I loved the idea and enjoy incorporating it into ritual when I can.

WHEN DRAWING DOWN JUST DOESN'T WORK

One of the things that most Witch books don't mention is that drawing down the moon is not always successful. Heck, I'd go even further than that: most attempts to draw down are failures. I can count on my fingers and toes the total number of mind-blowing "I just met the Goddess!" moments I've had in over twenty years of Witchcraft. The rarity, and not the frequency, of the truly exceptional drawing down experience is what makes it so powerful.

There are a whole host of reasons why a drawing down might come up short. It could be that we just aren't in the right physical or mental state to deal with a deity floating around in our bodies. It could be that the goddess or god we are trying to invoke has better things to do. Drawing down the moon is an *exceptional* thing, and exceptional things don't come around all that often.

Most books that feature a drawing down the moon ritual immediately follow that with "The High Priestess reads the Charge of the Goddess," and for good reason. The Charge was written to be read when a drawing down was not successful. It eventually became a standard piece of Wiccan liturgy, but that wasn't its original purpose. I don't want to call it filler, but it was the backup plan, and all good Witches have a backup plan.

Several years ago my wife and I attended the esbat ritual of a local coven. There was a drawing down that night, but for whatever reason it didn't take. I remember the High Priestess just shaking her head and saying, "She's not here," and moving along with the ritual. On our way home that night Ari commented on this and told me just how impressed she was by it. My wife wasn't impressed by the invocation not working; she was impressed by the honesty of the High Priestess in that situation. The Priestess could have pretended that everything had worked as planned just to impress the guests, but she didn't. Our respect for that woman grew that night because of how she handled the situation.

I have been in circles where the High Priest or High Priestess fakes a drawing down. I'm sure there are lots of reasons in their minds for justifying such a thing. Many Witches suffer from the delusion that the people they circle with are looking for a show, so they attempt to provide them with one. But Witchcraft is not a show, and doing something false even with the best of intentions doesn't make it suddenly right. Faking a drawing down cheapens the experience for everybody down the road and probably doesn't gain us any favor with the gods either.

Over the years I've run into many talented Witches who for whatever reason have trouble with drawing down the moon (or sun). Perhaps there's some sort of internal block there, or perhaps their relationships with the gods aren't as deep as they need to be. I don't know the reasons, but I do know that it's no reason to judge them. Even if one never gets the hang of drawing down, they can still work magick, perform ritual, and engage in all sorts of other Witch activities. Drawing down the moon is one part of Witchcraft, and we all have different skill sets and things we do well inside the circle.

Most of all, drawing down the moon is never about the person who draws down the deity; it's about serving the other members of the coven. It's not something we do for personal glory. We do it to bring our friends and chosen family closer to the gods. The greatest drawing down experiences I've ever had were when I got to talk to the Goddess, and not when the God was operating inside of me.

So when a drawing down doesn't work, there's nothing to worry about! It's really very common. Sure, there are Priestesses who are successful almost all the time, but I think they are the exception and not the rule. When it doesn't happen (and there will be plenty of times when it doesn't), have something else ready to read, and move forward with the ritual. Just because a drawing down didn't quite work doesn't mean that the Goddess and God aren't there in circle, because they most likely are. And the next time they choose to show up during a drawing down, the experience will probably be even more powerful because of the time off.

Part Five

The Great Rite

CHAPTER FIFTEEN

The Great Rite, Present and Past

Rituals, even those crafted with the best of intentions, sometimes leave you wanting more. That was the case for my wife and I many years ago at a Midsummer rite just north of Port Huron, Michigan. The rite had been intensely silly (instead of using an athame, my friends had cast the circle by driving a bright yellow car named after and resembling a Pokémon around our campsite), and I remember laughing at the absurdity of it all. Laughing is often a welcome companion during ritual, but on this particular night it wasn't enough.

Much of that was because of just how beautiful it was outside. When presented with an absolutely breathtaking sky as a ritual backdrop, you sometimes find yourself wanting a serious ritual. As midnight approached, the sun continued to grasp onto its spot in the sky, its light mixing with that of the moon and the stars. Without much in the way of speaking, my wife and I both grabbed our Books of Shadows and a blanket and set off for a small hill a ways away from our friends.

We spread our blanket on the ground and looked up at the sky on that night of the longest day. After a period of silence I asked my wife if she would read the Charge of the Goddess for me. While reading the Charge, Ari's voice began to change, and soon she sounded less like my wife and more like the Goddess of the Witches. When she was done, she asked me to read the Charge of the God, and I complied.

Somewhere in the middle of that reading, time and space began to slip away from us. I'm sure I finished reading my Charge, but I don't remember doing so. What I do remember are our shared kisses, and how they felt both urgent and sensual. We felt compelled to kiss, as if a higher power was pushing us forward, both of us unable to say no. There were no thoughts of our friends, work, or anything else, but just one another, our Craft, and the natural spaces above and below us.

Our shared kisses soon began to be replaced by other expressions of lust, longing, and love, and I swear that I could see the Lord and Lady in the sky above me mimicking what Ari and I were doing on our blanket. I could feel the power of the Horned One near and inside of me. It wasn't a full drawing down, but he was lending his energy to our coupling, and I felt the power of the Goddess do the same with Ari. It was sex, but it was also an intense spiritual exercise, and it was wanton and loving and everything I'd hoped to experience in such an instance.

When we were done, some of our friends applauded our coupling. (Apparently we weren't as far away from everyone as we'd thought.) But there was no shame or embarrassment. We had shared something magickal and joyous, and our coupling had been more than sex; it had been the Great Rite, perhaps Witchcraft's greatest mystery.

What Is the Great Rite?

In its simplest form, the Great Rite is a celebration of union. It's about two different and distinct forces coming together to create something new. Many Witches express this idea using the male-female sexual dynamic, and until recently that dynamic was what most conversations about the Great Rite revolved around.[209] But the Great Rite is about more than just female-male coupling; it's about every conceivable kind of coupling, and all sorts of other things.

In its most traditional form, the term *Great Rite* was used to describe sacred ritual sex enacted and enjoyed by Witches. To most Witches sex is a pleasurable and welcome activity and is not seen as some sort of

---

209. That was the way of things in most every Witchcraft book published up until the 2000s. The book currently on my lap, *A Witches' Bible* by Janet and Stewart Farrar, describes the Great Rite as a ritual of male-female polarity (page 48).

strange cosmic challenge posed by a vengeful deity to test how much self-control we have. Humans are sexual beings, and many Witches revel in that aspect of themselves.

This does not mean that Witches enjoy sex in an irresponsible manner —just the opposite. Sex is a divine gift, and gifts should be well taken care of. But gifts should also be used. What's the use of getting a new book and then not reading it? Sex is something to be enjoyed, and it's also possible to enjoy sex while engaging in it on a deeper level.

It's also worth noting that many of the gods and goddesses honored by Modern Witches are sexual beings. There were no Pagan gods born to virgin mothers; in fact it was just the opposite. In many stories used today to explain the Wheel of the Year, sex also plays a major role. Instead of sexless beings, our gods are often sensual beings, and they celebrate sex in a variety of ways and with a variety of partners.

So yes, the Great Rite can most certainly be a sexual celebration, but that's not all it is. It's also an acknowledgment that there are a number of powerful forces at work in our universe. We can enact the Great Rite in ritual without taking off our clothes. In most Witch circles the Great Rite is performed *in token*, meaning the Great Rite is symbolically enacted and/or acknowledged at some point in ritual.

When performed in token, the Great Rite is still about two forces coming together to create something new, but it also becomes about acknowledgment and thanks. We acknowledge the gods and the earth, and the roles both forces play in the world's fertility and in our lives. And because we have food to eat, roofs over our heads, and things to drink, we thank the earth for her bounty and thank the gods for our good fortune.

Many Witches focus only on the sexual aspects of the Great Rite, but I believe that's a shortsighted way of looking at the world. The universe did not begin with sex; it began with the Big Bang, an intense explosion of energy and matter over 13 billion years ago. The grass growing in my backyard is a combination of many things, most visibly the sky (sun, water) and the grass seeds that have sprung from the earth. The union of land and sky is what creates the green growing places, and that, to me, is an expression of the Great Rite.

Almost everything we do that creates something new requires the union of at least two forces. It's easy to express that idea with "woman and man create baby," but this universe is about far more than populating the earth with tiny humans. There is no night without day, and no new day without the night. Limiting our world to penises and vaginas is silly because the world just doesn't work exclusively that way.

Even masturbation, with its creation of a new and unique orgasm every time, requires the union of two forces. That orgasm doesn't exist without my sexual organ, along with some friction and imagination. Even some of our most personal and private moments require the union of two or more forces.

The Great Rite is a celebration of the earth's fertility (we wouldn't be here without it), but it's a mistake to think that the Great Rite, by extension, is simply about male-female sex. Unless the individuals doing the coupling are actively trying to conceive a child, the Great Rite is always to some degree symbolic. If it were only about reproductive sex, the Great Rite would be limited to people of childbearing age who are not using contraception. That would exclude 99 percent of Witches I know due to age or not wanting to conceive a child.

The Great Rite is for everyone. It presents an opportunity to get caught up in the power and energy that fuels the universe, often while engaging in one of the most sensuous and indulgent of human experiences—sex. Sex is indulgent because it involves nearly every aspect of our existence—our bodies, our minds, and our emotions—and when we combine sex with the Great Rite, we activate the spiritual part of ourselves as well. Taken together that's nearly world-shattering, and not just because of the orgasms.

When we celebrate the Great Rite physically, we are tapping into some of Witchcraft's ultimate mysteries. Around us we can feel the universe, the gods, magick, and the powers that create new things. During the actual Great Rite I feel absolutely connected to the person I love the most in the world, and that connection is then shared in a physical, emotional, and spiritual way.

Even when enacting the Great Rite "just" in token, we are connecting to things so much greater than ourselves. We are connecting to the process that turns grapes into wine and wheat into bread. The Great Rite in all its forms connects us to the fertility of the earth and the universe's power to create. It also connects me to my coven, my Craft, my tradition, and the greater Pagan community.

In the course of writing this book, I've also come to the conclusion that the meanings behind the Great Rite in token and in truth are very different. There are ideas expressed by the symbolic Great Rite that I often neglect when experiencing the Great Rite naked with a partner. And not surprisingly, the goals and aims of the Great Rite performed in truth are very different from those that surround the Great Rite in token.

Sacred Sex In History and the More Modern Origins of the Great Rite

One of the inspirations for the modern Great Rite is the *hieros gamos*, or sacred marriage. In the sacred marriage a human being (generally a king or other high-ranking person) is "wed" to an individual representing a goddess or god. The two then have sexual intercourse, with the sex act bestowing blessings upon the leader and ensuring fertility for the land they rule. Sacred marriage did not exist everywhere in the ancient world, but it was a very real practice, existing in (at least) ancient Sumer, Egypt, and Cyprus.[210]

The first literary reference we have to sacred marriage is a 4,000-year-old poem from ancient Sumer. In that poem the goddess Inanna tells the tale of how she made love to the shepherd Dumuzi, who himself eventually rose to the level of deity. The poem of Inanna and Dumuzi either inspired the sacred marriage or at least set it to verse, and is wildly explicit.[211] Like many ancient pagan cultures, Sumer was extremely sex-positive, which extended to how its deities were portrayed in myth.

The term *hieros gamos* is also sometimes used to refer to the practice of sacred prostitution. In ancient Babylon the goddess Ishtar proclaimed herself "a prostitute compassionate am I," and when her joy-maidens made love to clients, those men were thought to be engaging in something sacred

---

210. Burkert, *Greek Religion*, 108.
211. Dening, *The Mythology of Sex*, 48.

and divine.[212] (It's also worth noting that there are several modern scholars who discount the idea of sacred prostitution in its entirety.[213]) Ishtar, along with Astarte, Inanna, and Aphrodite, are the goddesses generally referenced when people discuss sacred prostitution, but Aphrodite's association with the practice is a bit problematic.

Aphrodite was most certainly revered by courtesans, and sex with a female prostitute was even called *ta aphrodisia,* but the evidence for sacred prostitution involving Aphrodite is a bit scanty.[214] The Greek geographer, historian, and writer Strabo (64/63 BCE–24 CE) is generally used to link Aphrodite to the practice of sacred prostitution, but his work is full of contradictions. In his work *Geography* he references a major temple for Aphrodite in the Greek city of Corinth that "was so rich that it owned more than a thousand temple slaves, courtesans, whom both men and women had dedicated to the goddess. And therefore it was also on account of these women that the city was crowded with people and grew rich."[215]

But in this particular instance he's referencing something from Corinth's past, and there's never been any archeological evidence found in Corinth suggesting such a structure to Aphrodite. A temple with "more than a thousand slaves" would have left a large footprint, and it's just not there. And just a couple of paragraphs later Strabo references "a small temple of Aphrodite," omitting any reference of a gigantic temple complex.[216]

A more poetic interpretation of sacred marriage can be found in Homer's *Iliad,* when Zeus and Hera make love upon Mount Ida:

> So speaking, the son of Kronus, caught his wife in his arms. There underneath them the divine earth broke into young, fresh

---

212. Dening, *The Mythology of Sex,* 54.

213. Budin, *The Myth of Sacred Prostitution in Antiquity.*

214. Rosenzweig, *Worshipping Aphrodite,* 104.

215. Strabo, *Geography,* chap. 6, http://www.perseus.tufts.edu/hopper/text?doc=Strab.%208.6.20&lang=original.

216. Strabo, *Geography,* chap. 6, http://www.perseus.tufts.edu/hopper/text?doc=Perseus%3Atext%3A1999.01.0198%3Abook%3D8%3Achapter%3D6%3Asection%3D21.

grass, and into dewy clover, crocus and hyacinth

so thick and soft it held hard ground deep away from them.

There they lay down together and drew about them a golden

wonderful cloud, and from it the glimmering dew descended. [217]

In later Greek poetry the earth and sky's union that comes from the falling rain was described as a marriage that ensured the fertility of the world.[218]

Taken as a whole we can be confident that many ancient pagans revered sex for both its physical pleasures and its ability to help individuals touch the sacred. Union, outside the bounds of penises and vaginas, was also seen as an important component of a well-functioning earth. Sex was not always sacred, but it always had the potential to be, and it was not something to be vilified or embarrassed about, at least until the Christians took over.

Sadly, sacred sex, along with the sacred marriage, disappeared for several centuries in a spiritual sense due to the prominence of Christianity. People still had sex for enjoyment obviously, and I'm sure that some of it was even transcendent, but it was not something spoken of in polite company. The closest we get to anything resembling the sacred marriage are allusions to the lance and the Grail in the stories of King Arthur. But sacred sex would make a triumphant return in the nineteenth century, largely due to the efforts of one man.

History has very little to say about Paschal Beverly Randolph (1825–1875), but he would ultimately have a tremendous impact on modern magick and, indirectly, Modern Witchcraft. That Randolph was a free man of color (his mother was of African descent, his absent father a white man) makes his accomplishments all the more extraordinary. Randolph's life reads like an adventure book. He visited every continent in the world with the exception of Antarctica, was a part of numerous fraternal and esoteric orders, and wrote over a hundred books. His work would influence generations of occultists, including Helena Blavatsky,

---

217. Homer, *The Iliad of Homer*, trans. Richard Lattimore, 303. Line spacing in the original.

218. Burkert, *Greek Religion*, 108.

Theodor Reuss (one of the German founders of the O.T.O.), and Aleister Crowley. He was also a confidant of President Abraham Lincoln.

Randolph wrote extensively on magick, Spiritualism, mythology, and other occult topics, but he is best remembered today for his writings on sex magick. Randolph saw sex not just as a way to build up magickal energy but also as a "physical substance" made up of three components: electrical, magnetic, and chemical.[219] When the female and male versions of these substances combined during sex, Randolph believed they created an aura around the couple, an aura capable of attracting higher powers.

Randolph also saw sex as a power capable of revealing the secrets of the universe. He believed that if a man and a woman orgasmed at precisely the same time after an extended session of lovemaking, "germs of knowledge, knowledge itself, and magic power descend to, and find lodgment in our souls, the mystic doors of which are then instantly opened and as suddenly closed again."[220] Just what entered a pair of lovers' souls was dictated by what they were thinking of at orgasm. Evil thoughts invite evil energies, but Randolph generally thought of this operation as a positive one.

Randolph's belief that sex served to attract higher powers and could be used to experience the divine roughly parallels the modern Great Rite, yet few Witches today are aware of Randolph's contributions to the modern Craft. When people comment on the more modern origins of the Great Rite, they tend to invoke the name of Aleister Crowley, who would refine many of Randolph's ideas and make them an essential part of many twentieth-century occult and Pagan practices.

In his day Crowley was notorious for practicing "sex magick," but as modern commentators such as Lon Milo DuQuette have pointed out, Crowley's goal with sex magick was both creation and ecstasy. Orgasm reveals a moment of absolute truth where we become divine, and in that moment of divinity we can create anything with our com-

---

219. Alexandrian, *The Great Work of the Flesh*, 39.

220. Paschal Beverly Randolph, "Appendix A: The Ansairetic Mystery," in *Paschal Beverly Randolph* by John Patrick Deveney, 316.

bined wills.[221] Like the Great Rite, Crowley's exploration of sex magick was about the celebration of something new and becoming one with a higher power. Crowley most certainly saw his practices as open to everyone, as his sexual adventures were not limited to any one gender.

Crowley also took his ideas about sex magick and put them into a more poetic (and publicly acceptable) form in *Liber XV: The Gnostic Mass* (generally known today as simply the *Gnostic Mass*), the central rite of the O.T.O. In the Gnostic Mass, bread and wine are used to represent what is created when two forces come together through sexual union. The Gnostic Mass is one of Crowley's most beautiful pieces of liturgy. It's also rife with sexual imagery if one knows where to look ("By the virtue of the Rod! Be this bread the Body of God!"[222]).

Writing in an age when explicit sexuality on the printed page was still mostly verboten, Crowley peppered his magickal writings with references to cups, rods, lances, grails, roses, and rods—all allusions to penises and vaginas obviously. The language of "the grail and the lance" would later be used by Witches engaging in the symbolic Great Rite, linking that particular practice directly to the sex magick of Crowley.

Not surprisingly, something approximating the Great Rite also turns up in Leland's *Aradia*. After the goddess Diana has been conjured, the Witches of the Italian Witch-cult were said to do the following:

> All shall sit down to the supper all naked, men and women, and, the feast over, they shall dance, sing, make music, **and then love in the darkness**, with all the lights extinguished; for it is the Spirit of *Diana* who extinguishes them, and so they will dance and make music in her praise.[223]

The Witches of *Aradia* aren't exactly performing the Great Rite in this instance, but they are looking upon sex as something sacred, and that sex is also being engaged in while Diana and her partner are present.

---

221. Crowley, *The Best of the Equinox: Sex Magic*, intro. Lon Milo Duquette, xi.
222. Ibid., 19.
223. Leland, *Aradia*, 14. Emphasis Mankey.

Today Witches who perform the Great Rite look for inspiration in the paganisms of antiquity, along with the more modern interpretations shared by Crowley and Randolph. Because the Great Rite encompasses so many different aspects of creation, places to find inspiration for it are limitless. Just like there was no one particular way to celebrate the *hieros gamos* in the ancient world, there is no one particular way to celebrate the Great Rite today, but some ways are more common than others.

CHAPTER SIXTEEN

The Great Rite in Token

The Great Rite is most often performed *in token,* usually in conjunction with the ceremony of cakes and ale (or cakes and wine). The Great Rite in token serves as the symbolic representation of two forces coming together, and most often involves the athame and chalice (with the chalice containing wine or some other liquid). I have a lot of friends who call this rite "the knife in the cup," and this representation of the Great Rite is so widespread that it's become a nearly iconic expression of Wiccan-Witchcraft.

Traditionally, many Witch tools were categorized by what type of energy they were believed to contain. "Aggressive" tools such as athames and swords were said to have masculine energy, while more delicate tools such as the chalice (or cup) were said to have feminine energy. So the knife in the cup was seen as the symbolic union of male and female energy, with all the accompanying thoughts of male-female fertility. As gender identity has become recognized as more fluid over the last twenty years, there are many Witches who have grown uncomfortable with the knife in the cup.

Witchcraft is an inclusive spiritual tradition. It does not discriminate and accepts all sorts of sexualities and gender identities. If someone is uncomfortable with the athame and chalice being used in the symbolic Great Rite, they are free to discard and/or modify it. Witchcraft is *always* about what works for the individual Witch or coven. People who discard the cup and knife aren't fundamentally changing Wiccan-Witchcraft, and they deserve to be supported.

However, an athame is not a penis and a cup is not a vagina. When my wife plunges her athame into our coven's chalice, I don't picture a vagina being penetrated by a penis in my mind's eye. I simply see two forces coming together. It's true that for many people the athame is connected to the God and the chalice is connected to the Goddess, but that's only one interpretation. The great thing about symbols is that they can be interpreted in a whole host of ways.

Female-male copulation is a part of nature though, and there's certainly nothing wrong with celebrating that. Most of us have a mother and a father after all. And there's also nothing wrong with celebrating female-female and male-male copulation either, for they are also a part of nature. There are also humans who are completely asexual and organisms that reproduce asexually. There are all sorts of sexualities, and I believe that all of them are expressed in the Lord and Lady (and all that lies between them).

I find it useful to get past the sexual symbolism that's often incorporated into the Great Rite and get down to what the rite truly expresses. In ritual, the symbolic Great Rite has a multitude of meanings and is used to celebrate several different though related things, such as the following.

The Union of Two Forces. For a long time this was often expressed by the Goddess and God and implied sexual intercourse, but any two aspects of deity work here, along with more metaphorical concepts such as sun/moon, earth/sky, land/sea, and night/day. Any two things that come together and create something new are worth celebrating. And anytime two hearts unite, they create a new relationship and a new love.

The Natural World. Everything that we see around us in nature essentially comes from the combination of at least two forces. The Grand Canyon, for instance, was shaped by water and eroding rock. Without each force, that wonder would not exist, and everything that grows in our backyard is a combination of various forces and elements.

I've heard the line "worlds are born" used in conjunction with the symbolic Great Rite, and it's an expression I absolutely love. Our earth is just one piece of a much larger natural universe, and one that wasn't created by sex. We aren't here strictly because of human procreation; we are here because stars exploded and worlds were born. When we enact the symbolic Great Rite, we are connecting to the things in our backyard and to the vast cosmos above us.

The Triumph of Life over Death. In my coven's Great Rite ceremony, we use the line "Life is more than a gift; it is a promise. All that dies shall be reborn." For me the Great Rite is a reminder that no matter how bleak the world may look in January, life will eventually return. Nature teaches us that there can't be new life without death, and that both stages of existence are important natural processes.

I will die, and you will die, but because of the Goddess and God we will eventually be reborn and return to this world that we love. When we enact the Great Rite we are acknowledging that to live is also to die. The natural world is full of death, and so are many of the myths that make up the Witch's Wheel of the Year, but in both instances life does eventually return.

The Blessings of Fertility. Despite humanity's best efforts over the last two hundred years, the earth remains a remarkably fertile place. Humans produce nearly four billion tons of food every year, and that is in addition to what is produced by the very fertile natural world around us every day.[224] The fact that most of us, at least in the industrialized world, are well fed and have enough to eat is a true blessing. It's easy to simply equate fertility with the creation of babies, but fertility encompasses more than our ability to reproduce; it's linked to the ecosystems that sustain and maintain our lives on this earth.

When I enact the symbolic Great Rite, I stop to think of all those wheat and corn fields out in the Midwest, California's Central Valley (where most of my produce comes from), and England's apple orchards,

---

224. "Key Facts on Food Loss and Waste You Should Know!," Food and Agriculture Organization of the United Nations, accessed October 13, 2018, http://www.fao.org/save-food/resources/keyfindings/en/.

which produce the hard cider I love so much. The world is a very fertile place and it's a fertility that should be celebrated.

CAKES AND ALE

In many Witch circles today the symbolic Great Rite is performed in tandem with a part of ritual known as cakes and ale (or cakes and wine). Because the Great Rite in token usually involves wine (or ale or some other beverage), the two rites dovetail nicely and even share some of the same sentiments. While many Witches quickly rush through cakes and ale, I find it to be a vital and important part of coven ritual for a variety of different reasons.

Cakes and ale involves the sharing of food and drink, most often near the end of ritual. While the ceremony is called cakes and ale, any sort of food stuff works as a "cake." Over the years my coven has used all manner of baked goods as cakes. Cookies, rolls, bread, and cupcakes all come to mind, along with fruits and vegetables. For ale we've used wine, cider, mead, beer, milk, and sparkling grape juice. Any kind of liquid can be used as ale, though wine is probably the most traditional. A completely alcohol-free cakes and ale ceremony is acceptable and is a must for covens with recovering alcoholics. (I have a great deal of sympathy here since my own mother is an alcoholic.)

At its core, cakes and ale serves as a celebration of the abundance and fertility of the earth. We are able to eat cakes because the earth provides us with grain and all the other things necessary to turn that grain into something edible. Most of us also see cakes and ale as a tangible gift from the gods.

Because they are a gift from the gods, cakes and ale serves as a moment of thanksgiving during Witch ritual. We thank the gods for what they've given us, and our thanks help to sustain them in turn. When handing out cakes and ale, I'm reminded of all the other gifts that my Lord and Lady have given me over the years (my coven, the Craft, and dozens more). We should be thankful for what we've been given, and cakes and ale provides an opportunity to do just that.

The Pagan group the Church of All Worlds has a saying that I've always found applicable to cakes and ale: "Water shared is life shared."

While my coven's cup is generally filled with wine instead of water, the sentiment is still valid. Groups that share food and drink with one another generally stay together. Sharing cakes and ale is a way for a group to bond and forge the ties that will keep them together.

The phrase *cakes and ale* is a traditional English one that means "the good life," [225] and there are few things better in life than enjoying good food and drink with chosen family while in a magickal space. The phrase first showed up in Shakespeare's *Twelfth Night* in 1602 in the line "Dost thou think, because thou art virtuous, there shall be no more cakes and ale?" Because of the deeper meaning of the phrase cakes and ale, I find it preferable to cakes and wine, though the latter is nearly as common in witchy circles (with wine also being more common in my own chalice).

Cakes and ale serves another purpose in ritual: it's a great way to ground. After an hour of raising energy and praising the gods, putting some food and drink in the belly is an easy way to come back down to earth, so to speak. Eating and drinking help reconnect us to the physical world, which is so easy to forget about while in the magick circle. In the few instances when I've left a ritual without receiving cakes and ale, I've found myself a little out of sorts.

Before being consumed in ritual, the cakes and ale should be blessed by whoever is leading the ritual. When with my coven, I generally use the beverage that was activated in the Great Rite and then pass that cup around the circle. At large gatherings I use individual cups for everyone, blessing them with my athame, which still usually has a bit of the liquid held by the cup in the Great Rite. My wife suggests passing around the cup before the cakes to avoid food particles getting in the wine.

TRADITIONAL WITCH CAKES

There is no one "traditional" Witch cake, but there's one that comes close. In Charles Leland's *Aradia* there are instructions for a Witch's supper, with some rudimentary guidelines for specific Witch cakes. The exact recipe is not given, but the cakes should be made of "meal and salt,

---

225. The Phrase Finder, https://www.phrases.org.uk/meanings/257200.html.

honey and water." [226] Incantations to say over the meal and salt are also given, along with conjurations for the deities Cain and Diana.

The most well-known conjuration from *Aradia* is to be said immediately before the cakes are baked:

Conjuration of Diana.
I do not bake the bread, nor with it salt,
Nor do I cook the honey with the wine;
I bake the body and the blood and soul,
The soul of (great) *Diana*, that she shall
Know neither rest nor peace, and ever be
In cruel suffering till she will grant
What I request, what I most desire,
I beg it of her from my very heart!
And if the grace be granted, O *Diana!*
In honour of thee I will hold this feast,
Feast and drain the goblet deep,
We will dance and wildly leap,
And if thou grant'st the grace which I require,
Then when the dance is wildest, all the lamps
Shall be extinguished and we'll freely love! [227]

Parts of this invocation are quite lovely, but the idea of baking "the body and the blood and soul" of Great Diana has always struck me as veering dangerously close to ideas about the Catholic Eucharist. I know very few (if any) Witches who believe that eating a ritual cake counts as eating the soul of a deity, but that doesn't take away from the fun of chanting Italian Witch incantations while baking. It's also possible that the invocation is simply equating eating grain with eating the soul of the earth, which to me is far less creepy than "body and blood."

The threats toward Diana are out of place in most Witch traditions today, but such refrains are still common among many Catholics. "Saint shaming" is a very real practice, and effigies of saints are sometimes sat

---

226. Leland, *Aradia*. Opening of Chapter 2, page 136 in the Phoenix Publishing edition.
227. Leland, *Aradia*. Page 140 in the Phoenix Publishing edition; quote from the original Leland translation.

in corners, drowned in water, buried, or placed upside down if devotees feel that the saint is not working hard enough for them.[228] It's possible that threats toward Diana stem from this tradition.

While Leland did not leave us with detailed instructions on just how to make a Witch cake, it's easy enough to make cookies containing salt, honey, water, and meal. Here is a recipe to make something equivalent to what the Italian Witches of 1899 might have been eating.

Ingredients

1 tablespoon honey

½ cup white or red wine

½ cup brown sugar

⅓ cup oil or melted butter (I prefer butter)

½ teaspoon baking powder

¼ teaspoon salt

2 teaspoons spring water

2¼ cups flour (I've seen some recipes that call for half this amount of flour, substituting an equal amount of oatmeal.)

You can also include any spices you might like, such as ground cloves, cinnamon, ginger, or anise seeds. Sugar granules can also be sprinkled on the tops of your cakes if you so desire.

Instructions

Preheat oven to 350 degrees Fahrenheit.

Mix all the ingredients together minus the flour. Slowly begin to add in the flour while saying:

I conjure thee, O Meal!
Who art indeed our body, since without thee
We could not live, thou who (at first as seed)
Before becoming flower went in the earth,

---

228. Rollin, *Santa Muerte*, 50–52. I love this book, and I love Santa Muerte, and she's been especially helpful to me while writing this book. (I'm also far too frightened of her to ever engage in saint shaming.)

Where all deep secrets hide, and then when ground
Didst dance like dust in the wind, and yet meanwhile
Didst bear with thee in flitting, secrets strange!
I conjure thee so that I might make a cake in honor of Diana,
She who is the Great Lady and Queen of the Witches. [229]

Once all the flour has been added, add any extra spices, and knead the dough on a well-floured surface such as a cutting board.

Knead for ten minutes, adding extra water or flour as needed. If your dough is too dry, add a few drops of water. If it's too gooey, add some more flour.

Drop about a teaspoon of the dough onto a well-greased cookie sheet and shape into a crescent moon with your hands.

Before placing your cookies in the oven, say one final conjuration:

We did not bake the bread, nor with it wine,
We did not cook the honey with the vine,
We baked the body and the blood and soul,
The soul of Diana who makes the years roll.
She knew neither rest nor peace,
In cruel suffering no torments cease.
Until she granted what we most desired,
The arch of magick growing ever higher.
We begged it of her from our very hearts!
And in that grace was granted by her mighty arts.
In honor of thee we hold this feast. [230]

Bake the cookies for about twenty-five minutes, turning them over once about halfway through to prevent scorching on the bottom. If you want to sprinkle a little extra sugar on top of them, do so when you flip them over.

This is a very simple recipe and can be easily adapted. For sweeter cakes add a bit more honey or sugar. I also like to use hard apple cider instead of wine in the fall. Any sort of water can be substituted for

---

229. Adapted from *Aradia*, with a lot left out. It's a really long invocation!
230. Adapted from *Aradia* by me, because I like everything to rhyme when possible.

spring water, but I like using natural sources when I can. And the cakes pack a bit of an extra punch when water from a sacred spot is used in their creation.

LIBATIONS

Because the gods share with us, we also share our cakes and ale with them. This is known as a libation, and most covens keep a libation bowl on their altars to collect offerings for the gods. In my coven we reserve at least one healthy drink of our ritual wine for deity, along with a couple of cakes or slices of bread. Post-ritual we take that libation outside and leave it near our lemon tree as an offering to the gods and the fairy folk who reside in our backyard.

Libations serve as a way of offering thanks to the gods for all they have given us. They are a token of our appreciation, but they power the gods as well. Back in 1954 Gerald Gardner wrote that "our gods are not all-powerful, they need our aid. They desire good to us, fertility for man, beast and crops, but they need our help to bring it about; and by our dances and other means they get that help." [231]

For many Witches it's strange to read that the gods have limitations, but just like Gardner, I believe they do. Just as there are limits to what human beings can do, I believe the natural world imposes some limitations on the gods as well.

Presenting the Lord and Lady with libations empowers them. The gods don't consume their cakes and ale like we humans do, but I believe that they receive the essence of that food and drink when we offer it to them, and through that essence they receive power. Libations aren't the only way to empower the gods, but they are an easy way to do so.

Libations can be offered to the gods in several different ways. The most common way is to leave whatever offering you have outside in a rather secluded place. Many of us don't have a large backyard (or sometimes any yard at all), and that's just fine. Bushes, tree trunks, grassy patches, and bodies of water are all fine spaces for libations. In some traditions it's considered good luck to leave your offerings at a crossroads or

---

231. Gardner, *Witchcraft Today*, 91.

other liminal space, but what's most important is to leave your libation safely and discreetly.

In many ancient pagan cultures fire was used as an instrument to send offerings to the gods. It was believed that the offering was being accepted if the smoke from the fire went straight up into the air and that it was being rejected if the smoke did not. When I'm at an outdoor festival, I will often pour my libation onto a fire, but it's far less practical to do this when I'm at home.

Another alternative is to throw your libation into the garbage, sink, or compost pile after an appropriate amount of time. If this is my only alternative, I like to leave my libation upon my altar for at least an hour or two post-ritual to ensure that the gods receive the essence of what I've left for them. I believe the gods "consume" my libation when I take it outside, so if I have to dispose of my offering indoors, I believe it's important to wait a while before doing so.

There are many covens who won't consume their cakes and ale until they have been offered to the gods and placed in the libation bowl. This is not necessary, but I think it shows deference and respect, feelings the gods certainly appreciate. When we operate in sacred space, the gods are often equal partners in our magickal endeavors, so sharing the food and drink they helped us to receive is the least we can do.

Most covens mix their offerings of cakes and ale in the libation bowl, but my wife frowns upon this practice. As she's said to our coven many times, "Would you like to eat bread soaked in wine? I didn't think so." So instead of putting our wine into the libation bowl, we leave a little bit at the bottom of our chalice and then take it outside to give to the gods. When it comes to libations, there are no absolute right or wrongs. Just show some respect and be thankful for the blessings in your life.

SYMBOLIC GREAT RITE RITUALS

Though the Great Rite in token is symbolic, that doesn't mean it's devoid of magick or energy. Because the Great Rite is a celebration of creating something new, the people participating directly in the rite should charge their athames, cups, or whatever other tool they will use while performing it. When I enact the symbolic Great Rite, I actively focus on opening myself up to the energy of the natural world around me. I then channel that energy and place it in whatever tool I'll be using. When that energy mixes with the energy of my High Priestess and the wine in our cup, we've created something new.

I've heard some people call the symbolic Great Rite "drink and dunk," but it's no empty gesture; it's about creating a new energy and getting in touch with the powers of creation. The Great Rite doesn't have to involve a huge amount of energy, but it should never be treated as a mundane act.

The Great Rite can be performed alone, provided the individual Witch has access to at least two different tools. The first version of the Great Rite I ever enacted was as a solitary Witch at my dedication ritual. I simply used one of my fingers as an athame, dipping it into the bottle of wine I had taken with me to that rite.

The Basic Great Rite/Cakes and Ale

Tools Needed: Athame or wand, cup full of wine or some other beverage

High Priest: *Life is more than a gift; it is a promise. All that dies shall be reborn.*

High Priestess: *And now we celebrate the most ancient of magicks, the magick of joining.*

High Priest: *The athame is to the sky*

High Priestess: *As the cup is to the earth.*

The High Priest plunges their athame into the cup.

Both: *United in life and abundance, blessed be!*

High Priestess (holding the cup up in the air): *May the Lady and Lord bless this drink as they have blessed this coven. So mote it be!*

Another covener takes the plate of cakes and holds them up between the High Priestess and High Priest. The High Priest dips his athame into the wine, and upon removing it, lightly touches each cake with the athame.

High Priest: *May the Lord and Lady bless these cakes as they have blessed this coven. So mote it be!*

The High Priestess and High Priest drink from the cup and then pass it clockwise to the other coveners. Then they each take a cake before passing the rest to the other coveners. Libations are put in the libation bowl. Cakes and ale continues for as long as the High Priestess wishes.

This version of the Great Rite comes directly from my coven's Book of Shadows, and when I originally wrote it I thought it would be temporary and that I'd eventually come up with something better. Seven years later this is still the version I'm using, and for good reason. It hits all the high points for me: triumph over death, rebirth, joining, and the joy of creating something new. Several years ago my entire coven started saying it aloud with my wife and me while we performed it, which is a great way to involve an entire group in the Great Rite.

The line "The athame is to the sky as the cup is to the earth" is one that can easily be amended, depending on what works best for the Witches in attendance. Some covens might want to use the more traditional sounding "The athame is to the Lord as the cup is to the Lady." There's no right or wrong here, but only what's best for each group or Witch.

The Great Rite/Cakes and Ale, All Chalices Edition

This version of the symbolic Great Rite requires three different chalices, along with three different humans to hold those three cups. (I will use High Priestess 1, High Priestess 2, and a High Priest in this version.) Because this rite involves pouring the contents of two chalices into an empty one, I like the two glasses to be filled with a different liquid. This can be something simple, like water and wine (which is how the Greeks drank their vino), or it can be more elaborate, like champagne and orange juice (which is especially appropriate if your ritual is in the morning).

High Priestess 1: *Within our hands we all hold the power of creation.*

High Priestess 2: *Now let us celebrate that power with the greatest of rites,*

High Priest: *While remembering that all who die shall be reborn.*

High Priestess 1: *We now celebrate the original magick,*

High Priestess 2: *The magick of joining.*

High Priestesses 1 and 2: *When two become one*

The two High Priestesses pour the contents of their chalices into the empty cup held by the High Priest.

High Priestesses 1 and 2: *And worlds are born.*

All: *May it ever be so.*

The High Priest then holds up his now full chalice and asks the Lady and Lord to bless its contents.

High Priest: *Gracious Goddess and Horned Lord, we ask that you bless this drink. May it serve as a reminder of your power and grace. Blessed be!*

High Priestess 2 then takes the tray of cakes and lifts them up in front of the High Priestess 1. High Priestess 1 then dips her fingers or athame into the High Priest's chalice and blesses the cakes.

High Priestess 1: *Gracious Goddess and Horned Lord, bless these cakes and may they ever connect us to you both and the beauty of this world. Blessed be!*

The High Priest hands the wine to the High Priestesses, who then pass it along to the rest of the coven. The cakes are passed out in a similar manner, with cakes and ale lasting for as long as the coven desires.

CHAPTER SEVENTEEN

The Great Rite in Truth

In my twenty-plus years in Witchcraft, I have had dozens of conversations about nearly every topic related to Wicca and/or Paganism, with the exception of the Great Rite in truth. For a long time it was something that existed only on the printed page in my world. It was a topic written about in Witchcraft books, but generally in a very clinical and uninspiring way. Sometimes writers would explain why it was being celebrated beyond the obvious, linking it to historical events or fertility, but exactly what the individuals doing the celebrating were getting out of it was left unsaid.

The Great Rite is a rather taboo subject in a lot of witchy circles, and much of that is because sex itself is still rather taboo in Western society. As a whole, Witches do a lot better than most people when it comes to the subject of sex, but it still sometimes leads to awkward conversations. The Great Rite is the most intimate of Witchcraft's mysteries, and many people just don't like sharing those kinds of experiences with others.

The Great Rite suffers from other problems too. Because many people perceive it as an exclusively heteronormative practice (an idea that I and many other Witches disagree with), there are some Witches and covens who want nothing to do with it. There are also people who have abused and sullied the idea of the Great Rite, using it as an excuse to coerce unwilling sexual partners into the bedroom.

In my own practice the Great Rite, along with drawing down the moon, are the greatest of Witchcraft's mysteries, and both are the hardest to fully achieve. There are most certainly rites for these two practices (such as the ones in this book), but simply saying the words in those rituals doesn't make drawing down the moon or the Great Rite happen. There are rituals for the Great Rite because those rites help to set up the experience, but the acting out of a ritual script is not the experience. The words in a ritual are there to help facilitate the experience, but the words themselves do not create the experience.

To fully draw down the moon or experience the Great Rite relies on a great many factors, and many of them are out of our direct control. Both rely on the cooperation of deity, and sometimes the Goddess and God just don't want to show up. They are both also activities that require our body and mind to act in concert with each other and with the gods. My partner and I might want to enact the Great Rite, but if one of us can't breathe due to a head cold, it's probably not going to work. Sexual activity requires breathing, and if one of us can't breathe, things are not going to go as planned, no matter how badly we might want them to.

Activities like the Great Rite also require cooperation from the world around us. On a Saturday night when Ari and I were planning on performing the Great Rite, our neighbors were having a party, and it was impossible to concentrate while just fifteen feet away forty people were listening to awful music and having inane conversations. Sometimes the distractions are even more mundane. For example, it's hard to be in the mood for the Great Rite when it's 100 degrees outside and your home lacks air conditioning.

The Great Rite can be hard to do, and it's something that people don't often talk or write about, but it's still something worth doing because the results are extraordinary. It provides a transcendent moment where we become one with our deities, our universe, our earth, and each other. This sounds like a pretty big event, and it is, which is why it's difficult to do sometimes. But Witchcraft was never meant to be easy, and the greatest mysteries are often the ones that are the most elusive.

When I'm asked what makes a good ritual, I often reply with the word *connection*. Witch ritual is most often about connecting with the earth, the gods, the coven, the turning of the seasons, the ancestors, magick, and many other things. The word connection also applies to the Great Rite. There are obvious reasons for this (two bodies penetrating each other are certainly connecting), but when we participate in the Great Rite we are connecting to other *bigger* things too.

Connecting with a Partner (or Partners). Ari is more than just my wife and best friend; she's my magickal partner. In circle we act like extensions of each other, and we often know what the other is thinking before we think it. The Great Rite has been essential in drawing us closer together as working partners. To share magick and energy in such an intimate way deepens the bonds between partners.

Sex is something that can most definitely be a need shared between two people. I've had sex for the sake of having sex, but that's not the Great Rite. When we perform the Great Rite, we most often are inviting our gods and the watchtowers to join us in that experience, and that's not something most of us do on a day-to-day basis. Not only am I naked and vulnerable with my partner during the Great Rite, but I'm also sharing my gods with her (or him), allowing them to catch a glimpse into my spiritual self, and they are doing the same with me.

"Two becoming one" is something that sounds so clichéd, but it's what we are attempting to do when we practice the Great Rite. Just where you end and your partner begins should be hard to grasp. Obviously bodies are joining, but so are hearts, minds, and spirits. When I'm truly lost in the magick and mystery of the Great Rite, the two of us do become one, if only for a little while.

Connecting with the Natural World. It's become harder and harder to connect with the natural world in the age of cell phones, but Witches do it better than most, and one way to do it is through the Great Rite. I don't know of any creatures in the wild that read books or watch TV, but almost every living thing on this planet copulates (or at least wants

to). Does the history of the world from the smallest single-celled creature to us today flash through my mind during the Great Rite sometimes? Yes, it does.

I think we touch something deep in our genetic code when we participate in the Great Rite. We are connecting with everyone and everything that has come before us. In those moments my partner and I are
one with the natural world. Instead of fighting nature, I embrace her
and the joys, instincts, and freedom of choice[232] she has given me and
every other living creature throughout the ages.

Connecting with the Greater Universe. I always come back to the
phrase "and worlds are born" when thinking of the Great Rite. While
the earth has certainly played a large role in our existence today, we
wouldn't be here without greater forces colliding, expanding, and transforming throughout the cosmos. We don't think of it very often, but we
are made of stardust, and our world is just one among possibly millions
or even billions of others.

Opening up our consciousness to energies beyond the terrestrial
earth is also a part of the Great Rite. It's not necessary to imagine yourself as a moon or a star while making love, but we are connected to
those bodies just as we are to our backyards or the rivers and oceans we
live near. We journey through the world on our feet, and we journey
through the universe on our blue marble of a planet.

Connecting with Our Deities. The Great Rite also serves as a way to
connect with the goddesses and gods we worship, honor, and interact
with. During the Great Rite we aren't drawing them down necessarily (we want to remember the experience after all), but we are opening
ourselves up to their energy and their presence. It's an experience we
share with them, and while we are experiencing it we further our understanding of them.

I'm not the god Pan during the Great Rite, but I can feel him hop-
ping around in my brain. He shares his lustiness, prowess, and energy
with me, all while allowing me to remember doing the Great Rite and

---

232. That freedom of choice can just as well be the choice not to have sex, which is also
    perfectly natural.

connecting with all those other powers that are a part of it. At the same time, since I'm one with my partner, I can feel her goddesses (generally Aphrodite) within and without her too.

Sex is a sacred and holy act, something most Witches are cognizant of. In our myths, our gods have sex, and their sex often powers and changes the world. Celibate deities are deities that don't understand the human condition. The Great Rite is not something just humans participate in; I'm sure our gods do it as well!

The Great Rite helps us tap into a multitude of different energies, with some being more dominant than others, depending on the individuals involved and the reasons behind the rite's enactment. Sometimes during the Great Rite I feel very close to the Horned God, and sometimes it brings me closer to the natural world, and other times all I can see in my mind's eye are swirling spiral-shaped galaxies. No experience is ever the same, which only adds to the ritual's power.

One of the reasons the Great Rite is so effective at creating these experiences is because *sex is an altered state of consciousness.* When people think of altered states, they often think of drugs and alcohol or perhaps some sort of deep meditative state, but sex works too. Much of our rational brain shuts down during sex (think about where the blood goes!), opening our minds up to other worlds and experiences.

Sexual activity is also a magickal powerhouse. When we build the cone of power, we often think of dancing, music, etc., as a way of creating it, but sex can do that too. For two people who are intimate with each other, sex might be the best way to create the cone of power! The energy created from sex comes from our wills but also the muscles we use to grind, thrust, lick, kiss, and tease. There's a third energy that's often a part of sex too: the energy that comes from anticipation and excitement.

Energy builds differently during sex too. For many of us it builds slowly, with every kiss and caress. The energy is finally released during orgasm, a powerful piece of magick in its own right. Sex has been used in magick for centuries (or longer), and the Great Rite is a way to tap into that magickal energy when it's needed most.

The Great Rite doesn't have to be used for a specific magickal purpose, but it can be if that's what's required. The best thing about the Great Rite is that it serves many different functions. It can be a way to unite with various powers and energies, and it can also be used to enact change in our lives. Our sexuality is a gift from the gods, not a curse, and the Great Rite celebrates that, because sex can be a celebratory act.

When I engage in the Great Rite, my partner and I are paying homage to our trust in each other. The idea that someone would want me to share my gods and body with them is such a beautiful thing! Why shouldn't it be honored with ritual, energy, and magick? The Great Rite is a gift, and how each of us experience it is going to be different, which is one of the reasons it's a mystery.

The Great Rite in Truth: When and Where

The Great Rite is unlike any other ritual in Modern Witchcraft. It's something my wife and I perform both in and out of the circle, during private rites involving just the two of us, and both before and after ritual with the coven (but not with the coven). No time is wrong for the Great Rite, and since it's such a personal (and generally private) act, the whens and wheres will differ from couple to couple.

When I draw down the moon, build the cone of power, or initiate someone, I do so inside a well-constructed magick circle, but I don't always hold to this standard when performing the Great Rite. Sometimes a couple will just feel the need to engage on a deeper level, and be lucky enough to find themselves in circumstances where they can participate in the Great Rite without prying eyes or causing a scandal. Because of this I've done the Great Rite outdoors in the moonlight and in my own bed (and I'll admit to my bed being the more comfortable of the two). When performing a more spontaneous Great Rite, there's usually no higher magickal purpose beyond our coupling than becoming closer to each other and our gods.

There are also times when I do the Great Rite in a properly consecrated magick circle. In those instances I'm generally engaging in the Great Rite for a specific purpose. Perhaps my wife or I need to conjure up some very specific magickal energy, and sex feels like the right avenue to do so. Performing the Great Rite also draws us closer to the Lord and Lady, and sometimes we want as much of their energy as possible in our circle when performing certain rites or charging a ritual tool.

I'll also admit that sex in a magick circle just feels extra sacred and adds extra power to our lovemaking. All that sexual energy that builds up stays right there with us, intensifying the experience. I've never cast a circle and said "Let's do the Great Rite!" just because of the extra spice it adds, but I've been tempted to do so a few times.

In most instances Ari and I engage in the Great Rite a few hours before or after a coven ritual. Doing it before a rite in the space where the coven will be meeting charges our ritual area to the extent that people can feel the sexual energy when they enter temple space. This is an especially powerful magickal trick when trying to conjure up the reproductive and sexual energies that are associated with sabbat celebrations such as Beltane. Like attracts like, after all, and nothing attracts more sexual energy than actual sex.

Because the Great Rite provides a deep link with the deities we honor and worship, performing the Great Rite before ritual brings the energies of the Goddess and God closer to us. I find it easier to draw down the Horned God within a few hours of the Great Rite because he and I have already actively engaged with each other on some level that day. I find that my wife draws down the Goddess much more easily after the Great Rite for similar reasons. When we stir up the energies of the gods, those energies don't just go away entirely after a drawing down or after the Great Rite.

For this reason, engaging in the Great Rite after ritual is an incredible experience. I'd never claim that I was "making love to the Goddess" after performing the Great Rite post-ritual, but her energies are definitely in there after the coven has done a drawing down. Those energies are different from what we experience on a day-to-day basis and add a level of power and gravitas to the Great Rite. If a Witch is performing the Great Rite for some sort of magickal purpose, it also adds the power of the gods to whatever they are working on.

Though it's not something my wife and I practice with our coven, there are many Modern Witches who perform the Great Rite during coven ritual. In such instances the coven is generally cut out of the circle and led some distance away from the ritual space before the rite begins. With everyone gone, the individuals leading the ritual perform the Great Rite, letting everyone in the circle back in when they're done.

Enacting the Great Rite in truth with the coven is generally done in times of great magickal need or perhaps to create a certain type of energy that can then be used by the entire coven. It can also be done to invoke certain deities. For instance, a coven might need the assistance of the Horned God at Samhain and use the Great Rite as a way to tap into his mysteries. The energies that are created during the Great Rite vary from couple to couple and group to group. The more the rite is practiced, the more likely it is for groups to find a need for the energies that come with the Great Rite.

In addition to performing the Great Rite in the middle of a ritual, there have been groups that perform the Great Rite in truth in front of the entire coven. This is not a common practice these days, and if you encounter a group that does this, I'd be cautious and ask for an explanation. If none is forthcoming, I'd head for the nearest exit. However, this technique can be used to raise a tremendous amount of power, so it's not entirely unjustified.

When it comes to the whens and wheres of the Great Rite, there's one absolute truth: *The Great Rite is always about informed consent.* The Great Rite shouldn't be done while drunk or with a partner who is reluctant. Since the Great Rite requires at least two participants, those two people need to be in sync when it comes to wanting to enact the Great Rite. The Great Rite is not something that should be associated with potential regret.

The Great Rite is also not a rite that is required of anyone in Modern Witchcraft. Every year I read stories of "High Priests" requiring their students and/or initiates to perform the "Great Rite" with them in order to advance in the Craft. Such claims are absolute bullshit, and anyone making them is unethical and a liar. *There is no sex in the circle without consent.* The Great Rite is meant to be performed by partners who are looking to connect on a deeper and more magickal level. Anyone who would use the idea of the Great Rite in order to coerce someone to have sex with them is not acting on a deeper or more magickal level.

THE GREAT RITE WITHOUT SEX?

Because sex creates an altered state of consciousness, indulges the physical senses, and requires a good amount of physical activity, I'm not sure the Great Rite can be completely replicated without it. However, there are rituals that can be done that create at least some of the feelings that are experienced during the Great Rite. Since I believe much of the Great Rite is about connection, any rite that fosters a deeper sense of that feeling will include at least some of what is felt during the Great Rite.

The following rite can be done with any working partner you are looking to grow closer to. It does not require the use of a magick circle, but I find that casting a circle and calling the quarters, etc., gives the rite a little extra oomph. Privacy and quiet are essential, so make sure to find a place where you won't be disturbed. A little incense or essential oil in a diffuser is also recommended. (I suggest rose, ylang-ylang, or sandalwood.)

This ritual can be done in place of a sexual Great Rite, and it can also be done as a prelude to the Great Rite in truth. I like using it as a "warm-up" to the physical Great Rite, but it also has connected me to people I would never have a sexual relationship with. I have many intimate friends I will never be intimate with in a physical sense, but I still want to grow closer to them. This rite is designed to help you do just that.

Soul to Soul: A Rite for Connection

Start by sitting in front of your partner, face to face, with legs crossed. You want to sit very close to each other, and if your knees end up touching, all the better. Each partner's left arm should be extended knuckles up, about even with their shoulder. Each partner's right arm should be extended palm up and sit about six inches lower than the left arm.

The rite begins with one partner saying "As above" and grasping their partner's right arm (or hand) with their left. When that hand or arm is grasped, the other partner should reply with "So below." This is repeated a second time (or a third or a fourth, depending on how many people are participating). Once your hands are linked, both of you should inhale and take a deep cleansing breath together.

Close your eyes and concentrate on the breathing of your partner. Hear their breath, and try to match your breath to theirs. When you have fixed upon their breathing, listen a bit more intently and try to hear their heartbeat. You also might feel that heartbeat in their hands or arms. Wherever you discover it, focus on it for a few moments and then open yourself up to it. Let your consciousness sink and focus just on that heartbeat and your partner's breath. Imagine yourself entering the light of their existence.

At this point you might encounter each other on a spiritual plane or you might simply feel connected to your partner emotionally. However you experience your partner, be sure to focus in on the connection. Imagine yourself connecting with your partner while opening up your own will so that they are able to experience the essence of you.

Once you have felt your partner on the spiritual plane, send your senses outward and feel the deities, guides, and/or ancestors around your partner. Feel their energies and reach out to them. They may want to meet you or invite you to partake in their energy. At the same time your partner should be becoming cognizant of the forces that help guide you in your own life.

Out past the powers immediately around your partner are the energies and magick of the greater world. Feel these too, and open yourself up to how your partner interacts with them. Are they attracted to water? Fire? How does the changing of the seasons affect them? Feel the earth through your partner's senses and try to understand their experiences.

Focus now on what lies beyond our planet, and project yourself up and out of our atmosphere into the greater cosmos. Visualize planets, stars, and asteroids, and feel your partner's energy and presence next to you while you do so. Know that you both are a part of the vast universe and that your spirits are free to journey where they like.

After feeling each other's energies out and beyond the earth, travel back the way you came. Go through the cosmos and back to the earth, touching your partner's gods and guides, and then once more simply focus on their energy. Concentrate again on their heartbeat and finally their breathing. When you both have returned spiritually to the ritual space, open your eyes and share what you've learned.

This rite relies on a physical and a spiritual connection and crosses over into what many call "astral travel." Astral travel is an out-of-body experience where our soul or essence experiences worlds and places beyond this mortal plane.[233] Many Witches visit this other space with a great deal of frequency, and others less so. No one has to believe in or experience astral projection to be a Witch, but for those who practice it, their experiences there are equal to and just as real as anything that happens in this world.

As a result, if you're limited by time and distance from actually physically being with a partner, the astral realm is a great place to engage in the Great Rite. For the experienced astral traveler, the results and sensations are the same as in our waking world. For Witches who already engage in the Great Rite on terra firma, practicing it astrally adds another layer to its magick and mystery.

THE RITUAL OF THE GREAT RITE

While I don't feel that ritual is completely necessary to capture the power of the Great Rite, I find that it does help. Putting ourselves in a "Witchcraft state of mind" during our work always increases the likelihood of success. I'm sure there are some couples and working partners who are capable of experiencing the transcendent nature of the Great Rite without any sort of ritual buildup, but performing the rites associated with it reinforces its value as a spiritual exercise.

Unlike drawing down the moon, which has a fairly standard set of ritual procedures associated with it, the Great Rite is much more of a blank canvas. I've read very little in the way of "Great Rite Rituals" over the years, and what I have read I have often disagreed with. Many of the instructions given for the Great Rite use language and terminology

---

233. If you're exploring the astral realm, I wholeheartedly recommend Devin Hunter's book *The Witch's Book of Spirits*, which was published in 2017 by Llewellyn. Devin includes techniques, along with descriptions of the places and things he's visited.

that excludes any pairing beyond male-female. Because I believe that the Great Rite is for everybody, I consciously avoid such terminology.

What follows is the rite I use with my wife when performing the Great Rite in a fully consecrated circle. I like to open with invocations to the deities we are close to, but that's not something required for the rite to be effective. Because this is the ritual I use with my wife, I'm using the terminology of "High Priestess" and "High Priest" in some places, though any combination of genders is appropriate. The Great Rite part of the ritual begins after the quarters have been called and the circle cast.

The last part of the rite involves kissing the invoking pentagram of spirit onto a partner. In my practice, "spirit" most often references everything in the universe and the cosmic glue that holds it together. Because the Great Rite allows us to become one with everything, its use feels especially appropriate here.

High Priest: *I call to the Great God, the Horned One of fertility and the wild spaces. Lend your energy to our rites so that we might grow closer to you. May we experience the mysteries and the wonders of this world through your power and might. Let us walk between the worlds and know what it is to celebrate life, the gods, and the joys that are the Craft! Be a part of our lovemaking as you are a part of our lives! Hail and welcome!*

After the God has been invoked, the High Priestess calls to the Goddess.

High Priestess: *I call to the Great Lady, the Mother of us all, she who has given us the blessings of life upon this earth! Touch us this night as we seek to explore your mysteries! Through your grace and your power may we grow closer to each other and this world that you have created! May we know what it is to go beyond ourselves, to touch the soul of another, and to touch what lies beyond ourselves. Bless and consecrate our lovemaking so that we might know you and the mysteries of the Craft! Hail and welcome!*

After the gods have been called, bless each other's body with this modified version of the fivefold kiss. Unlike the traditional fivefold kiss, this version is meant to be done slowly and to be enjoyed. Linger over the parts of each other that are pleasurable, and with every kiss know that you and your partner are experiencing something divine. There's no right or wrong about who is blessed first. Let the moment dictate what is appropriate.

High Priest: *And now we bless the most sacred of all temples, the body of you who is my High Priestess and Queen.*[234] *Within you lies the essence of all that I love and adore, and also the spirit of she who is Queen of all the wise.*[235] *With my lips I do cleanse and consecrate you!*

Blessed be thy feet that have brought thee to me this night.

Kisses feet.

Blessed be thy knees that have knelt at the sacred altar.

Kisses knees, first left then right.

Blessed be thy sex, source of all that is pleasurable and life-affirming.

Kisses genitals (and remember, you can do more than kiss here!).

Blessed be thy breasts, which are both beautiful and strong.

Kisses breasts/nipples, left first and then right.

Blessed be thy lips, which have spoken the truths of the Lady and Lord.

Kisses lips.

When both participants (or more, if you have several folks involved) have been cleansed and consecrated via the fivefold kiss, one partner should lie down on the bed or ground with their legs and arms outstretched (forming a star), with the other partner moving toward their feet. Beginning at the reclining partner's left foot, the invoking pentagram of spirit is drawn up the body, with kisses at the left foot, right hand, left hand, right foot, and finally the lips. This is repeated for both partners.

---

234. Alternatively, of course, "High Priest and King."

235. Alternatively, "and also the spirit of he who guards the portal between life and death."

Invoking Pentagram of Spirit

Starting at the left foot of the reclining partner, the partner doing the physical invocation begins to call upon the powers:

> *I invoke the mystery of mysteries, that which begat the universe and to that which we all return.*

Moving to the right hand, the rite is continued:

> *I invoke the power of the Great Goddess, she who is the beauty of the green earth and the white moon amongst the stars.*

The left hand is kissed and the Horned One is invoked:

> *I invoke the power of the Horned One, he who stands at the threshold of death and life eternal.*

The right foot is now kissed:

> *I invoke the powers of creation, the forces from which all worlds are born.*

And then the lips are kissed:

> *And finally I invoke thee, my love, for there is no part of us that is not of the Lord and Lady.*

Looking down at their partner, the one doing the physical invocation says:

We shall be as one with the universe and our gods. May the magick of joining empower us to fully walk between the worlds and experience something greater than ourselves. I shall be you and you shall be me, and together we will join together as one to feel the ecstasy and wonder of the universe. So mote it be!

The invocation is repeated for the other people, and after all the words have been said … well, what happens in the ritual circle during the Great Rite is a private matter. It's considered poor form to ever question another Witch about it.

THERE IS NO HOW-TO
WHEN IT COMES TO THE GREAT RITE

Unfortunately, there is no real how-to when it comes to the Great Rite. We can do all the rites associated with the practice, call to our gods, and then take off our clothes, but all of that is no guarantee that anything will happen on a deeply spiritual level. But I do think there are a few things that can be done to make a heightened experience much more likely.

Make It Special. Sometimes we end up performing the Great Rite without a lot of preparation because time and circumstances don't allow for it, but in most instances it's something we plan for. When that's the case, I like to build up to the event over several hours. I'll take a long, hot shower while listening to some music that puts me in a spiritual frame of mind, and spend a little extra time on my hair and pre-ritual wardrobe. (After all, I want my partner to find me attractive and desirable.)

My wife and I most often perform the Great Rite in our ritual room, which means moving a mattress onto the floor and getting out some extra bedding. While I'm setting up the "activity area," I'll also throw some rose petals on top of our blankets and place some crystals and stones around the area that stir up sexual energy. Some of the more common stones for this purpose include carnelian, sunstone, and yellow zircon.[236]

---

236. These suggestions are from *Cunningham's Encyclopedia of Crystal, Gem & Metal Magic* by Scott Cunningham.

Whatever you do here, just make sure that the touches you are adding appeal to you and your partner and whatever deities you might invite.

Other pre–Great Rite suggestions include a leisurely meal with foods that are either sacred to your gods or full of sexual energy. I also just like spending quality time with my partner beforehand, perhaps by going for a walk or sharing a nice glass of wine. There's no right or wrong here, but the more you think about the Great Rite beforehand, the better your chances for success will be.

Use Ritual Space. While I've certainly participated in the Great Rite outside of ritual space, it's always much better in a fully cast circle with all the usual accompaniments. I like to have the incense going, the candles lit, and my altar within view, along with the quarters and the Lord and Lady called to. The extra buildup that comes with creating sacred space will help put you in the right frame of mind for ritual.

If you find yourself in a place where it's not practical to create a fully realized ritual circle, you can still add a little bit of that energy to your Great Rite. Share the Charges of the Goddess and God with each other, or simply ask the deities you honor to join you in your lovemaking. Every little bit helps! Even just lighting a candle goes a long way. What's important is separating the Great Rite from your everyday way of doing things.

Cleanse and Consecrate. If you and your partner have taken a pre-ritual bath, it might seem redundant to cleanse and consecrate in the circle, but I highly recommend it. Cleansing the body is not quite the same as cleansing the mind, and a bit of "in ritual" cleansing helps me get into the right mindset for magickal work. Anoint each other with salt water or a favorite oil, and let the incense smoke wash over you. Both of you will feel refreshed afterward and ready for the Great Rite.

I find that the Great Rite works best when I release all of my inhibitions. I don't want to be thinking about things; I want to be doing the things! And while I do them, I want to reach out with my soul and spirit and see what's out there to grasp. That means trying to touch the earth, my partner, the cosmos, and my gods with the spiritual essence of my being. Turn off your conscious mind and rejoice in being alive and able to partake in the gifts that the Lord and Lady have provided for you!

Certainly you want to be responsive to your partner and focus on their pleasure, but this can be done without having to rely on the analytical parts of your brain. Sex is an instinct after all, not a learned behavior. We can let go of the mundane world during the Great Rite while still being attentive to our partner's needs. And sex can sometimes be ridiculous because our bodies are sometimes ridiculous. Don't be scared of sharing some laughter if it's called for.

Ultimately I find that the Great Rite is most effective when it becomes transcendent. That means I go beyond myself and no longer feel as if I'm in "just a room" or on "just a bed." I feel as if I've been transported to another place and that I'm experiencing something that exists both totally in the now and all throughout time. My mind drifts to moments throughout creation, and my heart feels linked and connected to my partner. The Great Rite, like so many of Witchcraft's greatest mysteries, is not something that can be described; it's something that must be experienced.

The Charge of the Goddess

The first draft of this book included a thorough history of the Charge of the Goddess, from Leland's *Aradia* in 1899 all the way through to Doreen Valiente's prose version written just over fifty years later. During the editing process of this book, I decided to drop my extended look at the Charge in order to shorten the page count and because much of that information is already online. For readers interested in the history of the Charge, that material can be found online by searching for "Charge of the Goddess History Mankey."

Though Valiente's original Charge is by far the most popular and well-known version, hundreds (if not thousands) of Witches over the years have adapted it to suit their own needs. The version of the Charge of the Goddess included here comes from my wife Ari's Book of Shadows and is the one we use in ritual. It's not a big departure from Valiente's version, but it does update some of the language, removing words such as *thinketh* and *seekest*. (Ari finds those words hard to pronounce.)

The Charge itself is traditionally divided into two sections, each one introduced by a narrator. The narrator can be anyone in the coven, though typically that role is filled by whoever is leading the ritual with the High Priestess. Many covens omit the narrator lines all together or have the High Priestess reciting the Charge read them. In our practice I tend to introduce the Charge ("Listen to the words of the Great

Mother…"), while we skip the "Hear ye the words of the Star Goddess" narration. Do what works best for you and your coven.

THE CHARGE OF THE GODDESS
BY DOREEN VALIENTE
(AS ADAPTED BY ARI AND JASON MANKEY)

Narrator: "Listen to the words of the Great Mother, who was of old also called Artemis, Astarte, Diana, Melusine, Aphrodite, Cerridwen, Dana, Arianrhod, Isis, Bride, and by many other names."

Whenever ye have need of anything, once in a month and better it be when the moon is full, then ye shall assemble in some secret place and adore the spirit of me who am Queen of all the Wise. There shall ye assemble, ye who are fain to learn all sorcery, but have not won its deepest secrets; to these will I teach things that are yet unknown. And ye shall be free from slavery, and as a sign ye be free, you may be naked in your rites; and ye shall dance, sing, feast, make music and love all in my praise.

For mine is the ecstasy of the spirit, and mine also is joy on Earth; for my law is love unto all beings. Keep pure your highest ideal; and strive ever toward it; let naught stop you or turn you aside. For mine is the secret door which opens upon the Land of Youth, and mine is the cup of the wine of life, and the Cauldron of Cerridwen which is the holy grail of immortality.

I am the gracious Goddess, who gives the gift of joy unto the heart of man. Upon the earth, I give the knowledge of the spirit eternal; and beyond death, I give peace, and freedom, and reunion with those who have gone before. Nor do I demand sacrifice, for behold I am the Mother of all living, and my love is poured out upon the earth.

Narrator: "Hear ye the words of the Star Goddess, she in the dust of whose feet are the hosts of heaven, and whose body encircles the universe." [237]

I who am the beauty of the green earth, and the White Moon among the stars, and the mystery of the waters, and the desire of the heart of man, call unto thy soul to arise and come unto me. For I am the soul of nature who gives life to the universe. From me all things proceed, and unto me all things must

---

237. My wife and I look at this line as optional in our practice.

return; and before my face beloved of gods and men, let thine innermost divine self be enfolded in the rapture of the infinite. Let my worship be within the heart that rejoices, for behold, all acts of love and pleasure are my rituals.

And therefore let there be beauty and strength, power and compassion, honor and humility, mirth and reverence within you. And thou who thinks to seek for me, know thy seeking and yearning shall avail thee not unless thou knowest the mystery; for if that which you seek, you find not within thee, you will never find it without. For behold I have been with you from the beginning, and I am that which is attained at the end of desire.

The Charge of the God

Nearly twenty years ago I went searching for a Charge of the God equal to Doreen Valiente's Charge of the Goddess in power and scope. When I was unable to find anything that appealed to me, I decided to write my own Charge of the God, and it's the version I've been using ever since. Most Charges of the God feel like a reworking of Valiente's Charge of the Goddess. I'm partial to my version because it's something completely unique.

My Charge represents the God of the Witches in his various guises throughout mythology and ritual. He's the god of death, the sun, the wild places, sex, and everything in between. One of the things I like about it is that it's adaptable. Verses can be easily dropped, rearranged, or read by a variety of people instead of one individual, depending on what one is using it for. Like Valiente, I've continually tweaked my Charge over the years, adding and dropping verses. What follows is the version I generally use today, along with a few extra verses that I've mostly dropped. Like the Charge of the Goddess, this is a great piece to use during initiations and/or elevations or perhaps before performing the Great Rite.

The Charge of the God by Jason Mankey

Narrator: "Revealed now are the words of the Great God. He is the ancient one, whose face has appeared in many roles throughout eternity."

I am he who abides in the deepest, darkest woods. It is my place to be with the creatures of the forest running in the cloak of blackest night. With bow strung across my back I make my home with the earth. I am the defender of the sacredness of nature. I am the Great God.

I am he whose light and warmth bring forth life from the soil. My warmth is the covenant of union between Lady and Lord. My brow is the radiant crown of summer, the glow about me my promise of eternal light. I am the Great God.

I am he who is magick, creator of eternal energy, the catalyst of beneficial change for all who would walk in the Old Ways. My whispers are those of tomorrows revealed and knowledge to be granted. I am the power to see and do all things. I am the Great God.

I am the trickster, scourge of all those methodical and overanalyzing. I am the trouble in the best-laid plans, the unexpected when all seems well. I am the chaos in a world of balance. I am the Great God.

I am he whose gift is the vine, the never-ending chalice of intoxication. My presents are those of joy: wine, dance, and the freedom to be without care. Merriment and mirth to me are great honor, for the joy of the folk is my reward. I am the Great God.

I am the cosmic god, one with all aspects of the universe. It is the stars that provide the sparkle in my eyes, a multitude of planets make up my body, and a thousand suns burn together as my heart and soul. I am the Great God.

I am he who abides in the skies, bringer of thunder and sender of lightning. I give the blessings of rain to the parched and hungry land. I command the winds that turn the seasons. I am he whose face can be seen amongst the clouds. I am the Great God.

I am the horned one, ancient god of fertility. It is my seed that brings forth life in the great womb. I am the bringer of physical pleasure, god of lust, god of the flesh. I give the joys of bodily union to all who ask. I am the Great God.

I am he who stands at the threshold of death, and life eternal. I welcome those who have departed your world and bid farewell to those who return to it.

I guard the mysteries of the end and the wonder of beginnings. I am the Great God.

Worship me side by side with the Lady. Honor me and I shall abide forever within you. For as long as tolerance, happiness, and righteousness exist, the true God will eternally reign. I am love, I am eternal, I am a part of all things. I am the Great God.

Extra Verses:

I am the sacrificial god. It is my blood that is poured out upon the earth so the soil may be renewed, and those that need forgiveness may receive it. I care naught for myself, only for those who serve me. I am the Great God.

I am the god of love. My arrows awaken desire in the hearts of women and men, and it is my poison that makes many foolish in the name of love. I affirm the commitment between those who choose to share heart, mind, body, and soul. I am the Great God.

Acknowledgments and a Final Note

Rituals are not meant to be read; they are meant to be done. I realize that the doing is often harder than writers like myself make it out to be. Finding a coven of reputable Witches can be an uphill task, and forming your own coven or circle is often even more challenging. The witchy world is more interconnected today than ever before, but we are still a relatively small part of the population and we can be hard to find away from large urban areas.

Time is a precious commodity too, and many of us do not have enough of it. A full work day with a commute might take anywhere from nine to twelve hours, and after eating, sleeping, and taking care of children or pets, well, there's not a lot of time left over for Witchcraft. I've been there and continue to be there now and again, despite what this book might imply.

Since the 1980s Witchcraft has been moving away from coven practice, and there are probably more solitary Witches today than ones who are part of an active group. That also makes it hard to *do* Witchcraft, but it's not an impossible obstacle to overcome. While initiation rituals might be out, that still leaves room for dedication rituals, building the cone of power, exploring our origins, growing closer to the gods, and celebrating our place both on this earth and in the grander scheme of things. In other words, there's still much that can be done on one's own, and the talented Witch finds a way to overcome all the obstacles in their path.

It's my sincerest hope that you'll try to find some time to actually do the rituals and rites in this book. I enjoyed writing them (and making my coven participate in them), but they only truly come alive when they are practiced. The mysteries of Witchcraft don't exist on the printed page, nor do they exist in our imagination; they most truly exist in the circle, surrounded by the Lord and Lady and a chosen family of other Witches.

I once remarked to a group of initiated (Gardnerian) Witches that someone could read our oathbound Book of Shadows a hundred times and yet come away with no real clue as to what we do. That's because our rituals aren't about the words; they are about the energies and experiences we have while in the circle. The biggest mysteries of Witchcraft lie in the doing, and as long as we keep doing, we'll continue to uncover more of them.

————

This was not an easy or simple book to write, and represents twenty years of reading, writing, researching, and most importantly "doing" in the Craft. I've been blessed to come across probably hundreds of Witches and other Pagans during that time, and most of them have contributed to the contents of this book in at least some sort of small way.

Not surprisingly, the most important person in my life is my wife, Ari, and she's a much better Witch than I'll ever be. My Craft is not my own; it's something I share heart and soul with my much better half. Thank you, darling wife. I hope I didn't embarrass you too much in the final chapter of the book.

After Ari, all the thanks in the world go to my father, Mick Mankey. My dad has been my biggest cheerleader over the last twenty years, and while he doesn't understand any of this stuff, he's always supported my desire to do it. Thank you, thank you, thank you, Dad! My younger brother Chuck has also always been supportive, as well as my new mom,

Therese! I share the craft of writing with my Aunt Donna and learned to be more curious about the world through my Aunt Marg. I love you both.

For the last seven years I've been a part of the best coven in at least Northern California: the Oak Court. Thank you all for letting me use our ritual space as my personal petri dish and for being a part of my many odd ritual experiments. I love and appreciate all our "Oak Nuts," past and present.

My earliest forays into the Pagan world took place primarily at Michigan State University and Green Spiral, the Pagan student group there. Many of the people I met in that group have been a part of my journey ever since, and though most all of us practice different things these days, the bonds still remain. "Thanks" doesn't do the entire Lansing Pagan Village enough justice!

Over the last eight years I've really come to treasure my connections in the Gardnerian community. My training in Gard has made me a better Witch and, most importantly, a better person and husband. The thanks here are extremely personal, so I'm sending out all the love in the world to Nina, Maggie, Michael, the rest of Wind Shadow, and Teresa and Eddie at the Walnut House of Cats, not to mention Ari and I's initiates in Oak's Shadow. I hope I've done you all proud with this book.

This book could not have been written without the fine work of Dr. Ronald Hutton and Philip Heselton. The history parts of this book are mostly a (poor) regurgitation of their much better ruminations on the subject. I'll admit to being a giant fanboy, now and forever! Thanks for telling Gardner's story to a modern audience.

To my fellow bloggers at Patheos Pagan—especially John Beckett, Mat Auryn, Gwion Raven, Angus McMahan, Phoenix LeFae, Lilith Dorsey, Astrea Taylor, Megan Manson, Niki Whiting, Jenya Beachy, Sonja Sadovsky, Thorn Mooney, Colin Davis, Christopher Drysdale, and Heron Michelle—thank you all for being such founts of knowledge and encouragement over the last several years. Beyond P Pagan, thanks to Heather Greene at the Wild Hunt and Anne Newkirk-Niven for always being supportive and enthusiastic about my work.

I owe everything to Elysia Gallo at Llewellyn, who gave me my first shot at writing a real book, and Andrea Neff, who edits my stuff and makes it so much better. Laura Tempest Zakroff encouraged me to get off my duff and submit this book to Llewellyn earlier rather than later. As is almost always the case, she was right, and you would not be reading this if not for her prompting.

I've been a Pagan festival warrior over the years and have Panthea-Con, ConVocation, Sirius Rising, Pagan Spirit Gathering, and Starwood to thank for me getting to this point in my life (along with probably the two dozen other festivals I don't have the space for here). If you've ever been to a workshop of mine at a festival or simply nodded at me reassuringly, you helped make this project a reality.

Lots of different individuals and organizations graciously allowed me to quote their work(s) in this book, a debt that I may never be able to repay. I got to quote the work of, and correspond with, Janet Farrar! This is a big deal for a Witch-nerd like me. Janet, thank you for your time and advice. Julia Belham-Payne and Ashley Mortimer at the Doreen Valiente Foundation allowed me to include the Charge of the Goddess in this book, something I'm especially grateful for. I can't imagine this book without Doreen's most well-known contribution to the Craft. Both the O.T.O. and the Society of the Inner Light were kind enough to speedily confirm to me (and especially my publisher) that Crowley's and Fortune's works are now in the public domain—perhaps not a big deal, but a lack of such confirmations would have resulted in a vastly different book.

And finally, this work is dedicated to the memory of my grandparents: Mick and Marie Mankey. I miss you both and hold onto your memory fiercely.

Brightest Blessings,

Jason W. Mankey

January 2018

Glossary

altar: The focal point of most Witch rituals, and where a great deal of spellwork is performed. At its simplest, an altar is simply where Witches put their stuff.

asperge: The process of sprinkling blessed and consecrated (salted) water around the circle for purification purposes. If an object other than one's fingers are used to sprinkle the water (such as a mini-broom or a feather), the object is called an *asperger.*

athame: A ceremonial knife or dagger used to project magickal energy. Athames are most commonly used to cast magick circles and for the rite of cakes and ale and the Great Rite. Traditionally the athame is a double-sided steel blade about five inches long, with a wooden handle. Athames are rarely used for physical cutting.

Beltane: A holiday celebrating the fullness of life, generally celebrated on May 1.

besom: A fancy name for a ritual broom. Besoms in ritual are generally used to sweep away negative energy.

boline: A knife exclusively used to tend to a Witch's magickal garden. Bolines are used to harvest vegetables, fruits, and herbs. The boline is often confused with the white-handled knife, and many Witches now use the two tools interchangeably. The blade of a boline can be either straight or curved like a sickle.

Book of Shadows: A book containing the spellwork, rituals, thoughts, and dreams of a Witch. If it's sacred and important to you, it can go into a Book of Shadows. The earliest version of the Book of Shadows was reserved exclusively for Witch ritual and instruction. Since then, many Witches have begun keeping their own personal Book of Shadows.

chalice (or cup): A cup or wine glass reserved for Witchcraft ritual. The chalice is generally used during the ceremony of cakes and ale and the (symbolic) Great Rite.

charge: To "charge" an item is to infuse it with your own magickal energy. In ritual, a charge is a firsthand written revelation from deity itself (such as the Charge of the Goddess). The term *charge* in this context was originally Masonic and indicated a set of instructions.

circle: A Witch's working space, generally created with personal and natural energies. A circle exists between the mundane world and that of higher powers. Circles can be cast anywhere. The term *circle* often indicates an open ritual group that performs Witch rites. The verb *circled* is used by many Witches to indicate the people they practice ritual with ("I circled with Phoenix and Gwion.").

coven: A Witch ritual group that acts in perfect love and perfect trust. Some Traditional Witch groups use the term *cuveen* as an alternative.

Cowan: A term for a non-Witch. This word was originally Masonic and referred to non-Masons.

creative visualization: A mental picture used in magickal work in order to apply intent to energy. Creative visualization is one of the building blocks of magickal practice.

degree: A symbol of rank and/or accomplishment in many initiatory Witchcraft traditions.

deosil: To walk or move clockwise. Clockwise is the default direction energy moves in and is how most Witches operate in sacred space.

downline: The initiates of an initiated Witch.

drawing down: The willful surrendering of consciousness to a higher power (generally a deity) so that the higher power can interact with the people around them.

elements: The powers of air, fire, water, and earth. Most substances on Earth can be broken down into these four broad categories, and contain attributes generally associated with one of these powers.

esbat: A Witch ritual performed on or near a full or new moon. Alternatively, *esbat* might be used as shorthand for "Witch ritual not connected to a sabbat."

greater sabbats: Shorthand for the cross-quarter holidays of Samhain, Imbolc, Beltane, and Lammas. The first Modern Witches celebrated only these four holidays, with celebration of the sabbats at the equinoxes and solstices coming later. These are perhaps called "greater" because they were the first sabbats celebrated by Modern Witches and were the holidays celebrated by the Celts of Ireland.

intent: The specific desired outcome of a magickal working.

invoke: An invitation to a higher power to be present at a ritual or magickal working. In some instances *invoke* is used as a synonym for drawing down the moon.

lesser sabbats: The sabbats celebrated at the solstices and equinoxes (Yule, Ostara, Midsummer, and Mabon).

Like attracts like: A magickal philosophy that encourages the use of items and ideas that are similar to the magician's end goal. For instance, to attract love you'd want to use ideas and items associated with love instead of the opposite. It also suggests that Witches will attract and find Witches similar to them because "like attracts like."

lineage: The family tree of an initiated Witch. Most lineages can be traced to the specific founder of a Witchcraft tradition.

Lughnasadh: The celebration of the first harvest, generally observed between July 31 and August 2. Spellings of Lughnasadh vary, and the sabbat is also called *Lammas* by some Witches.

Mabon: The name used by many Witches to indicate the autumn equinox. The term *Mabon* was first used by the Witch Aidan Kelly in the early 1970s and means "son of the mother." There were no ancient Mabon celebrations, though harvest celebrations were common enough. It's essentially a modern Witch holiday.

magick: Energy that is given a specific intention. Many Witches spell magick with a *k* to differentiate it from stage magic.

Midsummer: A sabbat celebrating the summer solstice, usually around June 21. Some Witches also call this sabbat *Litha,* which was first suggested by Aidan Kelly in the early 1970s.

Mighty Ones: A phrase used to indicate divine beings, generally deities. Some Witches also use the term *Mighty Ones* to indicate the watchtowers that are invoked at the quarters.

Pagan: Someone who practices a spiritual tradition that emphasizes the sacredness of the earth and calls upon pre-Christian deities. Because most Pagan traditions today utilize both modern and ancient ideas, practitioners are sometimes called Neo-Pagans.

pentacle: A round disc inscribed with a magickal symbol, traditionally used to invoke spirits, angels, or demons. In most Modern Witchcraft traditions it's viewed as a tool of earth and inscribed with a pentagram. It's generally used to bless the elements and serves as a gateway for both deity and magickal energy.

pentagram: A five-pointed star. The pentagram is most often depicted with one point facing up, which represents the triumph of the spiritual over the material. Many left-hand-path traditions use the star with two points facing up. In certain Wiccan traditions the upside-down pentagram (two points facing up) is used to indicate the second degree.

perfect love and perfect trust: The ideal coven is said to operate in a state of perfect love and perfect trust. Because of this, "perfect love and perfect trust" is often used as a password in Witchcraft rituals.

sacred space: The interior of a magick circle. Alternatively, a room set aside specifically for ritual or magickal workings, or an extremely powerful place in the natural world.

sabbat: A Witch holiday. Sabbats are most often associated with solstices and equinoxes, and the cross-quarter days that occur between them.

Samhain: A sabbat celebrated on October 31 commemorating the year's final harvest. Many Witches celebrate Samhain as the Witches' New Year. The modern Halloween is a descendent of the Samhain celebrations of the Irish Celts.

stang: A wooden stick, pole, or pitchfork used in many rituals by Traditional Witches. Stangs often function as the focal point of ritual, acting much like an altar, and can be decorated to represent the change of the seasons.

Summerlands: A place where souls go after death before reincarnating in this world. The term *Summerlands* comes to us via the Theosophical Society.

sword: Generally used to cast the magick circle. Anything one can do with a sword, they can also do with an athame, and vice versa. (Though using a sword to bless cakes and ale can be challenging due to its size!) Swords are often shared by a coven while athames almost always belong to the individual Witch.

tradition: A specific Witchcraft subgrouping that generally requires an initiation. Traditions often have their own Book of Shadows, and members can trace their lineage to a specific individual such as Gerald Gardner or Cora Anderson.

Traditional Witchcraft: A Modern Witchcraft tradition generally inspired by magickal practices such as English cunning-craft, Conjure, and other forms of folk magick.

upline: A Witch's upline consists of those who initiated the individual Witch as well as the initiators of their initiators. When thought of like a family tree, it's all the Witches above the initiate going all the way back to the tradition's source.

(the) watchtowers: The four powers that are invoked at the compass points of east, south, west, and north. They are generally associated with the elemental energies of air, fire, water, and earth. In the grimoire tradition, the term *watchtowers* referred to the angels Raphael (east), Michael (south), Gabriel (west), and Uriel (north). The energy provided by the watchtowers is generally thought to be protective.

white-handled knife: A knife with a white handle generally used for cutting or inscribing candles while in ritual space. It's sometimes known as a *kirfane* or a *kerfan.* The traditional white-handled knife is often confused with the boline.

Wicca: A Modern Witchcraft tradition that generally utilizes some form of the ritual structure first revealed by Gerald Gardner in the early 1950s. Wicca is probably best defined by its ritual structure and not by theological ideas.

widdershins: To walk or move counterclockwise. Widdershins energy is most often used for banishing or aggressive magickal workings.

will (or magickal Will): The sum total of all our experiences, emotions, and interactions with other people, deities, and the world around us. Our will often represents our purest intentions.

Yule: The name for the holiday celebrated at the winter solstice. Many Christmas traditions actually stem from ancient pagan holidays celebrated near the winter solstice. Some Pagans call the holiday *Midwinter,* as it falls between Samhain and Imbolc (seen by some as the start dates of winter and spring, respectively).

Bibliography

By the standards of today's Witchcraft and Pagan books, what you are holding in your hands is a pretty long book. It cites over fifty authors and contains nearly 200 footnotes—wow! (I'll stop patting myself on the back now.)

This book would not have been possible without the efforts of everyone cited within it, so to all the authors whose work I've regurgitated in these pages, thank you. In addition, since this is such a long book, I glanced over a whole bunch of stuff in some places that really deserved more of an extended look. Because of that shortcoming, I present to you this very long bibliography highlighting many of my favorite (and sometimes least favorite) authors. I hope some of the things I covered more quickly than I would have liked piqued your interest a bit and you pick up a couple of the following books.

Adler, Margot. *Drawing Down the Moon: Witches, Druids, Goddess-Worshippers, and other Pagans in America Today.* Boston, MA: Beacon Press, 1986. For several years the *only* Pagan history book was *Drawing Down the Moon*, and it did its job quite well. This is one of the most important books of the modern Pagan revival, and one of several game-changing American books published in the 1970s. Margot was also one of the nicest and most genuine Witches I've ever met.

Alexandrian, Sarane. *The Great Work of the Flesh: Sexual Magic East and West.* Translated into English by Jon E. Graham. Rochester, VT: Destiny Books, 2015. Originally written in 2000 and published in French. This is a deeply flawed book in many ways, but the write-up on Paschal Beverly Randolph was useful in putting together this book. (Just don't read the bits about Gardner and the Craft, as something was obviously lost in translation.)

Aradia, Sable, Lady. *The Witch's Eight Paths of Power.* San Francisco, CA: Weiser Books, 2014. This is an overlooked gem of a book that details several elements of Witchcraft not usually written about.

Aslan, Reza. *No god but God: The Origins, Evolution, and Future of Islam.* New York: Random House, 2005. I originally read this book two days after having all four of my wisdom teeth removed (and high on pain medication) and was surprised to see that it held up far better than I thought it would.

Bogdan, Henrik. *Western Esotericism and Rituals of Initiation.* Albany, NY: State University Press of New York Press, 2007. As far as I'm aware, this is the only book of its kind. Bogdan explores the rituals of the Masons, Rosicrucians, and Golden Dawn with a great degree of depth and understanding. It's written for an academic audience, so it's challenging in places.

Borgeaud, Philippe. *The Cult of Pan in Ancient Greece.* Translated by Kathleen Atlass and James Redfield. Chicago, IL: University of Chicago Press, 1988. Originally written in French, this is one of the few books dedicated strictly to my favorite goat-god!

Bowden, Hugh. *Mystery Cults of the Ancient World.* Princeton, NJ: Princeton University Press, 2010. I really only touch on the Mysteries at Eleusis in my book, but Bowden's book has insights into the mysteries of Mithra and Dionysus as well. Well written, easy to follow (rare in academia), and full of fabulous pictures, this is a must-read for anyone interested in the ancient mysteries.

Bracelin, Jack L. *Gerald Gardner: Witch.* London: Octagon Press, 1960. Bracelin probably did not write most of *Witch* (much of the credit goes to Sufi mystic Idries Shah), but ultimately its authorship doesn't matter all that much. Whoever wrote this book did so with the full cooperation (and oversight) of Gerald Gardner, making it a valuable historical document.

Broad, William, J. *The Oracle: The Lost Secrets and Hidden Message of Ancient Delphi.* New York: Penguin Press, 2006. This is a fun and quick read on the Oracle of Delphi.

Budin, Stephanie Lynn. *The Myth of Sacred Prostitution in Antiquity.* New York: Cambridge University Press, 2008. Though sacred prostitution is often spoken of as historical fact in modern Pagan circles, there are many who believe it to be a made-up idea unsupported by the evidence.

Burkert, Walter. *Greek Religion.* Cambridge, MA: Harvard University Press, 1985. Translated by John Raffan. First published in German in 1977. Burkert's book is not the last word on the gods and religion of the ancient Greeks, but it's a great start for the armchair scholar. Also cited is Burkert's *Ancient Mystery Cults.* Cambridge, MA: Harvard University Press, 1987.

Carey, Benedict. "A Neuroscientific Look at Speaking in Tongues," *New York Times.* November 7, 2006. http://www.nytimes.com/2006 /11/07/health/07brain.html?_r=0. This is a terrific article and one of the few sources I could find that looks at possession from a scientific angle rather than skepticism.

Clifton, Chas S. *Her Hidden Children: The Rise of Wicca and Paganism in America.* Lanham, MD: AltaMira Press, 2006. Somehow I don't think I cited Chas's work in this book, but *Her Hidden Children* is such a great piece of history that I think I must have thumbed through it at least a time or two while working on chapter 2.

Cicero, Chic, and Sandra Tabatha Cicero. *The Essential Golden Dawn: An Introduction to High Magic.* St. Paul, MN: Llewellyn Publications, 2003. Out of all the Golden Dawn introductory books I own, this is probably my favorite.

Conway, D. J. *Celtic Magic.* St. Paul, MN: Llewellyn Publications, 1990. This is not a particularly good book, but it was the first Witchcraft book I read as an adult. As a result, it's had a tremendous impact on my practice.

Crowley, Aleister. *Liber O.* Originally published in 1909. My edition was published in 1976 (in pamphlet form) by Samuel Weiser. Crowley can be a pain in the ass to read, but this is all easily digested and understood. Also cited is Crowley's *The Best of the Equinox: Sex Magick.* Introduction by Lon Milo DuQuette. San Francisco, CA: Red Wheel/Weiser, 2013. This is a great little volume featuring some of Crowley's better-known sex writings, including the original written version of the Gnostic Mass. Astute readers who go through the Gnostic Mass will find a whole host of "borrowings" from it that have become a part of many Witch rituals.

Cunningham, Scott. *Cunningham's Encyclopedia of Crystal, Gem & Metal Magic.* St. Paul, MN: Llewellyn Publications, 1988. Thirty years after its initial publication, this is still my go-to book for stones and crystals.

Davies, Owen. *Popular Magic: Cunning-folk in English History.* New York: Hambledon Continuum, 2007. After Ronald Hutton, Davies is probably the preeminent scholar of all things esoteric.

d'Este, Sorita, and David Rankine. *Wicca: Magickal Beginnings.* London: Avalonia Press, 2008. One of *the* books for anyone interested in the origins of Modern Witchcraft. When I cite something from this book, I'm probably omitting ten other equally fascinating things next to that citation. Also, Sorita is absolutely wonderful, and I shall forever cherish the memory of sharing several pints of cider with her one glorious August day in Glastonbury.

Dening, Sarah. *The Mythology of Sex: An Illustrated Exploration of Sexual Customs and Practices from Ancient Times to the Present.* New York: Macmillan, 1996. This is a beautiful book, and the history is pretty good for not being overly academic.

Deveney, John P. *Paschal Beverly Randolph: A Nineteenth-Century Black American Spiritualist, Rosicrucian, and Sex Magician.* Albany, NY: State University of New York Press, 1997. Deveney's biography of Randolph kicked off an era of renewed interest in one of America's greatest magicians and occultists.

Drury, Nevill. *Stealing Fire from Heaven: The Rise of Modern Western Magic.* New York: Oxford University Press, 2011. Upon first reading this book, I didn't get much out of it, but after reading it a second, third, and fourth time, I changed my opinion. A great look at traditions outside of Witchcraft.

DuBois, Thomas A. *Nordic Religions in the Viking Age.* Philadelphia, PA: University of Pennsylvania Press, 1999. I'm sure there's someone champing at the bit to tell me I'm wrong about Nordic religious practices, so thankfully I've got this book to back me up. Despite all the myths we have of the Norse gods (most written long after Christianization), we don't know as much about Scandinavian pagan practices as most people think. This is a great book.

Duncan, Malcom C. *Duncan's Masonic Ritual and Monitor.* Originally published by Dick & Fitzgerald in 1866. Today, *Duncan's Monitor* can be found easily and quickly online as a PDF, and it has been republished numerous times since 1866.

Farrar, Janet, and Gavin Bone. *The Inner Mysteries: Progressive Witchcraft and Connection with the Divine.* Portland, OR: Acorn Guild Press, 2012. I spend 20,000 words talking about drawing down the moon and related events in my book. Janet and Gavin wrote a whole book about it!

Farrar, Janet, and Stewart Farrar. *A Witches' Bible: The Complete Witches' Handbook.* Custer, WA: Phoenix Publishing, 1996. Originally released as *Eight Sabbats for Witches* (1981) and *The Witches' Way* (1984), the content of *A Witches' Bible* allegedly comes from an Alexandrian Book of Shadows. For anyone interested in ritual in the style of Gardner and other initiated British Witches, this is the closest one can get without joining a coven. I consult this book with much frequency in my own practice. Doreen Valiente contributed a great deal to this book and has a couple of essays in it.

Ferguson, Robert. *The Vikings: A History.* New York: Penguin, 2009. This is a nice little volume detailing the history of the people we today call Vikings. It's not particularly exhaustive, especially when it comes to their religious practices, but it's a good start.

Fortune, Dion. *The Sea Priestess.* Originally privately published in 1938. I use the Samuel Weiser edition from 1978. Fortune's novel is a must-read for anyone looking into the origins of drawing down the moon. The 1,000 words I spend on it in my book do not do it justice. Fortune had a profound influence on Witchcraft, despite not being a Witch.

Gardner, Gerald. *The Meaning of Witchcraft.* London: Aquarian Press, 1959. *Witchcraft Today.* London: Rider & Co., 1954. Most of what's in Gardner's books doesn't have much bearing on today's Witchcraft, but there are a few passages here and there that provide some insight into not just Gerald's beliefs but also possibly those of the original New Forest Coven. These are important books even if they are difficult reads.

Guiley, Rosemary Ellen. *The Encyclopedia of Witches & Witchcraft.* New York: Facts On File, 1999. Some of the historical articles don't hold up particularly well since its initial publication in 1989, but there's still a lot of useful information here. I use it far more often today than I did when it was originally released.

Hayden, Brian. *Shamans, Sorcerers, and Saints: A Prehistory of Religion.* Washington, DC: Smithsonian Books, 2003. This book is full of information and illustrations documenting the rise of spiritual and religious ideas in prehistory.

Heselton, Philip. *Witchfather: A Life of Gerald Gardner, Vols. 1 and 2.* Loughborough, Leicestershire: Thoth Publications, 2012. Heselton's research into Gerald Gardner and his probable membership in the New Forest Coven has been groundbreaking, and Philip has become *the* leading scholar of contemporary Witch history in the world. I can't recommend his work enough, and much of this book would not have been possible without his efforts. Also cited is Heselton's *Wiccan Roots: Gerald Gardner and the Modern Witchcraft Revival.* Somerset, UK: Capall Bann, 2000.

Hohman, John George. *The Long-Lost Friend: A 19th Century American Grimoire.* Edited by Daniel Harms. Woodbury, MN: Llewellyn Publications, 2012. The *Friend* (sometimes called *Pow-Wows*) is one of the most influential grimoires in American history. The Harms version provides extensive notes regarding the text and fascinating historical materials.

Homer. *The Iliad of Homer.* Translated by Richmond Lattimore. Chicago, IL: University of Chicago Press, 1961. Why this version of the *Iliad?* Probably because it was the one I read in high school and I still have it sitting on my bookshelf.

Howard, Michael. *Children of Cain: A Study of Modern Traditional Witchcraft.* Richmond Vista, CA: Three Hands Press, 2011. Howard wrote perhaps dozens of Witchcraft-related books before his death in 2015, and *Cain* is one of his better offerings. I don't think he's a very reliable historian, but his enthusiasm for all things witchy is contagious and he shined a light on many forgotten and/or overlooked Craft traditions. Also cited is Howard's *Modern Wicca: A History from Gerald Gardner to the Present.* Woodbury, MN: Llewellyn Publications, 2009. *Modern Wicca* is a must-read for history nerds since Howard was around for much of Modern Witchcraft's most formative years. He's also partially responsible for Lady Sheba.

Huson, Paul. *Mastering Witchcraft: A Practical Guide for Witches, Warlocks, and Covens.* Originally published in 1970. I use the Perigee edition from 1980. Huson's book is commonly seen as the first book about Traditional Witchcraft, but the last chapter of it was dedicated to something that looks very much like Wiccan-Witchcraft. Huson's book was one of the first books about Witchcraft to actually be useful.

Hutton, Ronald. *The Triumph of the Moon: A History of Modern Pagan Witchcraft.* New York: Oxford University Press, 1999. When this book was released almost twenty years ago as of this writing, it was a complete game-changer. People had speculated on the origins of Modern Witchcraft before, but never so thoroughly and eloquently. Some people can't get past the academic style of Hutton (a professor at the University of Bristol), but I love it! This is one of my absolute favorite books ever. Also cited is Hutton's *Witches, Druids, and King Arthur.* London: Hembledon and London, 2003. This book is a collection of essays dealing with several things related to modern Paganism, including Glastonbury, England, the Greek Magical Papyri, and C. S. Lewis (along with Druids and King Arthur obviously).

John of Monmouth. *Genuine Witchcraft Is Explained: The Secret History of the Royal Windsor Coven and the Regency.* Somerset, UK: Capall Bann, 2012. I don't know the true identity of John, but I do know that his book is a winner and one of the best Cochrane resources to ever see print. Highly, highly recommended.

Jones, Evan John, and Robert Cochrane. *The Roebuck in the Thicket: An Anthology of the Robert Cochrane Witchcraft Tradition.* Edited by Michael Howard. Somerset, UK: Capall Bann, 2001. Though I'll never be much of a Cochranite, many of his ritual techniques are effective, and I absolutely love everything ever written by Evan John Jones. This particular book contains several letters written by Cochrane, along with a few articles by Jones that were published in Michael Howard's *The Cauldron* magazine. Even more of Cochrane's letters were published in *The Robert Cochrane Letters*, with editing by Howard and a few essays by Jones. Somerset, UK: Capall Bann, 2003.

Kelly, Aidan A. *A Tapestry of Witches: A History of the Craft in America, Vol. 1.* Tacoma, WA: Hierophant Wordsmith Press, 2014. Aidan won't like hearing this, but I think he's a little unfair to Gardner in his work sometimes, and way too trusting of others who claim their Witchcraft is far older. This is an interesting read for anyone curious about American-born Modern Witch traditions.

Kurtz, Katherine. *Lammas Night.* New York: Ballantine Books, 1983. Though Kurtz's book is fiction, it still provides a fascinating glimpse into English occult practices circa 1940. Though the cone of power operation she writes about is probably very unlike the one Gardner and friends performed in 1940, it's still worth a read.

Lady Sheba (Jessie Wicker Bell). *The Grimoire of Lady Sheba.* St. Paul, MN: Llewellyn Publications, 2001. *The Book of Shadows* by Lady Sheba was originally published in 1971, with an expanded version published as her *Grimoire* in 1973. *Shadows* was rather revolutionary for its time, marking the first appearance in print of recognizable

Modern Witch rituals. Since Sheba broke her oaths to print her book, I won't say anything else about her or it.

Leek, Sybil. *The Complete Art of Witchcraft.* New York: Signet, 1973. Originally published in 1971. While Leek's book doesn't live up to its rather grandiose title, it was pretty revolutionary for its time. What Leek's book lacked, though, were rituals! Leek wrote literally dozens of books dealing with astrology and Witchcraft up until the 1980s, but her work is now sadly out of print. Even used paperback copies of her work sometimes fetch up to seventy-five dollars. My copy of this book is currently selling for about fifty bucks online. Apparently much of the demand for Leek's books comes from Christopher Penczak, who uses them with his students.

Leland, Charles Godfrey. *Aradia, or the Gospel of the Witches.* London: David Nutt, 1899. I think *Aradia* is the most influential book in the history of Modern Witchcraft, and many of its best lines are still a part of many Witch rituals. In 1998 **Mario and Dina Pazzaglini** released a new translation of Leland's text taken from his notes (Phoenix Publishing, 1998). Their edition of *Aradia* contains a wealth of background information as well. Chas Clifton, Robert Mathiesen, and Robert Chartowich also contribute to their edition. Also cited is Leland's *Etruscan Roman Remains in Popular Culture.* New York: C. Scribner's Sons, 1892. Though not as well known as *Aradia*, *Etruscan Roman Remains* is equally fascinating, and in some places even more so.

Lévi, Éliphas. *Transcendental Magic: Its Doctrine and Ritual.* Translated by Arthur Edward Waite. London: George Redway, 1896. This has been published by a whole host of different publishers over the years and can be found legally online for free. Lévi was one of the most important architects of the occult revival, even if he's not spoken about a whole lot in Witch circles.

Lomas, Robert. *Turning the Hiram Key.* Gloucester, MA: Fair Winds Press, 2005. It surprises me just how free the Masons are with their secrets these days, but it's probably good PR for Freemasonry. It's clear from reading this book that Lomas's initiation experience was moving and powerful.

Magliocco, Sabina. *Witching Culture: Folklore and Neo-Paganism in America.* Philadelphia, PA: University of Pennsylvania Press, 2004. This book—and Magliocco—have never gotten as much attention as they deserve, and both are a treasure trove of Witch and Pagan history. Also cited is Magliocco's essay "Aradia in Sardinia: The Archeology of a Folk Character," from *Ten Years of Triumph of the Moon.* Hidden Publishing, 2009.

Mankey, Jason. *The Witch's Book of Shadows.* Woodbury, MN: Llewellyn Publications, 2017. It's probably a bit self-serving to include my own book here, though in truth I'm only citing it in order to highlight the contribution written by my friend **Christopher Drysdale**.

Mitchell, Chaffin. "Do Full Moons and Supermoons Really Influence People and Animals?" AccuWeather. https://www.accuweather.com/en/ weather-news/do-full-moons-and-supermoons-really-affect-human -animal-behavior/61402994. Not my usual source material, but it's an informative article.

Murray, Margaret Alice. *The Witch-Cult in Western Europe.* Oxford: Clarendon Press, 1921. *The God of the Witches.* London: Faber & Faber, 1931. Murray was an Egyptologist by trade but began writing about Witchcraft during World War I when she was stuck in her native England. Many of her ideas aren't held in high regard by modern scholars, but she had a tremendous impact on Witchcraft and the modern Horned God construct. *The God of the Witches* is a much better and often more informative read than the more well-known *Witch-Cult.*

Nabarz, Payam. *The Square and the Circle: The Influences of Freemasonry on Wicca and Paganism.* London: Avalonia Press, 2016. I found this book to be a little disappointing, as many of the things written about by Nabarz can be found in the works of Hutton and others. On the plus side, this is a very concise version of those previous findings.

Randolph, Vance. *Ozark Magic and Folklore.* New York: Dover Publications, 1967. Originally published in 1947. Many people use this book to argue that there was a community of self-identifying Witches in the American Ozarks in the early twentieth century. I get just the opposite from his work, but no matter how you interpret this book, it's a fun read.

Regardie, Israel. *What You Should Know About the Golden Dawn.* Phoenix, AZ: Falcon Press, 1983. Regardie was the first person to make an attempt at printing the rituals and rites of the Golden Dawn, and during his lifetime he was universally respected as one of the foremost historians (and custodians) of modern ceremonial magick. Also cited is Regardie's *The Golden Dawn: The Original Account of the Teachings, Rites, and Ceremonies of the Hermetic Order.* Woodbury, MN: Llewellyn Publications, 2015. This is the seventh edition, revised and corrected by John Michael Greer. This is a giant of a book but is invaluable to the Golden Dawn historian/seeker.

Ridley, Jasper. *The Freemasons: A History of the World's Most Powerful Secret Society.* New York: Arcade, 2001. For anyone looking for an informed and less speculative history of Masonry, this is the book.

Rollin, Tracey. *Santa Muerte: The History, Rituals, and Magic of Our Lady of the Holy Death.* Newburyport, MA: Weiser Books, 2017. I love Rollin's book on Santa Muerte, and it's helped me foster a deeper relationship with the Boney Lady. While I would never summon Santa Muerte into a Wiccan circle, she's the subject of near-daily devotions in my house (by me).

Rosenzweig, Rachel. *Worshipping Aphrodite: Art and Cult in Classical Athens.* Ann Arbor, MI: University of Michigan Press, 2006. Though a mostly academic work, this is an easily read look at Aphrodite in Athens. Highly recommended! For readers looking for a challenge and to drain their bank accounts, I'm also a huge fan of **Stephanie Lynn Budin's** *The Origin of Aphrodite.* Bethesda, MD: CDL Press, 2003. This book is an exhaustive and extremely scholarly look at the origins of Aphrodite. It had a small print run, and my copy is now selling for about four hundred dollars online, which is crazy.

Society of Esoteric Endeavour. *The Society of the Horseman's Word.* Hinckley, Leicestershire, UK: Caduceus Books, 2009. Much of this book is full of contemporary accounts of the Horseman's Word, along with modern essays discussing their ritual techniques and beliefs. Sources such as Amazon and Goodreads list William Rennie as the author, though his name doesn't appear on the title page and is only included in the acknowledgments section at the end of the book. This book is also listed as *The Society of the Horsemen's Grip and Word* in most places online, though the title on the book's cover and spine omits the words *Grip and*, using only *Word*. Despite these oddities, this book is a treasure.

Stavish, Mark. *Freemasonry: Rituals, Symbols, & History of the Secret Society.* Woodbury, MN: Llewellyn Publications, 2007. This book is good reading, with easy-to-understand explanations of Masonic rituals and symbols.

Strabo. *Geography.* The exact date of composition for *Geography* is a matter of some scholarly debate, with dates ranging from 7 BCE to 17 CE (a period of over twenty years). For this book I used the Perseus Press edition edited by H. L. Jones and published in 1924.

Tann, Mambo Chita. *Haitian Vodou: An Introduction to Haiti's Indigenous Spiritual Tradition.* Woodbury, MN: Llewellyn Publications, 2012. It was almost as if Llewellyn knew I was going to need Tann's book to write my own. This is one of my favorite books on Vodou.

Valiente, Doreen. *The Rebirth of Witchcraft.* Tacoma, WA: Phoenix Publishing, 1989. To put it so simply, Doreen is the Mother of Modern Witchcraft, and *Rebirth* is her incredibly fabulous memoir. So much of what we say in the circle comes directly from the heart and pen of Valiente.

West, M. L. *Indo-European Poetry and Myth.* Oxford: Oxford University Press, 2007. This is a fantastic and extremely readable look at the origins of some of my favorite deities and their associated pantheons.

Zimmerman, Denise, and Katherine A. Gleason. *The Complete Idiot's Guide to Wicca and Witchcraft.* Indianapolis, IN: Alpha Books, 2000. This is a surprisingly good book, though the "Complete Idiot's Guide" fad of books didn't last very long.

Index

A

Alexandrian tradition, 153, 154, 199, 300, 354, 357

Anderson, Cora, 35, 36, 149, 151, 351

Anderson, Victor, 35, 36, 149, 151, 351

Aphrodite, 32, 80, 114, 262, 277, 279–281, 298, 321, 336

Apollo, 183, 240

Aradia (goddess), 42, 80, 272

Aradia, or the Gospel of the Witches, 41–44, 48, 49, 56, 59, 60, 211, 212, 271, 272, 301, 307, 308, 310, 335

archetypes, 248, 249

As above, so below, 170, 171, 185, 204, 209, 217, 219

astral travel, 36, 131, 179, 248, 249, 262, 327

athame, 84, 89–92, 95–97, 161, 169, 184–186, 201, 209, 219, 238, 282, 283, 285, 286, 293, 303, 304, 307, 313–315, 347, 351

Athena, 114

B

Beltane, 92, 284, 323, 347, 349

Besant, Annie, 19, 20

Besant, Mabel, 19, 20

Blavatsky, Helena, 17, 244, 299

To Write to the Author

If you wish to contact the author or would like more information about this book, please write to the author in care of Llewellyn Worldwide Ltd. and we will forward your request. Both the author and the publisher appreciate hearing from you and learning of your enjoyment of this book and how it has helped you. Llewellyn Worldwide Ltd. cannot guarantee that every letter written to the author can be answered, but all will be forwarded. Please write to:

Jason Mankey
⁒ Llewellyn Worldwide
2143 Wooddale Drive
Woodbury, MN 55125-2989
Please enclose a self-addressed stamped envelope for reply,
or $1.00 to cover costs. If outside the USA, enclose
an international postal reply coupon.

Many of Llewellyn's authors have websites with additional information and resources. For more information, please visit our website at http://www.llewellyn.com.